Walking in the Shadow

Ramina Wilkerson

The BRANCH Publishing

The BRANCH Publishing
Copyright © 2023 Ramina Wilkerson

All scripture references are taken from the New King James Version. Copyright © 1982 by Thomas Nelson.

All measurements are rounded based on the conversions from the metric system.

ISBN: 979-8-9888030-2-7

Cover design by RebecaCovers

Map design by Rodina Babani

www.raminawilkerson.com

PROLOGUE

The streets are empty. Abandoned. No one dares to disturb the silence, knowing what is coming, what always comes. Everyone takes shelter in their homes, praying for a peaceful and silent night. A restful night of sleep has been nearly impossible to come by as of late. A cold breeze funnels down the darkened street devoid of natural light. The stars and moon are absent, as if they, too, are in hiding.

As usual, our quiet evening begins with dinner as a family, followed by a bit of television and Dad ushering us to bed. But sleep is short-lived. The intense wails of sirens echo past our windows and walls, disrupting any notion we had of deep sleep. The sound coming from the sirens seizes the city, its cry rising and falling based on the direction of the horn. Baghdad, our home, braces for an attack.

"Wake up, wake up," my father insists, gently yet urgently shaking me. I roll over, slowly opening my tired eyes, when Dad lifts me from my bed, unable to wait for my confusion to clear. My body jolts with each stride as he holds me tightly against his chest and runs into the living room. He quickly moves to the wall, tightening his grip on me

1

and crouching against the corner. I can feel his heart beating against his chest. With his arms securely wrapped around me, I curl up into his hold, reality quickly sinking in.

My gaze frantically studies the room until I see my mother sitting in the other corner, protectively holding my younger sister, Sona. Despite her best efforts, my mother cannot conceal the fear clearly displayed in her eyes. Mere seconds pass before the loud, deafening explosions take over the sirens. Goosebumps cover my skin, and my stomach twists as I feel each explosion.

This evening is not unusual. Curling up in the corners of the living room, wondering if we will survive another night as the foundation of our home shakes, has become a familiar routine. It is the sixth year of the infamous Iran-Iraq War, and I am four years old. This is the only life I know. Too young and naïve to understand the chaos around me and too traumatized to envision how much worse things will become, I clutch onto the safety of my parents in this season as they are the only ones who grasp the significance of it all.

I cling to my father. With his arms wrapped tightly around me, I press my nails deep into his skin. The sirens continue their howling, serving as a warning for the city of Baghdad minutes before the earth-shattering missiles strike and destroy its beauty. The enemy bombings never take place during the day. They ambush in the darkest hours of the night, attempting to catch the country and its citizens off guard. The sirens allow the citizens enough time to jolt out of their comfortable, warm beds and scurry to the corners of the house. The sturdiness of the concrete and brick homes provides a safe shelter to withstand most bombings. The corners stand strong and tall, unwavering. Even though some houses collapse during the bombings, the cornerstones often remain, making them the ideal location to shelter as missiles go by. Many inhabitants' lives have been spared due to this well-known defensive tactic.

I cover my ears to lessen the wails of the piercing sirens. I can't help but think, *since I was born in a war, I will die in one. That much, I know.* It is something I have come to believe and accept. This is my reality. No child should ever have to think this way. However, this is all I have ever known, and it is hard to imagine anything else. I am forced to live life one day at a time.

Sitting in these corners feels like an endless sentence for a crime I have not committed. My parents try their best to hide their emotions, to keep my sister Sona and me calm, but I cannot help but notice the look of sheer terror plainly displayed on their faces as we feel the ground beneath us shake. Each missile sends a shock wave through my body as I tremble from head to toe, trying to stay motionless. Crying is for the faint of heart. Although every cell in my body wants to shed the pent-up tears inside and scream, *I DON'T WANT TO DO THIS,* I know that will only add more strain to my parents' already stressful situation, so I stay quiet.

Our undeserved "time-outs" in these corners last anywhere from a few minutes to several hours. The sturdy concrete and brick are not the only materials keeping us safe during the attacks, however. We have an additional layer of protection—duct tape. Each room has one or two windows, and on the inside of each window is a duct-taped "X" running from one corner to the other. As bombs and missiles strike, they cause quakes large enough to rattle and shake the house, potentially shattering windows. The tape keeps the house free of glass by forcing the broken window panes to shatter outward. Using duct tape on windows has become good decor, and every home prudently displays it.

Darkness confronts me as I look past the tape and out the window, fighting despair, trying to think of better times and happier moments. Positive thoughts are hard to conjure up as all I can focus on at the moment is the proximity of the explosions. The further the sound, the further the explosion, and the safer I am from that particular

3

missile. Despite this last one being more distant than the previous missiles, the comfort is fleeting as each attack is unpredictable.

I sigh in relief at the howl of the second siren, a welcoming annoyance that means the attacks are subsiding for the night, and my life is spared yet again. Until tomorrow night, that is. This has become our nightly routine.

"Jesus Christ Himself being the chief cornerstone." Ephesians 2:20

BAGHDAD - 1982

A hot summer day that starts like any other takes an unexpected and dire turn. Early in the morning, July 26, 1982, Madlen, a clothing and accessories boutique employee, is abruptly awakened by labor pains. As they intensify, so do her fear and anxiety. Although she is not entirely alone, she feels alone. Her husband, James, deployed shortly after marrying Madlen. In all reality, he was drafted and shipped off to an undisclosed location to fulfill a gruesome assignment ordered by Iraq's president, Saddam Hussein.

"I need to go to the hospital!" Madlen shouts. Her mother-in-law, Marna, rushes to her side. It is a bittersweet moment as they scramble a few belongings before rushing to the hospital, fully aware James is missing the experience and joy of the birth of his firstborn. Although war brings so much sadness, the citizens of Iraq have found a way to maneuver around the pain. They have learned that any circumstance, no matter how dire, can be overcome with a bit of ingenuity and a lot of perseverance.

There is no time to feel sad, Marna tells herself as she rushes Madlen to Ilwiya, a maternity and childbirth hospital.

With each passing minute, the contractions intensify as the labor slowly progresses. After twenty hours of labor, the doctor mutters, "It is time," and he motions to the nurse to make the necessary preparations.

"In a few moments, you will be a mother," Marna states.

But those moments turn blurry for Madlen, followed by darkness as she begins hemorrhaging. What seems to have been a smooth labor quickly turns to confusion and chaos. "Blood! We need blood!" The doctor yells emphatically.

Due to the war, the hospitals are overwhelmed with wounded soldiers, including Ilwiya. They are at full capacity and have depleted their blood supply to treat the soldiers. No blood is available for a transfusion to sustain Madlen, and the doctors have no hope of saving her without it.

Desperate, the doctor looks to Marna and one of his nurses. "Storm through the hospital and see if anyone is willing to donate blood." In tears and fearing for Madlen's and the baby's life, Marna and the nurse frantically run through the hospital corridors, looking for hope. Long, white hallways seem to get colder with every step, slowly closing in with each "no" they face.

From a distance, a soldier, pacing outside a room, notices their distress and desperation as they trudge through the hallways. He darts towards them, "Is everything alright?"

"No," Marna cries as she relays the situation to him, and immediately, with tender eyes, he looks at the nurse and asks for Madlen's blood type.

"A-positive," she replies.

He gazes into the hospital room where an elderly woman lies, pale and seemingly lifeless. He looks back at Marna, "You can have the blood allocated for my mother's transfusion. She's in the final stages of life with no hope of saving her, and she no longer needs the blood."

Quickly thanking the soldier, the nurse disengages the bag of blood from the stand near his mother's hospital bed and sprints to Madlen's delivery room as Marna tries to keep pace. Moments later, the transfusion begins, and Madlen's pale body slowly regains color. Despite the country's sorrow, people have not lost their humanity. The soldier's act of kindness saved Madlen's life. And mine.

It is July 27. I have arrived, yet my father has no indication of the news nor the traumatic experience my mother endured. James, born and raised in Baghdad, Iraq, but of Persian descent from his maternal side, is gone often. However, shortly after my birth, my grandparents send a message of the news to him. A few weeks later, as the evening darkness settles in, there's a faint knock on the door. My grandfather opens it only to find my father standing tall, dressed in his green military uniform, carrying a small bag. His army unit sergeant was gracious enough to grant him a one-week leave to visit his family and meet his daughter.

* * *

"Before I formed you in the womb I knew you; before you were born I sanctified you." Jeremiah 1:5

BAGHDAD - 1981

My parents met at a party, neither one expecting fate to run its course one cool summer evening. My mother, Madlen, a petite young lady with hazel eyes and lighter hair than many Middle Eastern women, was dancing with her sisters and girlfriends when she noticed the vocalist staring at her. My dad, James, a mathematics teacher and a lead singer of an Assyrian band, was drawn to Mom immediately. Throughout the party, the two subtly flirted with each other until my dad summoned enough courage to ask my mom for a dance. During the slow dance, the two casually shared information, but then lost contact for two years. One day, out of the blue, as Mom was leaving a friend's house, she ran into Dad on the street, and immediately, their connection rekindled.

After two years of friendship and three months of dating, Dad's family asked for Mom's hand in marriage, as is customary. Dad did not propose to Mom. Instead, his family sought permission from her parents. In the weeks leading up, my paternal grandparents requested a meeting. Once the request was accepted, a date was set.

On the day of the proposal, influential family members brought flowers and presents to display honor to Mom's family. The two were not present during this gathering, as it was a time for the parents to discuss all the details before finalizing their decision. Soon after her father accepted, her sister ran to the bedroom to notify Mom of the news. Dad anxiously paced outside the apartment building. He straightened up as Mom leaned over the balcony ledge outside her bedroom and shouted, "They said yes!" Wedding planning commenced promptly, but not before my maternal grandparents hosted an elaborate engagement party.

On July 9, 1981, my parents, James and Madlen, celebrated their wedding three months after their engagement. The wedding included more than two hundred guests and a fifteen-layer cake. My paternal grandparents established an endearing tradition with their best friends. Each time a member of the two families marries, the other family provides the best man and the maid of honor, and vice versa, starting with my grandparents. This tradition has been ongoing for several years. In addition, they also provide the wedding cake for each other. With each wedding, they add two additional layers to the cake, showcasing the expansion of the family. This unique tradition keeps the two families connected and involved in each other's happiest days. Unfortunately, this tradition ceases to exist. With so many Assyrians dispersing across the globe due to the war, the family friends escaped to another country, and we lost touch. Had the tradition continued, my wedding cake would have been twenty-three layers tall.

Five weeks after the wedding, on August 15, the army drafted Dad, leaving Mom behind with his family. Ideally, he is allowed one week off every twenty-five days, depending on the severity of the war. If the war intensifies, his ability to break away from the Army extends between two to three months. When he is gone, contact is limited. Family members can send letters with other soldiers on leave if they are in the same unit. Soldiers serving in units together build a strong bond, and each time one is on leave, the rest send letters to their families.

* * *

"Therefore what God has joined together, let not man separate." Mark 10:9

Interlude - Assyrian Weddings

Weddings are fun-filled events. That's right; I said *events*. They consist of several affairs leading up to the big day and sometimes days to follow. After the initial meeting, the parents discuss the potential future, starting with the dowry. In a large city such as Baghdad, the dowry is monetary, ranging from one hundred dinars to a thousand or two. In villages, however, it can vary and include flock, farmland, or money. Once the agreed-upon dowries are paid, the bride's parents will host an engagement party where the couple exchanges wedding bands. Both will wear a simple gold band on their right ring finger to signify their engagement. The groom's family will also shower the bride with gold jewelry, mostly 24-karat gold, as it is considered precious—it is pure and contains no other elements. The more jewelry pieces, the better; this is a sign to everyone that the bride is valued and will be well taken care of.

In the weeks leading up to the wedding, female relatives of the bride gather at her house to assemble a large honeymoon blanket for the couple. The older women sit around and pass the needle from one woman to another while the younger ones dance traditional Assyrian dances. In the days leading up to the wedding, there is "the washing of the groom." All the male family members and friends gather at the groom's house, shaving and cutting his hair, giving him an outstanding head-to-toe scrub, followed by a shower. These rituals symbolize the removal of evil. During the festivities, everyone gathered can be found cheering, singing, clapping, and eating. It's an all-out celebration.

The groom's family fully funds the wedding, including the bride's wedding dress. The wedding day is packed full. The groom's family and friends will gather at his home as they celebrate with music and dancing before driving to the bride's house to pick her up. A parade of vehicles will travel to her house, where she is surrounded by family, friends, music, and dancing, similar to the festivities at the groom's house. The bride awaits her groom to escort her to church. When the groom and his family first arrive, they perform a chant declaring they are here to take her, and her family responds with their portion of the chant. After a few dances performed by everyone present, the groom attempts to escort the bride out of the house, but not before she is held for "ransom." Usually, a male relative of the bride blocks the front door of her home and refuses to let her leave without receiving a monetary payment from the groom's family. The amount varies at the discretion of the family member asking. In return, the groom's family takes something of value from the bride's house for ransom. Most times, amid the chaos and craziness, the item isn't identified until the family figures it out days later. Once the bride is released, the couple is escorted to the church, where the groom leads his bride down the aisle.

The wedding ceremony differs from village to village and lasts one to four hours. Along with the maid of honor and the best man, the bride and groom remain standing for the entire ceremony. In some ceremonies, the groom is pricked with a needle to deter evil spirits. In others, the couple must walk around a small altar seven times. In some cases, the priest ties red and white ribbons on the bride and groom's arms, and they keep those ribbons on for the remainder of the events to signify their unity. Usually, the bride and groom's close family and friends attend the ceremony, while the extended family and friends skip this portion of the day. Once the ceremony is concluded, the bride and groom leave the church as traditional Assyrian dances are performed by everyone present. Rice, coins, and sweets are thrown at the couple as they walk toward their car before driving to the reception hall.

The couple waits for the guests to enter the reception hall first. The reception festivities will not begin until all the family members and most friends have entered the banquet hall. Then, the bride and groom are greeted at the door with music and dancing. The bride and groom's entrance is one of the day's biggest highlights. The more exuberant the welcome, the better. Memorable songs are composed just for this portion of the reception. Family and friends stand at the door and dance as they lead the bride and groom to their seats in a traditional Assyrian dance called Khigga, where everyone holds hands, forms a long line, and dances in a big circle. They use handkerchiefs called Yalikhta that are edged with beads and small bells to make noise, along with walking canes wrapped with white fabric and decorated with beads and bells called Kopali—we are boisterous people. The dancing welcomes the happy couple into the reception hall, and everyone breaks into traditional Assyrian dances once the couple arrives at their table. Most receptions continue until two or three in the morning, and some don't stop until sunrise. Assyrians are known for their extravagant and lively parties.

In some villages, people gather at the groom's house the night after the wedding for more celebration. This is a more casual event and comes with more dancing and eating. In other villages, this ritual continues for seven straight nights. Weddings are a significant event in my culture. They are one of the largest celebrations, from the fancy reception halls to beautiful gowns, unlimited food and cake, and endless hours of dancing.

* * *

"Rejoice with those who rejoice." Romans 12:15

BAGHDAD - 1983

"You were about a year old," Mom says as she retells one of her favorite yet disturbing stories. It was 2 a.m. when I woke up hungry, stood in my crib, and called for my mom. When she finally awoke, she turned the bedroom light on. "I will never forget the horrific sight," she grossly explains. Cockroaches covered the walls and the curtains behind me. They were nasty brown creatures, some dark, some with red spots that flew around the room, flapping their loud and long wings, traveling from one wall to the next. Terrified and disgusted, Mom reached for a towel, swatting them away from me. "I was mortified, but I tried to stay calm for you," she tells me as I chuckle despite feeling somewhat repulsed by the story. As a baby, I found the situation amusing as I laughed hysterically, thinking she was dancing to entertain me. Mom says my laughter eased her stress and made the night more bearable.

Mom has endured much during the first few years of marriage. When she returned from her week-long honeymoon, she moved into a small apartment with my father and his family. Thirty-one days later, he is drafted just as she discovers she is pregnant. Changes are taking place rather quickly and leaving very little time to adjust. But she learns that she is a strong woman who can overcome anything, facing each day as it comes.

It is customary for a newly married couple to move in with the groom's family for at least the first year of their marriage, if not longer. The tiny two-bedroom, one-bathroom apartment is shared with my grandparents, an aunt, and an uncle, who all sleep in one bedroom, while my mom and I live in the second bedroom. The apartment comes with a spacious living room. One part has a couch set with a small entertainment center that stores a small vintage television. The other part holds the dining table and a small freezer (most homes in Iraq have a small stand-alone freezer). There is also a small kitchen with a tiny refrigerator, eight cabinets, and four drawers. The apartment building has a broken elevator and is infested with giant, gruesome cockroaches that hiss and fly. As the cockroaches manage to find their way into almost everything, all the dishes, pots, and silverware must be washed before each use, even though they are clean and stored correctly in their cabinets. While Dad, the family protector, is in the Army fighting the ongoing war, Mom and I are left in this room with a bunch of filthy insects. Spending my first two years in this apartment and seeing them daily has left us with katsaridaphobia, or in simpler terms, a fear of cockroaches.

The cockroaches, however, are not the only distressing part of this apartment building. Friday morning, my family and I, along with hundreds of others, are awoken by a Mullah, a highly educated man in Islamic theology and sacred law. Our apartment building is located next to the mosque, one of many where Muslims gather for worship. Each city has multiple mosques with enormous speakers on each side of the building. One of these speakers is on the same story as our apartment and faces our bedroom.

In Muslim countries, Fridays are considered official holidays as they are Muslim's high holy days. Islam views Friday just like Christians view Sunday as a holy day. Every Friday morning, from eight until noon, the Mullah reads from the Qur'an for four hours. The readings are chanted and broadcast live from all the mosques. Living so close to the speaker makes Friday mornings, everyone's only day off, extremely challenging. All windows and doors are tightly shut, but the blaring mantra still weaves its way in. Everything we have tried has failed to tune out the piercing sound.

Being an Assyrian family in a Muslim country is highly frustrating as we are forced to endure this chanting every single Friday. Still, it is part of the norm and something we have accepted.

"Not by works of righteousness which we have done, but according to His mercy He saved us, through the washing of regeneration and renewing of the Holy Spirit." Titus 3:5

BAGHDAD - 1984

L iving in the shadow of the Iraq-Iran War, I do not have the opportunity to spend time with my father or genuinely get to know him for the first few years of my childhood. Due to his deployments, I have only seen him a handful of times. When he visits during his short leaves, he is a stranger to me, especially with his bald head, as it is customary for military men to shave their heads. This is different from the look I am accustomed to.

He is home again and has one week to cultivate our relationship. He tries to hug me, but I maintain my distance as I run to Mom and hide behind her leg. Seeing that Dad is struggling, she proposes a proven way to win me over. "Chocolate!" she suggests. "You should take a quick trip to the store and buy her chocolate; that will solve this problem."

With no hesitation, he immediately leaves and purchases several bars. He walks through the door, and my eyes meet his hand holding the delicious, heavenly delicacy. I am intrigued. He crouches down and extends a hand, offering the candy, but he wants a hug in return. Immediately, I agree as I wrap my arms around his neck, snatch the chocolate bar, and rush to the couch to enjoy it. He is slowly gaining my trust and love, but it isn't easy, and it's not happening quickly. It has taken him several visits and many chocolate bars to spark a connection. I am growing up fast, two years old, walking and talking, and he's missing it all. With his limited visits, he has to be creative, and chocolate is all the creativity he needs. This is the perfect beginning to a beautiful relationship as he always returns from war with chocolate.

I am one of the many children who live without their father. But unlike others, I am one of the lucky ones who get to welcome him home, as countless others aren't as fortunate. The Iraqi army always needs more soldiers to sustain the lengthy and destructive war that has been transpiring for the past five years. Thus, the government launched ongoing drafts of boys and men of all ages to aid the military and carry out Hussein's grudge against Iran. Boys as young as thirteen are taken out of school, given a rifle, and forced to fight for their country. Hate and anger are instilled in them at an early age. Their innocence slowly slips away with every use of the heavy artillery they are burdened with. Each bullet drains the life out of both the victim and the shooter. Parents cannot object to such atrocities as opposing the government's orders results in immediate execution. Week after week, I notice fewer boys in my neighborhood and more grieving mothers as they hug their innocent children, fully aware the next time they see them, their youthful spirit will be replaced with trauma, fear, anger, and hatred. Very few can avoid the military draft.

* * *

"I will be a Father to you, and you shall be My sons and daughters, says the Lord Almighty." 2 Corinthians 6:18

BAGHDAD - 1984

The city of Baghdad is overwhelmed by the darkness, the sirens, the explosions, and the blood each night. Despite the tragedies, the number of funerals each day, and the horror that covers my city every night, life resumes its normalcy during the day. While the Iran-Iraq War is playing like a movie in the background, I have to continue living with the rest of Iraq's citizens. I have to make the best of the hand Hussein has dealt me.

Saddam Hussein, a Sunni Muslim, is an intelligent and well-educated man who has faced suffering in his upbringing. Sunni is one of the two sects of the Islamic religion, the second being the Shia. Both sects worship Allah, follow the same ritualistic pillars, read the same holy book—the Qur'an, fast for Ramadan, and celebrate other religious holidays. However, the two sects have been at odds for ages. Following the death of the Prophet Muhammad, the founder of Islam, a dispute erupted regarding who should succeed him in both political and religious office. Sunni is the sect that believed Abu Bakr, a friend of Muhammad's and the father of his wife, Aisha, should succeed him. Shia is the sect that believed Muhammad's cousin and son-in-law, Ali, should succeed him. Their disputes continue to this day. Over time, the dissension has become less religious and more political.

Saddam prefers to be called "Uncle Saddam," a term forced upon me and everyone else in the country. I watch my family members of all ages address him as such out of fear. I never know who is listening to my conversations as Saddam has spies and secret agents throughout the country. It is much safer to submit and use the term imposed upon me than to defy and face torture and even execution. Uncle Saddam was born in 1937 to impoverished parents in a town just north of Baghdad. His father disappeared before Hussein's birth, making things even more challenging for his mother. Reportedly depressed at the time of his birth, she gave him the name Saddam, which means "one who confronts" or "one who frequently causes collisions." He grew to live up to his name. Because his home life with his mother was unstable and she could not care for him, Hussein moved in with his uncle, Khairallah Talfah, in Baghdad. Talfah was a former military officer and was politically active. His uncle's political ideology strongly influenced Saddam early in life.

As a young man in 1959, Hussein participated in a bloody, failed attempt to overthrow the prime minister and had to flee to Egypt for refuge. He attended law school there in the capital city, Cairo, until he could return to Iraq. Upon returning, he was given jail time for his previous political actions; however, that did not dampen his aspirations. After his release, his political career grew, and his influence increased. His ideas and leadership seemed promising and gave the citizens hope.

In the early years, before establishing his position as president, Hussein developed and implemented systems and programs that advanced Iraq and generated wealth for the country. He modernized the infrastructure, industry, and healthcare system. He positively impacted agriculture, education, and social services. Further,

Hussein nationalized the oil industry, which led to a massive revenue stream for the country. His efforts expanded his influence, enabling Iraq to stand apart from other Arab countries. The nuclear weapons program he developed increased attention to Iraq amongst other countries.

Hussein's charismatic and caring personality earned him the citizens' trust and love. He dedicated his life and career to building and improving Iraq. People pledged allegiance to him and enjoyed the many benefits of his policies. Early on, people were loyal to him as well as in agreement with the aspirations he had for the country. They had no reason to doubt. Soon, though, the facade of peace and progress would come to a screeching halt, with citizens left astounded by what they heard and saw. The seemingly abrupt shift from political savior to tyrant came as a shock to everyone.

Hussein's presidential support rested on the minority Sunni in Iraq, which made the Shia a threat to him. Events close to home fueled his fear of losing power when a Shia revolution erupted in Iran, a neighboring country, in 1979. The revolution was led by Ayatollah Khomeini, who then became Iran's supreme leader. Hussein feared the Shiites would rebel against him as they had in Iran. To prevent this, he declared a territorial dispute over a waterway and ordered an invasion of Iran on September 22, 1980. This developed into a bitter and bloody war.

* * *

"Like a roaring lion and a charging bear is a wicked ruler over poor people." Proverbs 28:15

Interlude - Being An Assyrian

Situated in the land between the two infamous rivers, the Tigris and Euphrates, are enormous ruins of cities that once made up a large empire with one of the strongest armies in the world. It was known as Assyria, an ancient civilization in Mesopotamia that unified tribal communities, established new ways of governing and developed advanced iron weapons ahead of its time.

The Assyrian Empire began as a regional power in the second millennium B.C. but later grew in size, power, and stature until its fall in the late seventh century B.C. at the hands of the Babylonians. The heartland of Assyria began in present-day northern Iraq, northeast Syria, southeastern Turkey, and northwestern Iran. Their history spans around 6,760 years. Assyrians speak Suret, a dialect of Aramaic, the language Jesus spoke.

The rich history is not only documented with much influence in urbanization, agriculture, and so much more but has also been referenced in the Bible on many occasions. In Isaiah 10:5-19, God calls the Assyrians "the rod of His anger." God also used the

Assyrians to punish the Israelites. One of the most recounted Bible stories concerning the Assyrians is the story of Jonah.

> "Now the word of the Lord came to Jonah the second time, saying 'Arise, go to Nineveh, that great city, and preach to it the message that I tell you.' So, Jonah arose and went to Nineveh, according to the word of the Lord." Jonah 3:1-2

Jonah, a minor prophet in the Old Testament, was called by God to travel to Nineveh to preach the message given to him. At first, Jonah refused and attempted to escape to another city in a boat. During the journey, the sea provided anything but smooth sailing. A great wind swept through the sea, resulting in a violent storm that threatened to break the ship and caused fear among the sailors. Though the ship crew lightened the boat by tossing their cargo into the sea, it was to no avail. Nothing helped until Jonah confessed; knowing his disobedience in running away from the Lord had caused this. The instant Jonah was thrown into the water, the raging sea calmed. A large fish swallowed Jonah, and he was in the belly for three days and three nights. While trapped, Jonah repented for his disobedience and was rescued from the fish and thrown onto dry land.

Jonah approached Nineveh and preached God's message. Nineveh's people, including the king, listened and turned from their evil ways back to God. In honor of God and their repentance, they fasted for three days. A three-day fast called "The Nineveh Feast" or "Somat Baoutha" is revered every February, honoring Jonah and God's mercy on the Ninevites, the Assyrians. Nineveh, Assyria's capital, is now called Mosul, located in modern-day Iraq. Assyrians celebrate these three days by fasting and praying—also considered "pleading"—to commemorate God's deliverance of Nineveh. At the end of the three-day fast, Assyrians attend a church service dedicated to Jonah and the citizens of Nineveh. The service is often long, and most hymns and readings are in the old Assyrian dialect, which is sometimes difficult to follow. Growing up, I'd often find myself zoning out during these lengthy services only to feel a nudge from my mother, letting me know it was time to stand in line and receive communion. Once the church service was finished, the congregation would gather in the church's open court, where a lamb was sacrificed, cooked, and served. To fast and attend church was considered a great honor for everyone in our church congregation.

Part of fasting in the Assyrian culture, be it a small one in honor of Jonah or Lent in honor of Christmas or Easter, excludes eating any animal products, thus becoming vegan during these fasts. Lunch and dinner consist of rice served alongside a vegetable dish. However, breakfast is more challenging as it is often served with eggs, yogurt, cheese, and bread. Breakfast is always offered with hot tea, as is customary in every Assyrian home. Serving tea brings a little humor as households commonly steep loose tea leaves in a small kettle, which rests on a larger kettle with boiling water. Once the two reach boiling temperature, a tea strainer filters the leaves before serving it. Every so often, a few stragglers travel into the cup. Floating tea leaves in a cup are jokingly interpreted as a sign that guests will visit that evening. Short leaves mean a short guest; long leaves suggest a tall guest. Often, when neighbors visit, family members exclaim, "See, your tea indicated you would have guests tonight."

Assyrians were among the first to accept Christianity in the first century A.D. through the Apostle Thomas. Despite the challenges Assyrians have faced and the subsequent conquest by Islam, they maintained their Christianity. Assyrians are Christians by birth and attend the Assyrian Church of the East. Though I have been taught many references to Bible verses and stories like Jonah, I have never read the Bible at home, nor have I witnessed my parents or any other family members, for that matter, reading the Bible. I'm raised to believe the Bible is a holy book that brings blessings onto the house, and I am not holy enough to hold it and read it. I am not allowed to move it from its sacred shelf and cannot write or highlight any parts of it. But as a child, knowing Assyrians are in the Scripture brings those stories to life and helps me better understand myself and my history.

My culture is distinctive in many ways. It has its traditions and rituals, some of which I am fond of, while others I find questionable. Nonetheless, all are uniquely ours.

For example, the Bible teaches that God completed the creation in six days and rested on the seventh day. Most Christian communities observe Sunday as a day of rest. The Assyrians also do this; however, our day of rest begins on Saturday evening, around sundown. Not only do we refrain from completing any tasks during the rest, but we also are not allowed to use scissors. Using scissors is thought to invite evil's presence.

Whenever we toss water from a cup, bucket, or anything else, we have to say, "Shi-mit Allah," which means "in God's name." We must say the same thing when crossing a small creek to repel evil. I'm unsure where this tradition originated, but it has been passed down for generations.

In Matthew 5:13, Christ calls believers "the salt of the earth"; thus, Assyrians ensure we don't waste nor spill any salt, especially on the ground where people can step.

Assyrians consider the feet the least dignified part of the human body. Most people spend time sitting on the floor socializing, eating, playing, etc. Having our feet directly face someone is a disrespectful gesture we must avoid. If we cannot prevent this, the individual with feet up needs to apologize to the person they are facing. People avoid placing their feet on the coffee table, desk, or any other furniture that will expose them to others, even if they wear socks and shoes. When taking our shoes off, we ensure the bottom of the shoe is facing down. Soles facing up is a disrespectful gesture towards God. Whenever I see shoes with the soles facing up, my first instinct is to correct them and turn them right side up. The practice is ingrained in me and all other Assyrians.

The Assyrians celebrate New Year on April 1, also considered the beginning of spring. Various clubs and churches host festivities on this day to commemorate the significance of the day and the continuation of the Assyrian civilization. Most people attending the events dress in traditional clothes and dance for hours. The women's outfits consist of long-sleeve velvet and mid-shin dresses in different colors and patterns. We wear them with a silver metal belt of rectangular plates connected by round rings. Belts have chains that dip from plate to plate. A necklace is latched to the center of the dress and extended to both shoulders. They are made of silver coins and are interchangeable with different dresses. We often wear bracelets and anklets made of silver coins as well. Women also wear a head cover, a long thin black scarf wrapped around the head, and then covered again with another headdress made of silver coins and chains. All these chains and coins create a clunking sound; the louder the outfit, the better. Most people do not own a complete ensemble as it is expensive; however, they can combine the pieces by borrowing from others. It is not customary to dress in the traditional ensemble unless all the details are available, and it isn't precisely required but is expected.

As for men, their traditional outfits are made of linen, mostly in dark colors such as black and navy. The pants and shirts are loose with wide legs and long sleeves. The clothes are covered by a full or knee-length tunic, usually white, and decorated with Assyrian symbols. Each tunic is embroidered with several crosses on the back, shoulders, or upper arms. A wrap serves as a belt to hold the tunic and the shirt in place. The outfit is completed with a black wool hat and a feather attached to one side.

Since the fall of the empire, the Assyrians have been victims of persecution for centuries. As a consequence of religious differences from Islam, Assyrians have become a minority due to the Assyrian genocide, in which the Ottoman Turks killed at least 250,000 Assyrians during World War I followed by the Iranian Revolution in 1979, Saddam Hussein, and so many others.

One of the horrific genocides commemorated by the Assyrians is Martyr's Day or Premta d'Simele. August 7, 1933, was a documented day in history when horrific and gruesome acts were inflicted upon the Assyrians at the hands of the Iraqi government, resulting in the death of 3,000 Assyrians. Whether young or old, they were all slaughtered by appalling methods. Their land, crops, and cattle were all stolen. Martyr's Day has become a day of remembrance of all the lives lost. In many major cities, people gather in large banquet halls to honor the deceased by sharing poems, featuring musicals, and performing traditional dances through songs about Simele. Every year, preparations for this event begin months in advance. Thinking back on what people in my culture have endured is heartbreaking. Honoring those memories is noble as it ensures we never forget our history.

I take immense pride in being Assyrian. Of all the cultures God could have chosen, I am grateful he placed me in this one. I am incredibly thankful for the rich Biblical history that comes with it.

"Woe to Assyria, the rod of my anger and the staff in whose hand is my indignation." Isaiah 10:5

BAGHDAD - 1986

T he sun always gives me hope. Hope to take another breath and live another day. Baghdad is very peaceful during the day. My everyday life is happy from dawn to dusk. Fear escapes me when the sunlight strikes my cheeks and my surroundings, uncovering every shadow and melting all my worries away. Soon, the night will fall, and everything will change as the shadows eagerly await to come out and play. Darkness covers the streets with occasional sparks of light and thunder caused by explosions. It has been six years since the war began back in 1980. Despite the casualties continuing to rise, the citizens keep holding onto hope. Hope that someday the war will end, that someday our family members will return safely.

"Someday" arrives much sooner for my family than we anticipated. Dad has been released from the Army. The military drafts have impacted every household and every occupation, particularly the education system. Schools need teachers, especially the all-boys schools since all their teachers are male and most have been enlisted. Being a mathematics teacher has become a blessing that saves my dad's life. His school needs math teachers and has requested his presence, and the government granted their request.

Having him home again is a welcome relief as he immediately resumes his teaching job at Miqdam High School. Within days of being home, Dad receives an offer to coach volleyball at the Assyrian club in Baghdad. He quickly accepts. Coaching and playing volleyball have been two of my father's many hobbies. The club trains at a private center with outdoor and indoor courts, showers, lockers for both men and women and a small one-bedroom apartment above the indoor courts. In exchange for coaching and maintaining the center, our family receives free housing in the tiny apartment where we will reside for the next two years.

The timing of this couldn't be better as my uncle, David, has taken an interest in a girl and has asked his parents to reach out to her family to discuss a marriage proposal. The family accepts the proposal, and with that, as we move out, Uncle David will move his new bride into the apartment with his parents, as is customary.

Upon arriving at the facility, I notice that it is gated and that athletes must drive .4 kilometers (1/4 mile) from the gate to the building. Large trees occupy most of the open spaces surrounding the facility. In the evenings, these trees gently sway with the wind, causing the leaves to shake. To most, this is a soothing sound, but to me, the sound is frightening and often induces nightmares. Living with ample space yet limited lighting makes the distance look very dark.

I jerk up onto my elbow, shove the blanket off me, and look around the room. It's a dark bedroom faintly lit by the moon peering through the window next to my bed, its shadows stretching to the corner where my parents are peacefully sleeping. My skin is sticky, and the sheets are damp from my sweat. As I adjust my eyes and calm my mind, assuring myself that I am safe, I realize my recurring nightmare is the culprit. In addition to the war nightmares, I have developed a new one that centers around the trees walking toward the window beside my bed. They shrink and expand as they approach, moving their larger branches up and down. This disturbing recurring nightmare scares me to my core every night as it continues for the duration of our time at this club. While it is my least favorite place at night, daylight gives it a beautiful makeover. The open fields with their green grass provide a peaceful solitude. The tall, beautiful trees, so frightening at night, offer solace and a cooling shade in the heat of the day.

Dad loves playing volleyball as much as coaching it. This new opportunity brings a sense of security since Dad's life in the military brought so many unknowns. His passion for the sport shows through as he coaches the athletes. Watching him work has also inspired me to develop a passion for it. I have started learning how to play and have been training with Dad. I spend my mornings observing the training sessions, intently listening to his remarks and feedback as he works with the young athletes.

As he coaches me, he can't help but reminisce of a time when he was a teenager and of his glory days as an athlete. While he was playing recreationally at an athletic center, a Chinese coach was in attendance and observed Dad's playing. He immediately recognized Dad's talent and recruited him to play for his professional team. Dad competed professionally for the next five years, traveling to other countries like Libya and Egypt.

During Dad's two years of coaching the Assyrian club, the Iraqi professional team invited another coach from China. Upon his arrival, he selected the best coaches in Iraq, 150 coaches in total, including Dad. After intensive screening and testing, two are chosen from the 150, and again, Dad makes the list. The national newspaper printed an article about the two selected coaches and their upcoming travels to Japan for further training. The family is beyond proud of Dad and his achievement, but our pride is short-lived. Two days after the article is published, we discover that Dad's name has been removed from the list and replaced by another simply because Dad is Assyrian, and his mother is Persian. This is not the first time he's been denied an opportunity due to his ethnicity and culture, crushing his hopes and dreams.

* * *

"Hope deferred makes the heart sick, but when the desire comes, it is a tree of life." Proverbs 13:12

BAGHDAD - 1986

Dictatorship. Many are familiar with the term, but perhaps only those who live under its shadow fully comprehend it. Many understand the definition of the word: "a political leader that controls every aspect of the country, be it the public or private behavior of the citizens." But far fewer grasp the reality. Indeed, in our situation, every aspect of life is controlled by the government and Hussein—Uncle Saddam.

After one month in jail, Ramzy, our family friend, has been released. He was arrested based on rumors that he spoke ill of the government. Tonight, he is at my house for dinner. "Please go to your room and close the door while the adults converse. You're too young for this conversation," Dad commands as he motions toward my room, which is only a few steps away from the living room where they sit. My parents know whatever Ramzy has to say will be too traumatizing for me, and they are right. Being a curious child, I can't just walk away. *I want to know the story.* I step into my bedroom, leaving the door open just enough to peer out and listen, focusing on every spoken word. With each gruesome detail, my stomach turns, sending a shaft of fear shooting down my spine. My skin crawls as I cringe, yet I continue to listen.

"During my jail time, I was questioned frequently, starved, and beaten," Ramzy told my parents. "The agents in charge of my case took my torture one step further. They placed the tip of an air pump in my...," he pauses and shamefully continues; "...they placed it in my anus and pumped air inside of me." I gasp as I hear his painful experience described in detail. The government inflicted excruciating torment and pain onto him, doing whatever they deemed appropriate. They used humiliation as a weapon, along with physical torture. No child should listen to such news, but this is also the reality of my world. A month into his imprisonment, Ramzy was found innocent and released. Retaliating against the government will only land him back in jail with more suffering. "Lucky to be alive" is the standard response. It is better to take the punishment and retreat home quietly than oppose the regime.

I have so many questions. *Are people capable of such atrocity? How can human beings be capable of this much anger and hate?* Unfortunately, my questions are answered as I hear Ramzy's stories among many others'. A dictatorship requires both excessive power and fear-instilling tactics. For the people to submit to Hussein, they must fear him first. He induces fear through painful and gruesome tactics that leave everyone with physical, emotional, and mental scars. Suffering alone and in silence, we never know whom to trust and whom to fear. We must speak highly of and respect Hussein, whether or not we agree with his decisions. Our opinion is of no value to him. Taking action against any decision leads to torture and potential execution. As civilians, our duty is to submit and obey; it is not up to us to judge any matter.

When a civilian criticizes Hussein or his regime, that individual often disappears shortly afterward, never to be seen again. Simply holding a negative outlook on the president, his decisions, and the government will result in immediate execution. The government does not need facts to capture an individual for questioning; mere suspicion will suffice. Anyone deemed suspicious is arrested, imprisoned, and tortured. Often, the questioning methods include beatings, scourging, starvation, electrocution, and more.

Survival requires cooperation, obedience, and silence. We find temporary refuge in our submission and in containing our thoughts and feelings, including mourning the death of a loved one. When the government murders individuals, family members cannot mourn their deaths. It is considered a crime to grieve for people killed by the regime. One must suppress sorrow and emotional pain to avoid seeming suspicious, as that will result in jail time, questioning, and torture to "confirm" one's innocence.

"It is an abomination for kings to commit wickedness, for a throne is established by righteousness." Proverbs 16:12

BAGHDAD - 1986

The FIFA World Cup begins today, bringing much excitement to Iraq's citizens, young and old. Soccer is the highest-regarded sport in Iraq and the Middle East.

Soccer games are displayed on every television. The game brings us joy, giving us the illusion of escaping our current reality. We lose ourselves in the spirit of sport and competition during those ninety minutes instead of the war playing in the background. Since Iraq has not participated in the World Cup, most have gravitated to other teams to support and cheer for. That is, until this year. It is 1986, and Iraq has just made history by qualifying for the tournament.

My family gathers for these games, especially when Iraq is scheduled to appear, and we watch and cheer. We celebrate with food, drinks, and soccer. This is a historical moment, something to be proud of. It gives me hope that there is more to Iraq than the war I have grown accustomed to. But that hope quickly diminishes as we watch the Iraqi team lose and face elimination. Although the experience is short-lived, the excitement lasts longer as we continue to gather as a family to watch the remaining teams battle it out.

The pride in Iraq's soccer team quickly turns into sorrow and disbelief as the horrifying news spreads throughout the country.

Back in 1984, Hussein's eldest son, Uday, was assigned as Iraq's Olympic committee president. He, too, shares his father's cruelty in controlling people as he instituted a horrific campaign of torture and humiliation of the Iraqi athletes upon their return.

Uday is ruthless with the athletes, especially the soccer players. When the Iraqi soccer team lost, it was understood that torture would likely accompany their homecoming. Knowing they would likely be taken directly to jail, many athletes dreaded their return home after these losses. Within days, Uday made an example of them, and news of it entered our homes. Some had their feet beaten with sticks until they could no longer walk. Some had feces smeared all over their faces. Others were enclosed in small caskets with nails pointed inward so their bodies were punctured as they suffocated, while some were placed with wild dogs to be torn to pieces. Many athletes lost their lives in the name of "sport" this year.

The government forces people with athletic talent in soccer to participate. Declining to do so leads to jail and torture. Few athletes in Iraq have escaped Uday's barbaric regime after he was established in this role. Many are emotionally and physically mortified from the abuse they endured at his directives. Those who survived fled the country, while others were not as fortunate. Dreaming of becoming a professional soccer player is a dangerous dream. I am thankful my father's athletic talent is volleyball instead of soccer.

Uday's brutality doesn't stop with the athletes. Horror stories of his atrocities circulate almost daily. One of the many stories that has resonated with my family and me is of a young, Assyrian couple. Each weekend, there is at least a wedding or two taking place within the city of Baghdad. At this particular friend's wedding, Uday Hussein and his friends attended the reception unannounced. They can do so because Hussein, his family, and his officials have full reign across everything, and no one dares to object. Uday spotted the young couple at the wedding and noticed the wife's beauty. He sent one of his men to ask the husband if he would give up his wife for the night. The husband declined. Uday, being the relentless man he is, asked himself, and the husband, yet again, refused. A few hours later, the couple left the wedding reception. While waiting in his car, Uday sped up and ran them over as they crossed the street, killing them both. This was their punishment for denying him his request.

Hussein's control impacts almost every aspect of our lives; it also directly impacted my father. As a young man excelling in school, my father had high hopes of completing his college degree in the subject he was most passionate about, chemistry. As his high school years concluded, he anxiously awaited the start of college. In Iraq, to continue education, especially college years, is a privilege not experienced by most. In addition to the very rigorous and challenging educational system, most men are drafted for war or lose their fathers in the war. Therefore, they must drop out of school to work and provide for their mother and siblings.

As the end of summer neared, my father began planning his college days and what the future had in store for him. His anticipation grew each day, and soon, it was time to start his studies. Early August morning, shortly after walking into the university, he is greeted with the news that would wipe away all his summer dreams and anticipation. School officials announced that the college had shut down the chemistry program, and his major was changed from chemistry to mathematics. Since the government needed mathematics teachers and my father had earned a high score in math, they ordered that he become a mathematics teacher. He had no choice but to follow through with what was already determined for him. Thus, he became a math teacher for the following fourteen years.

A dictator can carry out anything he desires with little to no opposition. Hussein, his sons, and their most trusted government officials do not stop with civilians and athletes; they continue to push their brutality one step further every day. They seek ultimate fear and respect not only by torturing civilians but also by targeting soldiers. The government believes torturing soldiers will strengthen them and build their resilience. Their extensive training is often brutal and lasts hours. Each soldier has a specific job within their branch, and most tasks are painful and cause extreme suffering. However, a few are lucky enough to have tolerable assignments.

My father is one of the lucky soldiers; he has been chosen to join the team of cooks for his army unit, an assignment far more palatable than most. He spends the majority of his days cooking and cleaning after everyone. This is a huge blessing. My uncle, David, is less fortunate. With each visit, we notice new beating marks and large purple bruises from the electric shocks he continues to receive as part of his grueling training. In his most recent visit, he tells us of the latest training session, as his unit leader forced a group of soldiers to dig six-foot holes in the ground. Once they completed the task, the leader placed a scorpion, a snake, and several deadly insects in each hole. Then he ordered the soldiers to remove their boots and socks and jump into one of the holes. If they refused to jump in, someone pushed them in. Once the soldiers were in, they had to remain in the hole until they were bitten. Their loud cries of pain upon being bitten served as the signal to pull them out and administer medical treatment. This sadistic exercise was said to build their tolerance and perseverance. Unfortunately, this is just one of many examples of Hussein's cruel methods at play in the military. Each day, we wonder if my father and uncle are still alive. We wait for their visits to see them standing before us as our answer. Although they seem physically well, their vacant, distant eyes tell a different story.

Saddam followed in the footsteps of his uncle, Khairallah Talfah, who raised and influenced him. He referred to Persians as "animals

God created in the shape of humans." Hussein held even more hatred and anger toward Persian immigrants and anyone born to a Persian parent. My paternal grandmother, Nana Marna, was born in Iran and immigrated to Iraq around the age of ten. Every government document is stamped with a specific mark to identify that my father was born to a Persian woman, even though his father is an Iraqi citizen. When Hussein hates someone or something, so must everyone else; hence, people of Persian descent face much discrimination.

My father graduated in the top fourteen of his class after completing his bachelor's degree. The university recommended moving him along to continue his education and pursue a master's degree. He was asked to take a test that all graduate prospects had to successfully complete. Dad passed in the top ten in the country. This was an impressive accomplishment, and he was placed on the list to continue his education. However, the government stepped in and removed his name from the list because he was a Christian Assyrian, and his mother was Persian. Two strikes and he was out. They replaced him with a Muslim student whose father was a government official.

Individuals with Persian parents do not have the full "rights" of other citizens, even if they are born in Iraq and have Iraqi citizenship. This severely impacted the lifestyle my father and his siblings experienced growing up. Hussein even formed a military unit composed only of soldiers born to non-Iraqi parents, as he did not want them to be associated with the rest of the military. He forced them to march along the country's northern side, which is much closer to Iran, the most dangerous zone. This unit is secluded from the rest of the military and has to fight without protection from the army. Of course, this is my father's unit.

Listening to stories daily and watching my family members suffer has created a deep-rooted fear within me. *What if someday I stumble upon him? What if I am at a wedding, and he shows up? How will I protect myself? What will happen to me?* Fear of torture and death grips my mind. When most children my age are worried about their next day at school, their next outfit, or their extracurricular activities, I am concerned about survival. *How do I survive unscathed?*

*   *   *

"Her princes in her midst are like wolves tearing the prey; to shed blood, to destroy people, and to get dishonest gain."
Ezekiel 22:27

BAGHDAD - 1986

I take a deep breath as I realize my parents have begun searching for a new home, a bigger one, since my mother announced her pregnancy two days ago. Being an only child has had its benefits. I am my maternal grandparents' first granddaughter and my paternal grandparents' first grandchild. I experience the love most people can only dream of.

My "only-child" status will be revoked at three and a half years old. Still, I am overly excited to share my world with a sibling but also excited to move out of the training facility's tiny apartment. Moving means no more frightening trees at night. I can finally have a night free from nightmares. Despite the disruption the bombings have brought to our war-stricken lives, we have, in many ways, grown accustomed to them; bracing for them has become a part of our daily routine. Fearing them has become part of my existence. The trees, however, create a fear in me I cannot overcome as I battle that alone.

After a brief search, my parents find a house for rent 1.6 kilometers (1 mile) away. Excitement overwhelms me as I help pack our few belongings. Saying goodbye to the tiny one-bedroom apartment cannot come soon enough. No more bed by the window overlooking the terrifying trees; we will be gone within a week.

The two-story house we move into is designed for two families to occupy. The landlords, who are Muslim, live on the second floor with their two young children, while my family rents and lives on the first floor. We share the front door, but everything else is separate. Like most houses, including poor housing developments, this home is constructed with upscale marble tiles, as marble is easily found in the mountains and is financially accessible to most. It also has concrete and brick walls that help to maintain the heat during the cold winter days and stay cool during the hot summer months.

It is our first Sunday in this home, so it's time for our weekly family gathering this afternoon. This time, my family is the one hosting. In this new house, we have enough kitchen and living space to finally be a part of the house rotation for family dinners, a tradition that started years ago. My family gathers around food, drink, and music each Sunday. Mom is the fourth of six children. Two of her siblings live in America, and because they left before I was born, I only know of them. As for the remaining three aunts, I have grown up with them and their families.

My anticipation is high today because I will share my living space with some of my favorite people, especially my eldest aunt's three sons. Though they are older than me, we are best friends. Shortly after I finish helping Mom in the kitchen, I begin the preparations for my cousins' and my entertainment. I snatch the dish soap from the kitchen sink and squirt it throughout the shower room, covering the tiles. The shower rooms are built separately from the toilet room. Ours is a small 1.5 by 1.8 meters (5 by 6 feet) room with tiled flooring, a showerhead, and two faucet knobs extending from the wall. We rarely use the knobs to shower as they both produce cold water. Water heaters are a luxury only for the government elite and the rich. Typically, Mom warms water in a large pot over the stove, dilutes it with cold water, and pours it over me as I sit on a stool in the middle of the room.

On this day, I lather the floor with an abundance of soap. As soon as my cousins step foot in our house, they rush through the hall to find me and quickly strip down to their swim trunks, ready to slide. I splash the floor with water, and the fun begins. We slip and slide from wall to wall. The ground is soapy and bubbly, covered in foam. We are overwhelmed with laughter as we spin around the room. We spend hours playing, only stopping when someone gets hurt, usually from colliding with someone else or one of the walls. When the crying starts, the fun ends. This becomes a tradition for all future visits as our shower room is more prominent than others', offering us more space to slide and collide. Though injuries are inevitable, we willingly take the risk each time we're together.

My mother has a large family and an even larger extended family with endless cousins and relatives. Through our gatherings, I am beginning to learn the value of family and togetherness. With the war going on in the background, being with family brings a sense of security and, somehow, makes it bearable. I know I am not alone. I can look around the room at the smiling faces and know I am okay. Though fear cripples each person, our countenance portrays otherwise. There's an understood perspective we all hold to be true. *The war may ravage our country but will not fracture our family, bond, or routine. We will live a positive life despite everything happening in our environment because we have each other.*

Familiar and agonizing labor pains strike Mother, preceding the imminent arrival of my first sibling. At this point, I am unaware if I'll be getting a baby brother or sister. The medical industry does not have the advanced technology to identify the baby's gender or even their health, for that matter. Mother's pregnancy seems uneventful; even the birthing process is smooth and seamless compared to what she endured with my arrival. Better yet, my father is present, standing by my mother at the hospital. The moment my paternal grandmother, Marna, discovers I have a baby sister, she rushes to the hospital to make a request.

Since my parents' wedding, my grandmother has been hoping for granddaughters. Although grandsons are the preference in Iraqi culture, she sincerely wants at least one granddaughter to name after her own mother, my great-grandmother, Sona. The name means *seagull* in Assyrian. When I was born, Nana Marna didn't push to have me named Sona since I was my parents' firstborn, and she thought they should be free to choose my name. But when Mom's second child was another girl, all bets were off. How could my parents turn down such a sweet request from a petite woman who has suffered much in her lifetime?

* * *

"But above all these things put on love, which is the bond of perfection." Colossians 3:14

URMIA - 1941

"There was a bread-baking room in the quiet little village of Urmia," Nana Marna shares sorrowfully in her soft and gentle voice. Hearing her reminisce, I can't help but feel her pain as she recalls her heartbreaking childhood stories.

The town of Urmia, Iran, was primarily inhabited by Assyrians. The bread-baking room had a small hole in the ground where charcoal residue from the baking was ever-present. Every week, the villagers gathered sticks, dropped them in the hole, and lit them on fire. The familiar, comforting scent of fresh dough permeated the village, and everyone was familiar with the smell. No one in that little village ever imagined the baking room would be used to burn grown men alive.

Islamic Extremists often raided small Assyrian villages, and on one terrible day in 1941, Iranian Islamic soldiers invaded Urmia without warning. This time, they rounded up the men, one by one, and threw them into the bread-baking room. A soldier lit the fire, locked them in, and casually walked away. Screams rose from the women and children whose husbands, fathers, and sons were left to die. With the men out of the way, the women and children of the little village were left defenseless, alone, and at the mercy of the Islamic soldiers.

As the soldiers spread fear and terror through the village, a few seized several young girls. Kicking and screaming, girls were ripped from their mother's arms and dragged into the soldiers' vehicles. Some were pulled by their thick, dark hair, while others were simply scooped up and dropped into cars. With the men trapped and left to die in the bread-baking room, no one could defend the young women or fight for them. Even the government was no help as government agents carried out this raid. The Assyrian people were often left completely defenseless and hopeless.

Against the odds, Bejan, along with the other village men, put the fire out and escaped the bread-baking room. He returned to his home and family with great relief, only to learn what he had lost that morning— his young daughter, Mere.

Mere, sixteen years old, was one of the girls taken captive. Life would never be the same for her little family. She was the oldest of three sisters and one brother. Though her mother's days were sour and mournful after that awful morning, Sona, my great-grandmother, held out hope that her Mere was still alive, somewhere out there, waiting to come home.

One morning, years later, there was a faint knock on the front door. When Sona opened it, her heart leaped for joy to see Mere. Her long-lost daughter was standing at the doorstep with three young children, tears running down her face. Sona embraced her as tightly as she could, hardly believing that her daughter was alive and back home again. After the warm and tearful reintroduction, Mere shared the full story of the morning she was taken and the years that followed. The soldier who had captured her tossed her into his vehicle and later took her to his home, where his two wives and multiple children lived together. He repeatedly raped her, impregnated her, and eventually took her as his third wife. Defenseless and alone, she realized that she had to participate in the charade to survive, as fighting him only led to more beatings, abuse, and additional raping.

With her survival instincts heightened, she convinced him of her cooperation and obedience. She seduced him and caused him to fall in love with her. Soon, he loved her more than his first two wives, significantly improving her living conditions. Over time, she bore him three children: two girls and one boy. He never allowed her to leave, but he did provide her with a comfortable lifestyle. Mere did what was necessary to survive and protect her children. Eventually, her "*husband*" passed away from an illness, releasing her from captivity to return home with her three children.

Though her daughter had suffered for years, Sona was thrilled and grateful that she was alive, praising God for His grace and her daughter's safe return home.

Although this was a joyous occasion, not everyone welcomed Mere as her mother did. The rest of the family shunned Mere, especially her brother, because she had remained married to her captor until his death. They blamed her for not attempting to escape, even though they knew full well that doing so could have led to more punishment and, ultimately, her death. Mere's homecoming was bittersweet. Embraced by her mother and youngest sister, Flora, yet shunned by her brother, she also discovered that her other sister was gone. "Where is Marna? I want to see her and hug her," Mere inquired.

"She doesn't live here anymore. She moved to Iraq a long time ago." Sona replies with a mournful voice.

"How did that happen? What's in Iraq for her?" Mere asks. Shocked at the news.

"Shortly after your abduction, I received a message from your grandfather in Iraq asking me to send Marna to his sister's house so she could care for her."

Marna was ten years old when her mother, Sona, received this call. Sona's paternal aunt had broken her leg in an accident and needed someone to care for her as her children worked and could not meet their mother's constant needs. Since Sona was the oldest girl, it was customary for her to comply and fulfill her father's wishes. Children are culturally expected to obey their parents and their elders' wishes at any cost and at any age. Refusing to do so is considered disrespectful and unheard of. Sona packed her ten-year-old daughter's small suitcase and shipped her off to Iraq with a group of illegal smugglers who traveled between the two countries and were strangers to Sona and Marna. This was extremely hard for her to do, especially after losing Mere, but she found no other option. Sona was down two daughters, and her heart was distraught, but she had to find the strength to continue to care for her family.

When Marna arrived in Kirkuk, located in the northern region of Iraq, she was greeted by her grandfather and taken to meet her great aunt, Suren, and the family. She was a stranger to them, having never met anyone except for her grandfather, whom she had only seen a few times when he could endure the long journey between the two countries by crossing the mountains. Traveling between Iraq and Iran was limited, and it required more significant financial means.

In her new situation, Marna could no longer attend school. Instead, she had to meet Suren's every need: cooking, cleaning, laundry, and anything else asked of her. While growing up in Urmia, she had spent most of her days running and playing with friends on the various farms the families owned within Urmia's borders. She wasn't prepared for domestic life, nor did she need to be at this age, but almost overnight, her life had changed forever.

Marna had never cooked or washed laundry before, but now she had to learn, and she had to learn fast. She introduced herself to the neighborhood ladies and sought them out for advice and cooking lessons. She collected the laundry in a large basket and pulled it behind her all the way to the river to wash the clothes alongside the other women in her neighborhood. At first, Marna rubbed the clothes between her hands so hard she began to bleed, rubbing the skin off until one of the ladies saw the blood dripping down.

"Child, what are you doing?"

"My hands hurt, and they're bleeding."

"Oh, child...you should not rub the clothes against the palm of your hand. Instead, lay one side of the fabric on one palm and rub the other side of the fabric against that, not on the bare skin of your hand."

Marna also had to learn the language. Her immediate family spoke Suret at home, but the non-Assyrians in Iran spoke Persian, and in Iraq, people spoke Arabic. So, Marna had to learn Arabic to communicate with others and grocery shop for the family. Even though her cousins were older than she was by at least five years, she was the one who had to cater to everyone's needs.

Despite everything, one of the things she missed and craved the most was a mother's touch, especially after being separated from her mother at a young age. Looking for some affection, she would beg Suren to hold her and let her sleep next to her at night. Suren's answer was almost always "no." Occasionally, Suren allowed her to lie next to her for five minutes before asking her to get up and move on. Marna wasn't sure if these brief moments of comfort made her feel better or worse.

Having no choice, Marna quickly adjusted to her new life and made the best of it. After years of living with Suren and her family, learning a new language, and learning how to take care of a household, Suren and her husband decided to marry her off to their son, who was five years older than she was. Though Marna had no say in the matter, their son did, and he refused to accept their offer.

"She has been living with us for the past seven years. She's like a sister to me. How can you ask me to marry her after living with us for so long?"

Marna was relieved to hear his declaration and was grateful he did not want to marry her. Several families asked for Marna's hand in marriage after that, but Suren declined every one of them, hoping her son would change his mind. The neighborhood ladies were disappointed when they found out about Suren's intentions. Women talk—especially when they are out doing laundry together. Soon, the neighborhood women were revolted to learn that Suren only wanted Marna to continue serving them and maintaining the lifestyle the family had grown accustomed to. After learning this, the neighborhood ladies took Marna under their wings and cared for her as their own daughter.

"Child, you need to be careful. Suren doesn't have your best interest at heart. All she wants is to marry you off to her son so you can continue being the family's maid."

Marna was heartbroken and disappointed to find out the truth. After years of giving her life in service to them, this is how they were planning to repay her. Unable to provide for herself financially, she could not travel back to her home or family, nor did she have the ability to contact them to ask for assistance. "I don't know what to do. I have nowhere to go and no other family in Iraq," Marna told them in desperation.

"Are there any distant cousins or anyone close to your family living in Iraq?" the ladies prompted. Marna began searching for family, and after months of asking Suren and other Assyrians nearby, she located a distant cousin who lived in Baghdad and decided to visit her. Marna packed her bag and left the house with no intention of returning. She did not mention anything to Suren's family.

While staying with her cousin, a family friend came for a visit. He saw that she was lovely and took a liking to her, so he decided to ask for her hand in marriage for his nephew, Raman. Marna agreed to meet with Raman and found him charming and attractive. After a few outings, she agreed to the marriage proposal. Back then, dating was a foreign concept that rarely took place. Marna and Raman married on May 7, 1955, when she was seventeen. Raman became her prince, her rescuer who loved her unconditionally and provided her with the life she had dreamed of.

Although she happily married Raman, things were far from "happily ever after" with her in-laws. Her father-in-law despised Marna because she was uneducated and had lived much of her life as an enslaved person. He didn't deem her worthy of his educated, hardworking son. He mentally and emotionally abused her throughout the time they lived together. During his son's absence, his abuse took place since he knew Marna would never mention a word of it to Raman to avoid causing any disturbance within the family. His instincts were right; she kept it all to herself. She never told Raman when her father-in-law wrapped her long, dark hair around his hand and smacked her head against the wall because she had lost some of the dress shirts he asked her to launder and press. Later, she discovered he had hidden them and assaulted her because he despised her. After the beating, he kicked her out of the house with her two young boys. Crying, she carried her sons in her arms and walked to the home of a family friend who lived nearby. Raman knew nothing about this until he returned from work to a tranquil house that evening. When he demanded an explanation, his father briefly explained what had happened. Raman ran to where Marna was staying and begged her for forgiveness. He was mortified at what had happened in his absence and could not believe Marna's strength in enduring it all alone to avoid family disputes. Raman was able to convince Marna to return home with their two sons.

Not long after, tired of the abuse she endured, Marna's mother-in-law decided to leave her abusive husband, taking her daughter with her and leaving her three sons behind. Her abrupt departure forced Marna to care for her abusive father-in-law for the rest of his life. A few years later, he was diagnosed with cancer, and he became so helpless that he had to depend on Marna for almost everything. She cared for him as if he was her father and never treated him with anything but respect. As he lay on his deathbed, helpless, he sought her forgiveness. "After everything I have done to you, you have treated me better than most of my family members. Please forgive me for what I have done." She gracefully forgave him and cared for him until his final breath.

After eighteen long years of living in Iraq, Marna could finally return to Iran to visit her family. She took her two older boys—my father, James, and Uncle David. By the time she could visit, her father had passed away.

Although my grandparents have faced extraordinary challenges throughout their lifetime, they have a wonderful marriage and enjoy their life together. They make each other laugh despite the circumstances. She knows what makes him happy and what upsets him, just as he knows the same about her.

"Being married for so long, I can't think of a time when we've argued or had a marital dispute. We have a unique marriage. I stay clear of anything that provokes him, and he does the same for me. He always asks me if anything broke my heart so that he can repair it. He never wants anyone to break my fragile heart," my Nana Marna tells me.

Though my grandmother, Marna, led a life full of hardships, she always chose compassion over revenge and showed mercy where mercy was not expected. She often recites her and her sister's stories in a soft and mournful voice. I was four when I heard it for the first time, and since then, the tragedies have left a lasting impression. I can't even count the number of times I have listened to these stories, yet their impact is always the same. They leave me feeling sorry for Nana Marna and grateful for my childhood. Even though I am living through a war at a young age, I still have a better life than she and many other women have had.

* * *

"When my father and mother forsake me, then the Lord will take care of me." Psalm 27:10

BAGHDAD - 1987

It's Thursday morning, and I am spending the night at my paternal grandparents' tiny apartment, as I have done every week since we moved. These sleepovers are bittersweet but mostly sweet. Staying with Nana Marna means feasting on her delicious cooking. Her meals are always savory and rich in flavor. I look forward to her cooking, especially one of my favorite meals of white rice with carrots and beef stew simmered in curry. This is followed by my favorite dessert, Halwa, made up of three simple ingredients: flour, oil, and date syrup. They create a heavenly delicacy, and I savor each bite before swallowing.

Although I love my grandmother very much, my bond isn't as strong with her as it is with my grandfather, Baba Sawa, with whom I spend most of my time. My grandfather is an exceptional soul: gentle, loving, and cuddly. I affectionately call him Baba Sawa, which means "Old Dad." The name has caught on, and the rest of the family now uses it. He loves his name. Baba Sawa is a big teddy bear. He is tall and well-built. When he wraps his arms around me, I feel complete peace. His hugs are full of compassion and make me feel safe.

Being his first grandchild, he often reminds everyone I made him a grandfather. At their house, a long brown and green couch rests against the wall across the TV. To the far left, near the window, is Baba Sawa's favorite spot to sit. He is very particular about his spot as he leans against the carved wooden armrest. No one dares to sit there except for me. He allows me the freedom to push the envelope and get away with anything and everything. Whenever I take a nap, if anyone is home, they have to be extremely silent and tiptoe around the apartment until I wake. No one risks speaking loudly while I sleep. If they do, they have to answer to my Baba Sawa.

When together, we are inseparable. We spend most of our time playing card games, especially Koncan, similar to Gin. I don't understand most of the rules, but I have a workaround. I developed my own rules, and, unsurprisingly, since I made up the rules, I won every round. I don't think he's won yet. He follows the bizarre rules I invent and pretends to make sense of everything. I love sitting beside him while playing or watching TV and cuddling with him and my special blanket. He is my bodyguard, providing me with serene safety in a chaotic world.

This particular Thursday, Nana is doing laundry, the most dreadful house chore in my upbringing, but not for the reasons you may think. Yes, most laundry has to be washed by hand, rubbing the fabric between hands until all stains are removed, but that's not what bothers me. It is the drying process I dread. Clothes have to be hung on ropes using clothespins. Nana doing laundry means washing my blanket, Halla, an Assyrian word for "give it." Soft and fluffy with blue and white checkers and satin trim, Halla is the most important belonging in my life.

Nana just took my Halla from me. It doesn't take long for my restlessness and anxiousness to take over as I pace around the apartment. Cuddling next to Baba Sawa seems impossible now. After a minute of washing, which felt like an eternity, she hangs it on a rope on the small balcony. Sitting still is hopeless; pacing and looking out the window and onto the balcony is all I can fathom. So Baba Sawa, being the fantastic grandfather he is, steps towards me, takes my little hand, and leads me to the balcony. Hand in hand, the two of us walk back and forth through the skinny concrete balcony as I impatiently wait for my Halla to dry. Touching the satin each time we walk past it is soothing. It is not unusual for my grandfather to go out of his way for me like this.

However, there is one crazy quirk he is unwilling to break, not even for me, which sometimes makes my sleepovers bitter. He habitually does not allow us to drink anything, including water, while eating lunch or dinner. He is adamant that liquid will fill our stomachs and cause us to eat less. Therefore, drinks are only allowed after finishing our meal. I have difficulty adhering to this as a kid, especially when eating rice or bread and needing something to help me swallow. This habit is only carried out at his home, so I only have to adhere to it for twenty-four hours a week. Breakfast is the only exception, as we are allowed to have tea at this meal. Tea is a traditional staple beverage that is always served with breakfast. Despite his quirkiness and some of his silly habits, he is our family protector in the most loving way possible.

"Children's children are the crown of old men, and the glory of children is their father." Proverbs 17:6

BAGHDAD - 1988

Sharing a house with another family was never the long-term goal for my family as it has its drawbacks. The landlords have more privacy, living on the second floor while we watch them and their guests come and go, trudging through our living room each time. We enjoy living with them but don't enjoy the communal aspect of the house.

Teachers receive exclusive benefits from the government. One of which is land given as a gesture of gratitude from Hussein. My parents have patiently waited for my father's portion of land so we can build a home at no cost. It has been months since the application was submitted. Dad has witnessed so many of his fellow teachers receive their benefits, yet no land for us. Week after week, he finds out more plots have been distributed, but he and several Christian Assyrian teachers with Persian parents are still waiting. After several inquiries, Dad is informed he will not receive the land after all. Being a biracial, Christian Assyrian teacher has resulted in the benefit being withheld. The government has blatantly discriminated against my father and several other teachers, and retaliation will only endanger my family. This is where my parents consciously decide to seek the safer route, renting a house and paying for it ourselves.

In Mom's extensive search in our neighborhood and the surrounding cities, she stumbles upon a home in the same suburbs as our current one. This house is bigger than anything I have lived in. It has seven bedrooms and three rooftops used as additional living space, one shower room, and two toilet rooms. The toilet room is a small 1 by 1.2 meters (3 by 4 feet) space with a ceramic hole in the ground in the shape of the toilet seat, but not one we can sit on. Instead, we squat to pay our dues and then wash using the short hose attached to a faucet extending from the wall next to the squat toilet. Strong thighs and glutes are the byproducts of this tiny little room.

Again, it doesn't take long to pack and move, especially with so many cousins and family members. We complete the entire process in one day. Occupying the entire house means freedom, as we no longer have to share any part of it with others. The roofs are flat and surrounded by a concrete fence, standing at 1 meter tall (3 feet), preventing the neighbors from looking in. More recently, since the missiles and bombings shifted from Baghdad to cities and villages near the Iran-Iraq border, we are able to sleep on the roof in the hot summer. Most homes do not have an air conditioner, and the temperature can reach as high as 48° C (118° F.) Sleeping on the roof requires moving the bed frames, mattresses, pillows, and blankets to the roof before lining them up next to each other and hanging mosquito nets over each bed. During the day, we fold the bedding and cover it with a large blanket. In the evening, we lay the bedding out and lightly spray the beds with water as the cool evening breeze blows to speed up the cooling process.

This house is much more upscale than anything else I have lived in. The rent for this new house exceeds Dad's teaching salary. So, Mom, being an entrepreneur, launches a small daycare to earn additional income. She also finds random jobs she can do from home that pay by the number of pieces completed. For instance, she has our family paint the dots onto dominos. The factory mass-produces the white blocks with small circular indents. We cut and paint those blocks. My assigned task is filling the indentations with black paint using syringes as I gently place the needle in the indentation and carefully release one drop of color at a time. Every evening, as a family, we spend hours working. I nervously hold the syringe in my right hand and use my left one as a stabilizer. Spilling the paint outside the designated area will create a challenging mess to clean as the paint quickly stains the white plastic. I know this because I have made the mistake several times and have had to eliminate those pieces, which means no payment for them. This is a lot of pressure for a six-year-old to experience, but I push past my feelings as helping my family trumps everything. Once the paint dries, Dad uses pliers to clip each block off the plastic centerpiece that holds the blocks together. My parents, Sona, and I all participate in this family event. We produce hundreds of these pieces to satisfy the company's weekly quota.

Mom also designs decorative sandals to hang on walls. Using cardboard, she creates a template of an Arabian-style sandal. I help cut out the shapes and then cut fabric to glue onto the cardboard. Once the two pieces are glued together, Mom decorates them with various sequenced materials and beads. She always sells out of them. I take pride in seeing Mom's workmanship, with my assistance, hanging in homes as art. We creatively find ways to muddle along to stay afloat. All the hard work is worth our home and the freedom it brings.

* * *

"When you eat the labor of your hands, you shall be happy,
and it shall be well with you." Psalm 128:2

BAGHDAD - 1988

It's midnight, and I can't fall asleep; the anxiety of the first day of school is overwhelming. I'm tossing and turning for what seems like an eternity, but then my restlessness is disrupted by the dreaded siren. Within seconds, my parents are in the room Sona and I share. Lost in confusion, each parent grabs one of us and rushes to the living room, crouching in the corner, nervously waiting for the earth-shattering sounds of missiles that will soon continue demolishing my city. I sit in my father's lap, feeling his arms tightly wrapped around my body. With each thunder, our bodies jolt. No thunderstorm compares to the sound of a missile coming in contact with concrete. Darkness surrounds us but is occasionally pushed back by a brief burst of light coming from each explosion. My heart beats so intensely that it feels like it may burst through my chest. With each explosion, we face potential death. *When will the missile hit my house?* I must remind myself that the war has become a nuance that occasionally disrupts our lives and sleep. Normalcy will resume shortly after the second siren blares its resounding wail.

The siren finally sounds off at 3 a.m., indicating we can return to bed. We have three hours before we have to wake up to prepare for school and work. We must continue on regardless of our circumstances. Life in the daylight is good; it is happy, and most of our time is spent with family and friends. With the exception of a few newly demolished buildings that lay in ruins, we can go back to pretending everything is normal. But that "normalcy" recedes as the sun goes down on another day.

After the night we had, 6 a.m. comes relatively quickly. I am excited and groggy as I roll out of bed with a spring in my step. I promptly put on my uniform, a white button-down shirt and a sleeveless navy jumper that covers my knees. Schools nationwide require uniforms, including the boys who wear navy slacks with a white button-down or polo shirt. During the winter, girls wear white leggings, the only color allowed. Any type of jewelry, including necklaces, bracelets, rings, or earrings, is forbidden.

This is the moment I have been waiting for. War or not, I am starting school today. My parents excelled in school, so I have big shoes to fill, yet I am up for the challenge. Mom and I stride down the street. I hold onto her hand and listen to her reiterating the importance of my education. We reach my school minutes before the first bell rings at 7:30 a.m. I hug Mom and rush in without looking back. *This is my time to shine.*

I have heard numerous horror stories of the school system and its rigidity, but I only fully grasp the magnitude of it now. I remember Dad coming home and sharing the reality of expelling a student from his math class for using a calculator, despite the repeated warnings not to do so. The Iraqi government has forbidden calculators from schools. Any student found with a calculator in their possession receives a warning. If this behavior becomes a repeated offense, they are expelled and fail the grade. Being a mathematics teacher at Miqdam High School for fourteen years, my father encounters many students with a calculator despite knowing the consequences. Unfortunately, he cannot show leniency as it will be considered a violation of government rules. Instead, students must use the blank paper they are given to solve the problems and show their work.

My elementary school is co-ed, which is the only level of education where the two genders are together. The rest of the levels are separated. This is another rule imposed by the government that no one dares to defy. My school begins in early August and finishes at the end of May, with finals taking place during the first week of June. I have to learn to prepare for finals as early as first grade. The class schedule is announced on the first day of school and remains the same for the remainder of the year.

Silently walking into the room, I stand against the wall with the rest of the students, waiting for the next set of instructions. "This is your new classroom; now, I will determine your seating assignment," the vice-principal tells the class. "You may not change seats without my permission," she continues. The structure is beginning to feel like a prison. Listening to my parents and other family members discuss the rigorous school system is one thing, but experiencing it myself is entirely different. It's hard to comprehend the *"child prison"* I've been subjected to. I feel my childhood freedom slowly slipping away, but I keep telling myself, *It's okay. It's nothing I can't handle.*

"Ramina." I hear my name called. My heart slams against my ribs. "Here," I softly answer, avoiding eye contact.

"Take a seat," she says, pointing to the middle-row front desk, her face stoic as she visually inspects my uniform. My desk is made of wood, big enough to seat two students, with two compartments to store my belongings and no back support. I use the desk behind me to prevent leaning forward all morning. I feel sad for the girls assigned to the back row, who have to use the cold concrete wall as their backrest.

Lost in my thoughts, I hear the name, "Naima," and watch her slowly saunter to my desk and take a seat. We smile at each other and accept our fate as deskmates for the year. I quietly sit up straight and watch each girl nervously walk to her assigned seat. My outcome has been decided; this is now my second home.

Everyone is seated, the room is quiet, and tensions are high. The vice-principal has one more task—assigning class monitors. Each classroom will have two monitors. Usually, they are selected based on attendance, attitude, and academic achievements. However, in first grade, the monitors are chosen based on relation to the vice-principal or other school staff. Since the teachers are the ones who rotate between classrooms, sometimes they are late or will skip attending class altogether. It is the class monitor's responsibility to stand in the front and maintain order within the classroom, ensuring everyone remains quiet till the teacher arrives.

I begin to feel dread rising within me. Fear is no stranger, but this is different. The anxiety the school system inflicts is directly affecting me and my every thought. One wrong move, and there will be consequences. I can't have that. Luckily, my love of education supersedes my fear of school.

The bell rings, and my first teacher steps into the classroom. Immediately, we stand up straight in honor of her presence, as is customary in all classrooms. She motions us to sit. She calls every student's name and gives us our textbooks. Hussein controls education. Students across the country learn the same subject at the same time and pace. There is no time to slow down for others to catch up. There is only time to keep up or fall behind and drop out. Teachers must follow guidelines and schedules set by the government. They also issue the same textbooks nationwide, passed down year after year until revised by the government. We all study the same material our parents did. After receiving six books on my first day of school, I am given one week to wrap them to preserve their condition. Failure to do so leads to a beating from the vice-principal. Luckily, most stores sell a variety of colored book-wrapping paper and plastic bags for added protection. Those who cannot afford wrapping paper must use brown, paper grocery bags to avoid the humiliation of being beaten with a stick.

I watch the clock tick, patiently waiting for it to strike noon. I am mentally exhausted and emotionally drained, and it is only day one. I must endure this for five more days before I can revel in my only day off, where I will be having a sleepover at the grandparents' house. Living in a Muslim country, citizens of all religions and belief systems must adhere to the governing Islamic rules and policies, including following their school and work schedules. Since Islam observes Friday as their holy day and only day off, school and work take place Saturday through Thursday for everyone.

I feel a sense of dread as I look down to see the white paper the vice-principal has just placed in front of me—my class schedule for the year. I have math and Arabic every day; everything else is set for twice a week. A ten-minute break between each class is all we get to use the restroom and eat a snack. Food and drinks are not allowed in classrooms and must be consumed in the hallway before the bell rings for the next class. Using the restroom seems next to impossible with three hundred girls released for break simultaneously and only one large bathroom with five stalls available. Stepping into the classroom after the bell rings leads to a scolding at the hands of the teacher. I have been free to eat and move about for six years, but now I must adjust and shift my mindset.

Starting with the first grade, students are introduced to subjects such as math, Arabic grammar, science, history, geography, and social studies. Each subject requires rigorous memorization. As my week slowly unfolds, I am beginning to absorb what my parents and family members spoke of. My math and Arabic teachers take the necessary time to teach each topic and ensure the students understand the material, allowing a bit of time for students to ask questions and interact with one another. As for the remainder of the classes, there is too much to be reviewed throughout the year to maintain pace with the government's schedule, so the focus is mainly on disseminating the information as quickly as possible, regardless of comprehension.

During the first class with each teacher, we are assigned several pages to learn at home for the next time we meet. Reviewing the material, I quickly realize this is more about memorization and less about comprehension. The following class, moments after her arrival, she poses a question and scans the room, looking for raised hands and students eager to answer the question. She calls on one of my classmates, and the student recites the answer verbatim to the book. Nodding with approval, she continues asking question after question. Occasionally, she calls on the students whose hands are not up. In doing so and in their subsequent failure to recite the material, she reaches for her wooden stick and asks them to extend their hands. I hear several snaps against the skin, followed by whimpers. At an early age, obedience and hard work are ingrained in students. Children are not allowed to be children at school; that is for home life. In school, we are programmed to be little soldiers of education.

My schedule also includes a mandatory Islamic religion class for the Muslim students only. The class is conducted twice a week. All non-Muslims must leave the classroom during this time. My Assyrian classmates and I stand in the open concrete courtyard in the middle of the school during the Islamic course, regardless of the weather and temperature. During the coldest days, we find shelter by huddling together, shivering, and anxiously waiting for the bell to ring so we can go back inside. Despite the cold reaching 5° C (41° F), I have found a blessing in this—it gives me time to study for my next class, especially if I have an upcoming quiz that day or week.

Even worse than the pressure my classmates and I experience daily, the two major tests we have to take each year are ever-lurking in the back of our minds. The first test occurs shortly after New Year's Day; the second is in June, at the conclusion of the school year. Passing these tests is crucial as we are not allowed to advance to the following grade without a proficient score. The first one includes the material we have absorbed from the first day of school in August until test day in January. The second one encompasses the entire school year from August to the last day of school in May. The second is the most important of the two, as failing this test results in failing the entire grade. If a student fails this one test, even if they receive high grades throughout the year, they will be required to repeat the entire grade.

There is another high-stakes element to these tests. A student who fails a subject at the end of the year must retake everything, including all of the courses within that grade, even the ones the student passed. It impacts every subject with no mercy. I already fear failing the test, and it's only the beginning of the school year. I am determined to study hard to prevent that from happening. Despite this stressful situation, I am grateful the government grants students one week off before finals to allow them time to study and prepare for such monumental exams.

The school allows students to retake a grade three times. If a student fails a class or one of the cumulative June tests three years in a row, the school expels them with no hope of returning. No reason is considered good enough to be granted an exception. Unfortunately, this system prevents many from completing their education.

My time off during the school year is very limited outside of Fridays. The most extended break occurs during the Eid al-Fitr Islamic holiday, which roughly translates to "Festival of Breaking the Fast." This is a week-long celebration where schools and businesses are closed for the entire week. In the month leading up to this holiday,

Muslims observe a fast called Ramadan, which occurs in the ninth month of the Islamic calendar. They fast in honor of the revelation of the Qur'an to the Prophet Muhammad. The fasting happens daily from dawn to sunset for twenty-nine to thirty days, depending on the month.

Although, as an Assyrian student, I enjoy having an extra week off as Muslims celebrate their holiday, the month leading up to it comes with a dreaded ritual. Muslim families wake up as early as 4 a.m. to prepare breakfast, which must be consumed before dawn. They then refrain from food and drinks until sunset. To ensure everyone is awake and cooking early in the morning, they have a unique alarm system—an individual with a bedug drum strapped around his neck, which he strikes with two padded mallets. The bedug drum is a barrel with leather padding on both sides, causing a deep, dull sound that can be extremely loud based on how hard the drummer thumps the mallets. The wake-up call only occurs during early mornings when bombings didn't happen the previous night.

Each neighborhood is assigned a drummer or two. Though the Muslims appreciate the traditional alarm, the Assyrians hate having their sleep interrupted by the awful sound, which is difficult to ignore. Often, the drummer knows which houses belong to Assyrian families, and he purposefully stands in front of those houses a bit longer out of spite. Most days, we attempt to sleep through the disturbing sound; however, some mornings, when the drumming pulls me out of a deep sleep, I wake up terrified, with my heart racing as if it will beat out of my chest. That feeling continues until the drummer finishes our street. Going back to sleep after that is always a challenge.

When I am unable to fall back asleep from the unpleasant wake-up call, I find the silver lining by using the time to review my homework. I can never be too prepared for school.

* * *

"For wisdom is a defense as money is a defense, but the excellence of knowledge is that wisdom gives life to those who have it." Ecclesiastes 7:12

BAGHDAD - 1988

Mom and Dad are Santa Claus? How is this possible? All the anticipation for my one present, expecting Santa to deliver it when it is actually my parents. I am six years old. How did I miss this?

I have been eagerly waiting for Christmas, which offers me an extended break from school. Much like all the Assyrian students and employees, we receive three days' leave to observe the holiday. Despite the teachers having to pause their lessons for those three days, the Muslim population continues with school and work as usual. Although Muslim students' school attendance is mandatory during this time, their learning is not.

Christmas Eve is my favorite night of the year. All the preparation, anticipation, and excitement are for this moment. The moment I fall asleep and wake up to a present and the traditional family festivities. I neatly lay out the new outfit, socks, and shoes my mother bought me, as she does every year per our cultural tradition. Unfortunately, I'm not allowed to wear this outfit until Christmas morning.

"The sooner I fall asleep, the sooner it will be morning, and the sooner I can have my present," I keep telling myself as I toss and turn in my cozy twin-size bed. I watch the fire flickering through the holes in the green gasoline heater. Mother left it burning as tonight seems cold. I hear footsteps and whispering in the room as 5 a.m. rolls around. As the steps slowly inch toward my bed, I quickly shift my position to my side. Facing the wall, I pretend to be fast asleep while intently listening to the whispers as they lay the present at the foot of my bed. Although we have a Christmas tree and ornaments, we don't store the presents underneath it. The tree is for holiday decoration only. My uncle, who escaped Iraq in the early eighties to avoid the mandatory military draft, lives in Greece and had a tree and decorations shipped to our house.

Only once the voices begin moving away from my bed do I dare to take a peak. *THE WHISPERS ARE MY PARENTS' VOICES.* I'm in shock. They fooled me all these years into thinking Santa Claus delivered my special present.

Daylight shines through my bedroom window, nudging me to wake up and confront my parents. I no longer have the desire to open my present; I want to tell my parents I know their secret. "You're Santa Claus?" I obnoxiously yell at Mom. She quickly shushes me. She places her index finger against her mouth and says, "Keep quiet. I don't want your sister to find out." She faces the sink and continues her tasks as if nothing has happened. Shaking my head in disappointment, I walk back to my room. My disappointment quickly dissipates when I notice the wrapped present waiting for me. I kneel on the floor beside my bed and tear through the wrapping. It's a large box containing wooden building materials where I can use my imagination and create anything.

I lay aside the present, quickly brush my teeth and hair, put on my new outfit, and rush to the kitchen to help Mom. Christmas breakfast is a feast as it breaks the twenty-five-day Lent. Since December 1,

Assyrians across the country have been honoring Jesus' birth through Lent, where we give up meat, poultry, and dairy, limiting our meal options to vegetable dishes with rice and beans. Lent is observed with high regard; even children honor it.

Christmas is a fun-filled holiday. Three days of nonstop festivities and celebrations begin shortly after breakfast when my maternal grandparents arrive. Holiday festivities mean more family time together, but first, the monetary gift from each grandparent, aunt, and uncle is opened and relished.

After I hide my cash, I reach for the unique bowl of candy and chocolate and pass it around. Each guest takes one piece regardless of their desire to consume it. Not participating in this tradition is considered disrespectful. Weeks before Christmas, Mom takes us shopping for candy and chocolate—the higher in quality and the more extensive the assortment, the better. After serving the candy, we serve tea in small, four-ounce cups and a special pastry called Kileche. This, too, is disrespectful to turn down.

I love helping my family bake my favorite pastry, Kileche. It requires many lengthy and intensive steps, but the end result is worth all the hard work and effort. In the month leading up to Christmas, most of the women in my family—the grandmothers, aunts, and cousins—gather at our house to bake endless Kileche for every family represented. We prepare the dough early in the morning and let it rest for several hours. Once the dough is ready, we split it into small balls and stuff them with random treats such as dates, walnuts, pecans, and coconut, each seasoned with sugar and cardamom spice. Then, we place the balls in a mold to form various shapes and sizes. Next, we put them onto huge silver trays and carry them to the nearest bakery to use the large wood-burning ovens because, like most homes, we don't have an oven. Each tray holds an average of thirty to forty Kileche. Every Assyrian household has the same project simultaneously and will use the various bakeries around the town and village, which can lead to very long lines outside the bakeries. At times, those lines can leave people waiting up to several hours.

I carry the eggs, a bowl, and a whisk to the bakery. When it's our turn, I whisk the eggs and brush the pastries with the liquid before baking. The bakery is large and can process several trays at once. After the Kileche are ready and emptied into bins we brought along, we carry them back to the house and separate them per household. Baking Kileche requires an assembly line with many people operating each station and exercising as we carry everything to and from the bakery. As painful as this process sounds, it is a tradition I and everyone else in the family look forward to and endure with a smile. The aroma of the warm Kileche fills the house each year, but I cannot consume them in honor of Lent; they contain eggs and butter, which forces me to wait until Christmas morning to take my first bite.

Now that everyone has gathered at our house for Christmas, it is time to celebrate with others by visiting their homes. Doing so requires no invitation. Unannounced visits are customary and display a sign of respect that the host appreciates. We spend three days wishing family and friends a Merry Christmas. Each household we visit follows the same tradition: a bowl of candy, a cup of tea, and Kileche. Declining any of these is highly disrespectful, but it is even more disrespectful to skip visiting someone's house. I love this tradition because my chocolate intake drastically increases during the three days.

"Therefore, brethren, stand fast and hold the traditions
which you were taught, whether by word or our epistle."
2 Thessalonians 2:15

BAGHDAD - 1988

Three days of celebration and candy quickly end as school awaits me tomorrow. I glance at my hands and realize my fingernails are painted red for Christmas. I frantically cry to Mom, "I must get rid of this before tomorrow." Nail polish and jewelry are banned in schools. If I arrive with nail polish of any color, it will result in punishment, which means a beating from the vice-principal or one of the teachers. The school often conducts random inspections of uniforms, jewelry, and fingernails, especially after a holiday, a time when children are more likely to commit an offense, unintentionally breaking the rules. The beating includes hits to the palm or the back of the hand with a stick. The number of hits is determined by the vice-principal, which is often unpredictable and can be swayed by her mood and the brightness of the nail polish. To be humiliated in front of my classmates is never a goal of mine. I strive to be the best and quietest student. Luckily, Mom successfully removes the nail polish, and relief washes over me.

Two months have passed since Christmas. Today's school day is no different than any other. It's stressful, but I am determined to get through it. As noon approaches, the day comes to a close, and I am ready for Mom's delicious lunch, homework, and then time with my friends. I usually walk home with my neighbor's kids, but Mom is outside waiting today. I can see the troubled look on her face from across the street. This is unusual because she never picks me up as the distance to my house is short. "What are you doing here?" I ask.

"Not now—we need to get home quickly." Her answer is short, followed by a deep sigh.

"Ok." I put my head down as I follow her, trying to maintain pace with her quick strides. We're moving so quickly, we appear to be jogging. She remains silent until we step into the house, and I learn of the matter. Earlier today, the news reported a gruesome incident at another elementary school in my city. Hussein and a few of his men arrived at the school and opened fire at the children with no remorse. I cringe as images of the sickening act play out in my mind. So many innocent children were executed today simply to keep the people oppressed and traumatized.

As I listen to the news anchor describe the horror, mixed emotions of heartbreak and relief wash over me. *Should I mourn for these children? Should I rejoice that it wasn't my school?* No first-grade student should have to feel this, yet here I am, caught in a world of such intense circumstances and juxtaposing emotions.

But the turmoil doesn't end there. Hussein's brutality and dark soul are a bottomless pit. On Friday, March 16, 1988, during the Iran-Iraq War's closing month, Hussein orders the Halabja Massacre in Iraq. Two days prior, Halabja, near the northern border between Iran and Iraq, was successfully invaded and held by the Iranian army. As a response to losing ground, Hussein decides to counter-attack. He first drops traditional rockets and chemical bombs of nerve and mustard gas on the town. The attack goes on for several hours. Once the bombing stops, the tiny village is left with the most horrific consequences—the genocide claimed the lives of 3,000 to 5,000 and injured 7,000 to 10,000 civilians. In the days to follow, appalling images of the attack circulate in the newspapers. Lifeless bodies of men, women, and children, both young and old, cover the streets. Reports declare some dying of "laughter." Some died a slow death, their bodies burning and blistering before collapsing. Others died vomiting a green substance, while some died quickly and mercifully from the direct impact of the bombs.

This was an intentional attack against the Kurdish people in the southern region of Kurdistan. Kurds are Iranian people who migrated to northern Iraq, Syria, and the southeastern part of Turkey. They are Muslim, but they are not considered Arab. They speak Kurdish, which is different from Arabic and Persian. Arabs and Kurds have had a long history of fighting that has yet to subside, and Hussein, an Arab, takes every opportunity to punish the Kurds. Days after the attack, he claims Halabja back from Iran and sends his troops in with nuclear, chemical, and biological (NCB) suits to determine the effectiveness of the weapons.

His actions and the actions of his men are heartless and beyond inhumane. They leave most people with mental, emotional, and physical scars that will never be masked or forgotten. These events are the backdrop of my childhood.

Fortunately, an unseen backdrop, more potent than Hussein's reign of terror, is also playing out unbeknownst to my family or me.

* * *

"Yea, though I walk through the valley of the shadow of death, I will fear no evil; for you are with me." Psalm 23:4

BAGHDAD - 1988

Hussein and his government's brutality reach a whole new level with torture, executions, and scare tactics designed to instill fear in everyone. Their cruelty and inhumane acts expand rapidly. I have no advocates, no protectors, and no defenders. I have a voice, but no one can hear it. A simple whisper can lead to unimaginable torture and possible execution. Mass graves across the country are evidence of his atrocities. But I can't let that fear stop me from living my life. I can hide inside, waiting for my time to die, or I can go out, live my life, and take the risk. For now, I choose to live and try to make the most of our circumstances.

It isn't long after I decide this that I experience a right of passage in growing up; I lose my first tooth. Dad walks me toward the wall that separates the kitchen from the bathroom and puts my tooth in a small hole in the concrete barrier. "This is where the tooth fairy comes at night. We place your tooth here...," Dad explains, "...and you will have your coin tomorrow."

As exciting as losing my first tooth is, it is nothing compared to my excitement about Easter. This holiday is a much bigger event than

Christmas and is held in even higher regard because it represents the celebration of Christ's sacrifice and resurrection. Without the resurrection, the Christian faith has no power. Just like Christmas, we honor Lent, except this time, it is for fifty days, giving up the same ingredients. We follow the same traditions with new outfits, candy bowls, and Kileche; again, we receive gifts from my parents and monetary gifts from relatives. To top it off, we get four days off from school instead of three.

To motivate the children to respect Easter more and fully honor Lent, the parents pay a few men from the village to dress in scary masks and costumes to frighten the children into fasting. This is called Somikka. The evening before the first day of Lent, these men knock on doors and warn the children that if they break their fast, the scary men from Somikka will come back and punish them with misery and hardship. Luckily, I respect my traditions, especially Lent, and never dare to miss a day.

Celebrating Easter means Kalu Sulaqa, Bride of the Ascension or Ascension Day, is right around the corner. This holiday is celebrated on the fortieth day after Easter, when Christ ascended into Heaven, and is distinguished as a joyous occasion. This day also coincides with an Assyrian historical event in 1401 A.D. Legend states that while the Assyrians were at war, the military wives and other women dressed in white and traveled to nearby towns collecting supplies to feed the men. One day, when the women heard of the potential fall of the Assyrians, the women joined the men on the battlefield instead of running away. They fought alongside the men and defended their land. It is said that the Assyrian leader, Malik Shalita, and his wife wore white when they battled side by side, and both lost their lives that day. Even though this event took place so long ago, it has left a lasting impression. Every year, this memory is commemorated. Girls from each village gather together. The Assyrian Club in the city chooses one girl to dress in a traditional wedding gown and parades around town asking for "gawzeh w-kishmeesheh/yabeesheh," which means "walnuts and raisins." Children from each village dress in white and knock on Assyrian doors, asking for walnuts and raisins. Sometimes, they are given other foods, and lately, people have been giving children money instead, primarily coins, which is what we always hope for.

Being grounded in my culture and roots is essential, especially in a Muslim country where it can easily be forgotten. But my parents, relatives, and even the Assyrian Church ensure that doesn't happen. In fact, during the summer, when the government-mandated school is finished, I still have another form of school to attend: the Assyrian School. It is hosted by the local church and offers classes each evening for all Assyrian students to learn the language, history, and cultural practices of the Assyrians. Since the public school is conducted in Arabic, the church ensures Assyrians never forget who they are and where they came from. This, too, comes with a lot of homework but, thankfully, no beatings. The teachers are more loving and compassionate, and I don't have a dress code to follow. The sole purpose is to ensure the Assyrian children develop a healthy respect and appreciation for our culture and history. I love attending and learning but also dread it because I never really have a break from school. It is draining, but it's not something I can avoid. Knowing all my Assyrian friends are experiencing the same thing gives me the hope and endurance I need to press on.

"But the wisdom that is from above is first pure, then peaceable, gentle, willing to yield, full of mercy and good fruits, without partiality and without hypocrisy." James 3:17

BAGHDAD - 1988

The end of school is fast approaching, which means I've come close to surviving my first year. This also means another favorite holiday, Musardel, is fast approaching. Occurring on the seventh Sunday after Ascension, Assyrians celebrate this holiday in honor of St. Thomas. As St. Thomas traveled through Urmiya, Iran, the power of Christianity was so influential that numerous people asked to be baptized by him. He performed the rite by sprinkling water on the crowd. Hence, Musardel is a day spent splashing around in the water. The night before, I and everyone else stash as many large containers and buckets as possible. The following day, the challenge is to be the first to wake up, fill all the containers, and start splashing the family with water. The goal is to get everyone, family and friends, as wet as possible. Since Musardel takes place in the early summer, we are sleeping on the roof. My mother manages to wake up first and quickly reaches for the water hose attached to the roof faucet and sprays us all. I am sopping wet in my bed before I even have the chance to brush my teeth. Most of our Muslim neighbors tend to join in on the fun. There isn't a dry soul on the block. Almost the entire country celebrates Musardel.

Though I love celebrating this holiday, I am even more eager for my summer break because it means I get my special time with Babi Matti, my maternal grandfather Matthew. Babi Matti means "my Dad Matti," a nickname the grandkids contrived. Tall and skinny with salt and pepper hair, he has a compassionate heart, a great sense of humor, and loves spending time with his family. I am the first granddaughter on my mother's side, and he cherishes that. He and I have an extraordinary relationship and a strong bond.

Completing first grade with high marks is something to be proud of. No one displays that pride better than he does. As I step into the house with a report card in hand, I find him in my living room, anxiously waiting for me. He steps toward me and reaches for the card. Every class is marked with a ninety or higher. Beaming, he tells me how proud he is of me. "Let's go," he says, "I'm taking you out on a special date, just the two of us." It doesn't take much convincing on his part for me to jump at the opportunity of alone time with him. Babi Matti is a very hard-working man who cares for everyone, including distant cousins and family members who travel from various villages throughout the country to stay with him and my grandmother. He opens his house and arms to everyone in need, never asking for anything in return. He is a soft-hearted man, and I strive to emulate him.

Our time together is exceptional. He doesn't own a car, so we walk to an ice cream shop where I pick my favorite dessert, Asbary, a fruity slushy. Shortly after, we walk to a jewelry store, and he surprises me with a gift. "pick a necklace," he says. To show pride and respect for someone, especially family members, 24-karat gold jewelry is the perfect gift. I chose a cross pendant hung on a 40 centimeter (16 inch) chain. I can hardly contain my excitement as he places it around my neck, his smile beaming. The brighter his face shines, the harder I want to work at school to maintain that radiant smile and pride. He is one of my biggest fans and motivators in school and life.

My Babi Matti has avoided the government drafts with minor medical procedures and surgeries. He doesn't want to serve in the military, as he is in his late forties, an age considered to be older. He has absolutely no military training and is physically unfit. Babi Matti is fortunate enough to find a loophole in the system that keeps him alive and safe. It is a huge relief that he is not drafted; I enjoy having him around too much. So many other men are less fortunate as they serve against their will and lose their lives.

My large extended family understands and supports Babi Matti's plan, but that does not stop the older grandkids from writing a song about him and all his medical procedures. Fortunately, he finds our little tune humorous and laughs every time we sing it. Everyone else joins in as soon as one person starts the song.

Babi Matti and Nana Younia, my maternal grandmother, do not have the most loving relationship. They co-exist, but their affection is almost nonexistent. Their relationship doesn't stem from love and respect but from pain and agony, especially for Nana Younia. Her life was forever changed at fourteen when her childhood was stripped away and replaced by womanhood.

"I have no greater joy than to hear that my children walk in truth." 3 John 1:4

DIANA - 1949

"Let's go to Hizeewe's house," Younia's parents told her. Hizeewe was an elderly lady, the mother of a family from Younia's hometown of Diana (Dee-yana), a tiny village in northern Iraq. Everyone in Diana lived close together at the base of the mountain that separates Iraq from Iran. As Younia and her parents walked around the corner and down the street, little did the fourteen-year-old girl know that her life will soon be changed forever. Upon their arrival, they were welcomed with tea and pastries. Younia interacted with the children in the household as the parents socialized. Her parents left shortly afterward while she remained behind.

At dinner time, Younia stood up. "I'm going home," she stated.

"What do you mean you're going home? This is your new home now," said Hizeewe.

"No, I need to go home. It's dinner time, and my parents are waiting for me."

"Don't you know? Your parents married you off to our son, Matti."

Just like that, Younia was handed over to another family and married to a young boy she knew only because they lived in the same small village. This arranged marriage was structured and executed without her knowledge or input. Stunningly, in a matter of hours, she was no longer a young girl on a play date but a married woman assuming domestic responsibilities she was unprepared for.

Soon, young Younia was pregnant. After several miscarriages, she had two girls and one boy before giving birth to Madlen, my mother. My grandmother, Younia, did not have an easy life. She lost her childhood at an early age, leaving school behind to be married and caring for her in-laws and the family. She also suffered at the hands of my great-grandmother, Hizeewe. Though Hizeewe was petite, her diminutive size concealed a rather harsh heart. She was known to be an aggressive and ruthless elderly woman in the village. Most aimed to stay in her good graces because they feared her.

Shortly after her impromptu marriage, Hizeewe restricted Younia's visits with her parents, especially her mother. She was forced to carry out the domestic duties of the house, performing daily tasks such as cooking, cleaning, and laundry by hand for eleven people. She also served her in-laws, husband, brother-in-law, and two sisters-in-law, along with caring for and raising five children.

Despite her arranged marriage and obstacles—serving a large extended family, facing the heartbreak of several miscarriages, and raising children very young—she managed to love and care for everyone. Most of her time was spent in the kitchen, catering to everyone's wishes as she worked non-stop, supporting her family through good times and bad. She was a very compassionate woman, always willing to help, and found joy in supporting her family.

My heart breaks whenever I hear my grandmothers share their struggles from an early age. I appreciate everything they endured because they produced generations of resilient, strong women. Their lives give me gratitude for the one I have.

* * *

"She is more precious than rubies, and all the things you may desire cannot compare with her." Proverbs 3:15

BAGHDAD - 1988

The Iran-Iraq War has just concluded; the war that has been ongoing my entire life, the war that has claimed nearly 500,000 Iraqi lives, is over. Despite the sacrifices the Iraqi citizens had to make, no borders were ever changed, nor were reparations made. Though the country is battered and beaten, the possibility of peace is overwhelming. The citizens are excited to welcome their family members back from the army. The nation celebrates by removing the duct tape from our windows. We can finally experience a full night of sleep with no interruptions. However, a peaceful country does not mean Uncle Saddam has concluded his brutality. His abuse continues regardless. We just continue to adapt, learn how to maneuver, and conform to anything he throws at us. Life continues irrespective of the government's barbaric ways.

Shortly after the conclusion of the war, Mother announces she is pregnant again. Despite our circumstances and living in the unknown, everyone is overjoyed by the news of my upcoming sibling. I want another baby sister, that much I know. I spend most of my free time with my three older male cousins, and although I love them and love playing marbles, Transformers, and Hot Wheels with them, at times, they can be rowdy and aggressive in their playing. I appreciate them including me in everything they do. Though I'm tiny, I rough-house with the best of them, evident by the many scars I have obtained through the years. I can't ignore the latest and largest scar on my knee I acquired after I face-planted on the pavement, leaving me with a giant cut. Limping my way home, I winced as the blood dripped down my leg. My mom and aunt cleaned my wound and found a rock wedged inside. I bit my lip as Mom dug it out and thoroughly sterilized it. Adventures like this one remind me that I don't want another boy. I am excited about this new addition, especially when Mom asks me to choose the name.

Each day I make a list of names I like and share them with Mom, but none seem to have a lasting impact. That is until I mention Rodina, which means "earthquake." The name quickly roots with us, and we keep revisiting it. May 29, 1989, is here, and my sister, Rodina, is born.

In the Assyrian culture, children are baptized as infants to bless the child and assign their middle name. My large family has gathered at the Assyrian Church to baptize Rodina. Dressed in a white gown, white socks, and shoes, she is tightly snug in my mother's arms. The priest begins his Assyrian chants as he waves a gold metal cross over my baby sister, motioning the Trinity symbol. He follows it with a few more chants before he asks Mom to remove Rodina's clothing. The priest then holds her frail body and dunks her in water; as she emerges, she cries loudly, gasping for air. Then he dunks her again and again, three times in total, representing Christ's death for three days. Mom rushes forward with a towel, wraps her up, and dresses her in a white gown. The priest concludes the ceremony by dipping his fingers in the holy oil and swiping it across Rodina's forehead, symbolizing the Trinity. He then announces her middle name will be Katrina. Each middle name assigned is in honor of a saint. Sona was given the name Phoebronia (Phoebe), and I have Mariam (Mary), the customary name given to every firstborn female in an Assyrian family in honor of Mariam, the mother of Jesus.

I love helping Mom take care of Rodina. Although I enjoy participating in the care of my sisters, it is also my duty as the eldest child in the family, an expectation imposed upon me culturally. At seven years old, I spend most evenings swaddling Rodina and rocking her to sleep.

I prepare Rodina for bed each night and place her in a wooden rocker bassinet. I use a long fabric that wraps around her and the cradle before I drape a white breathable fabric over her bassinet, creating solitude and ridding any visual distractions. Then I sing her a song as I gently rock her. Singing seems to soothe her, so I do so every night to rush her to sleep so I can run back outside and play. I have attempted singing various songs, but none have proven to work as much as "Ya Brati Khlita." It is a song about a man who loses his wife, and he's left with a young daughter whom he's putting to bed. I somehow correlate Rodina's attempt to sleep to this little girl who had just lost her mother. I'm unsure how the two equate in my mind, but it always works.

My mother entrusting me with so much responsibility has triggered feelings and instincts I'm not accustomed to, nor have I felt before. I have a tendency to check on my sisters often. Sometimes, I wake up in the middle of the night, feeling the need to ensure they are safe and sleeping well. Tonight is no different. While comfortably tucked in my warm bed, a gut feeling suggests I should check on Rodina, who is sleeping in her rocking crib. My baby sister loves cuddling with tulle, a plain white lace patch of fabric. She enjoys holding it and playing with it at every opportunity. Knowing this, a family member brought her a tulle swatch. Mom placed the fabric next to her as she swaddled her tonight.

Needing to reassure myself, I trust my instincts and step toward Rodina's crib. I lift the long drape and notice she is awake but has no reaction. She releases a whimpering noise as if she's gasping for air. Instantly I notice the tulle is missing. I search the crib and the floor with no luck. The gut feeling nudges me again to check her mouth. I gently push her lower jaw down and find the fabric lodged in her mouth. I pinch part of the tulle with my fingers and retrieve it. Instantly, Rodina calms down, and her breathing returns to normal. I rush to wake Mom and tell her what happened. She is shocked but grateful for my instinct. She's also proud to see my so-called motherly intuitions beginning to surface. This is a rite of passage into adulthood and becoming an official family caretaker. "We will pin the tulle to the mattress from now on to ensure this doesn't happen again!" Mom exclaims in her frantic, tired voice.

"Now thanks be to God who always leads us in triumph in Christ, and through us diffuses the fragrance of His knowledge in every place." 2 Corinthians 2:14

BAGHDAD - 1989

Firstborn children carry a heavier burden in the Middle East. An expectation is placed upon us from an early age that the rest of the siblings don't experience. Girls are expected to nurture the younger siblings, care for the domestic house duties, and aid their mothers with anything they need. Boys are expected to protect their siblings. They also join the workforce as early as thirteen years of age to help provide for the family and train to be "the man of the house." The cultural pressure we face prepares us for what's ahead; it causes us to step into any situation and react immediately. We face predicaments head-on. Carrying the responsibility of being the oldest child is a pressure we can't escape.

At seven years old, I take over caring for my sisters and the house duties full-time, including changing diapers, cleaning the house, cooking, and even tucking my sisters into bed. My parents work often and struggle with the constant stresses of war, finances, and trying to survive with their three young daughters. It is my duty to reduce their burden and pressure whenever possible.

I am happy to step into this role as with each task I complete, I feel a sense of accomplishment and one step closer to growing up and becoming an adult. But I don't give up my childhood that easily. Every so often, I tend to be my parents' worst nightmare with some of the unintentional mischief I cause.

Washing dishes after most meals is one of my many chores. As a child, I sometimes love playing with the soap, creating bubbles in the sink. After dishes today, I dispense a little bit of soap into a cup, add water and a skinny straw, and create a bubble machine as I blow air through the straw. It is a trick I learned from my cousins. I entertain myself for several minutes before Sona notices the mountain of bubbles forming and asks if she can join me. Being the cool, older sister, I agree. Giving her the cup, I say, "Blow into the straw." With her tiny hands, she secures the cup and proceeds to suck up the soapy water instead. She takes one large gulp and swallows it. Panic washes over me; in fear, I scream for my parents.

With tears streaming down my face, I explain what happened. In a swift move, Dad picks Sona up by her feet, holds her upside down, and gently taps her back, forcing her to regurgitate her drink. After a few scary minutes, she begins vomiting. Although the event had innocent intentions, it does not end well for me. My instincts are correct. It doesn't take long for my parents to calm down and for Mom to reach for her rubber sandal and use it to inflict a harsh beating on me. Each hit stings my skin, and the pain penetrates deeper. With every strike, I whimper, begging for forgiveness. After many hits that leave imprints on my arms and legs, Mom stops and continues her disappointment with a lecture on the meaning of being the oldest child and caring for my sisters. Begging for mercy during my discipline rarely leads to compassion. So often, when parents who are living in a constant state of trauma and anxiety are triggered, anger takes over, and logic is lost.

Rodina turned six months old recently, and my parents have decided our family needs a small dog the size of a Shih Tzu. I'm not sure what prompted them to do so as they attempted this a year ago and had to return the dog the following day because Sona and I were terrified. Here we are again, another dog, yet the same fear and anxiety for Sona and me. Most people in Iraq don't have pets. I can't think of a time when I walked into someone's house and found a dog or cat roaming around. They are few in number. Family members often remind me of the dangers of dog hair. Children are taught not to swallow dog hair as it can cause a deadly infection in the stomach. Statements like this keep me from wanting a dog.

This new dog, Lucy, soft, tan, with brown spots is with us much longer than I anticipated. My parents hope we will adapt to her. I wish that was the case. Instead, one afternoon, while Mom cleans, she puts Lucy on the stairs and blocks her with a gate. Rodina is crawling on the ground, and Sona and I are playing. I am unsure why, but I step towards the stairs and remove the gate, assuming Lucy cannot climb down the three steps. But, as luck would have it, she runs down immediately. Watching her move so quickly, I panic and run away, hiding in the bedroom with the door closed. Sona climbs onto my parents' bed, knowing the dog can't jump that high, while Rodina is left behind on the ground, screaming in sheer terror. The dog is excitedly licking her, but none of us understand what is happening. We assume Lucy is attacking Rodina instead of loving on her. Mom runs out of the kitchen to Rodina's screams only to find Lucy enthusiastically licking her. She snatches the dog, steps into the room I'm hiding in, and puts the dog on my head as a punishment. Trembling, I sit trapped in the corner between the door and the wall. I scream and cry, begging Mom to take Lucy off of me. She removes her and harshly strikes my arm for deserting my sister, leaving me with a slight bruise.

"This will teach you never to leave your sisters behind!" she yells. Since I am the oldest, I am naturally expected to step up whenever necessary, no matter the circumstances. In that instance, I failed to protect Rodina and paid the price. Lucy was gone that same day—my sisters and I never adjusted to her well. I feel guilty for Lucy, but I'm unsure how to overcome my fear of dogs, as having a dog has never been part of my reality or anyone's around me. Mom's discipline toward my mistake is rooted deeper than me leaving Rodina behind. All Iraqi parents endure stressful lives that are plagued with war and death, limited food supplies, Hussein's endless fear tactics, and numerous other struggles that inherently come with the territory. My parents function at a heightened level of fight or flight. Although they don't realize it, anxiety is always high, causing their reactions to their children's minor mishaps to be severe and unexplainable.

"Honor your father and mother, that your days may be long."
Exodus 20:12

BAGHDAD - 1990

August 1, 1990, is just another typical summer day. School is right around the corner, and I am dreading it. Since school takes up so much of my free time with homework and tests, I enjoy my summer the best I can. I spend most of my days playing outside with my neighborhood friends. Jump-roping, hopscotch, marbles, and beads are our go-to games, with the last being my favorite when my cousins are not around. Most girls in my neighborhood, including myself, have a jar full of random beads of all shapes, colors, and sizes that we use in a game. To play, we gather around and decide how many beads we're willing to gamble during each round, and then we set them down about 1 meter (3 feet) away from a hole in the ground. We gently tap the beads using our thumbs, hoping they land in the little hole. If we miss, then the next person takes a turn. If we tap them into the hole, we continue our turn until we miss. We tap one bead at a time until all make it in. The individual who lands the most beads into the hole wins the game and keeps all the beads in that round. Walking away with my friends' beads is the ultimate satisfaction. I spend more hours than I can count playing this game and never seem to grow weary of it. This is my game. I dominate, and more often than not, I walk away with everyone else's beads. Only today was not my day. I lost all my beads. I am very competitive in almost everything I do, and it is a very humbling experience watching one of my friends walk away with every bead I own.

I cannot bear the thought of not having any beads to play with. I have to find some soon to use them to earn everything back. I search high and low with no luck. I even probe Mom's clothing to see if any have beads I can cut off and use. Still, no luck. I only need one bead. As I'm extensively searching, I had what I thought was a genius idea—one of Mom's friends, Manal, has a beautiful collection of beads. I rush to Mom, begging her to allow me to walk to Manal's house and ask her for a handful of beads. After a few minutes of begging and reassuring, I promise Mom I will not be gone for long and will not derail from my mission. She agrees to let me go alone. I bolt out of the house on a serious task. My reputation is on the line, and I must earn everything back. I run down the street, make a right turn, cross two roads, make another right turn, and pass five houses before arriving at my destination. I gently knock on the door, out of breath and anxious, hoping Manal is home. After three knocks, Manal answers the door, surprised to see me at her doorstep without Mom.

"Are you willing to part ways with a few beads?" I ask after I greet her. Knowing this is a game most girls play, including her when she was my age, she smiles and replies, "Of course." She opens her sewing chest, showing a beautiful collection she uses to decorate clothing pieces. She allows me to make my selections. To my great delight, she offers me more than twenty beautiful beads. I am so excited. I quickly thank her and sprint back home, gasping for air. I find the friend who walked away with everything and convince her to play me again. She is on a high, feeling confident from her win, so she agrees. Little does she know I am on the verge of sending her home with absolutely nothing. I earn all my beads back and all of her beads as well. In the end, I walk away with over five hundred beads. *Oh, victory, how I love thee.*

After spending most of the day outside playing, 8 p.m. rolls around. The kids slowly disperse, and soon, the block is empty. Shortly after walking into the house, Mom calls me, "It's dinner time. Wash up and set the dining area." This isn't uncommon as most families eat dinner later in the evening, between 8 and 9 p.m.

My routine seems usual, nothing out of the ordinary. My bedtime is 10 p.m., although sometimes Mom and Dad let me stay up longer. Tonight is not one of those nights, as they need me to adjust to an earlier bedtime with school fast approaching.

* * *

"My grace is sufficient for you, for My strength is made perfect in weakness." 2 Corinthians 12:9

BAGHDAD - 1990

There's darkness all around. I hear the sounds of military boots stomping on the ground. The rifles clink while hanging from the soldiers' shoulders. The sirens begin again. Darkness creeps into my heart as much as it's present in the sky. Confusion blinds me.

Could it be wartime again? I ponder.

Agony takes root. War is all around, but not in a physical sense. I can hear and see the sirens, bombs, missiles, and the destruction. *I didn't know Iraq was fighting again.* The Iran-Iraq War ended almost two years ago on August 20, 1988. Yet, I am living through another war full of pain, blood, and suffering. Fear grips my heart, squeezing it tightly as I struggle to understand what is happening. My heart pounds against my ribs. I'm in shock, watching the horror unfold. I shift my body and stump my knee against a cool, hard surface. The pain jolts me from a deep sleep. I immediately sit up, gasping for air, attempting to slow my breathing. I wipe the sweat from my forehead as I feel my surroundings. Confusion slowly clears as my eyes adjust to my reality. *It was just a dream. Yet, it felt so real, as if I were there. I could smell the burning remnants of the bombs. I could hear the rifles, watching as they drained the life of every soldier and victim alike. I could see the blood flowing down the streets like a river.*

I lay back down, head resting on my thin, feather pillow, hoping to make sense of what I saw and experienced. If that was a dream, then it was unlike any other dream.

The sun has risen, but my world seems encased with gray clouds. I rush out of my room and hear Mom in the kitchen preparing breakfast. Dad has already left for work. Mom can see I am distraught. She approaches me with concern, puts her arm around me, and gently asks, "What's wrong?" Stunned by the images and crippled in fear, I struggle to find words to explain what I saw. Though the dream had occurred overnight, I felt as if I had lived through it for several months with so many details and specifics and no means of escape.

Mom tries to calm me down. "Would you please take a few breaths and slowly explain what's happening?"

"Okay," I reply while attempting to control my breathing. "Iraq invaded Kuwait last night."

She's stunned into silence.

"I think we're at war again!" I exclaim, examining her face and reaction. Mom stares at me with eyes wide open.

"What do you mean we're at war again?" She briefly pauses, almost as if looking for words, then continues, "That's impossible. Why would Iraq do such a thing?" she asks with a confused look.

The dream felt too real to be dismissed, too many details to be taken lightly. The emotions I felt as I watched the war unfold struck a chord, awakening feelings I had suppressed since the Iran-Iraq War. "We are at war again, Mom. The United States will be involved this time. The President of America will warn Hussein to retreat, but he will decline, and war will erupt. There will be bombings and missiles flying through Baghdad's sky, dead bodies spread across the country, and blood flowing down the streets."

As I describe the images of my dream, I notice Mom's face changing to a look of fear, confusion, and concern. Not only is she distressed to hear about these graphic images of war, but she is also unsure of what is happening to her daughter.

"Did you watch TV last night?" she asks. "Did you watch anything yesterday that might have triggered what you're describing?"

"No, how can I watch TV at night when no channels are available after midnight?" I answer. "I went to bed shortly after dinner, remember?"

"Good point..." Mom is trying to stay calm and positive for me. "Try to forget what you saw. Try to enjoy your day with your friends. We will figure this out." She then encourages me to change and prepare for breakfast.

I feel repulsed as the horrific images crowd my mind. I try my best to put them behind me. I brush my teeth, change from my PJs, and set up the dining area for breakfast. The aroma of scrambled eggs with warm, fresh bread shifts my focus from my troubling night, reminding me I need to eat. My attention is interrupted by a firm knock at the front entrance. I rush to the large wooden door and swing it open, only to find one of Dad's friends from school, a fellow teacher, standing in the doorway. "Is your Mom home?"

"Yes," I call for Mom. As she appears in sight, I can tell that she is surprised to see him at the door.

"Have you heard the news?" he asks with a frightened tone.

"No, what news?"

"Turn on the television, and you'll understand," he says. "James asked me to come by on my way home to have you pack a few bags in case you have to flee tonight."

Mom rushes to our fifteen-inch, vintage television with two silver knobs and a simple antenna. The antenna doesn't always work the best, so we strap a fork and tinfoil to the ends of it. Turning on the television is like turning my dream back on, except this time, I am watching it while awake. The news anchor announces the one thing the country dreads hearing. It is August 2, and Iraq is at war. Again.

Listening to the news, Mom turns around, looks at me, and asks, "How did you know? Are you sure you didn't watch TV last night?"

"I swear I was in bed all night."

She is in disbelief. Iraq is in the beginning phase of what I described to her this morning. The Gulf War has started, and my dream is no longer just a nightmare but a slowly unfolding reality. I have never dreamed of anything that felt so real, much less something that has come true. This is entirely new territory for me, and I don't know what to make of it. My dream and the Kuwait invasion took place at the same time.

My dream is a vision of future events.

How can that be?

I was afraid of what I had dreamt last night, but I am even more terrified as I watch it unfold in real-time on the television. It is a nightmare I am unable to escape.

I watch Mom pack a bag in the event we have to flee without notice to avoid the war. In wartime, Baghdad, the capital, tends to be the first target of attack. With the television playing in the background, as I listen to the warnings and predictions, flashbacks of the previous war begin to play in the back of my mind. I recall the horrifying sirens in the middle of the night and the loud, earth-shattering sounds of missiles and bombs exploding. Memories crash like the shards of a broken window. I am all too familiar with this trauma. Iraq just endured an eight-year-long war, and here we are again on the cusp of a new one.

Shortly after Hussein invades Kuwait, a small country bordering Iraq to the south and at the tip of the Persian Gulf, fellow Arab countries such as Saudi Arabia, Egypt, and others call on the United States to step in as Iraq resists the United Nations Security Council's order to withdraw. As the warnings are exchanged between the countries, the dreadful concept of another war begins to sink in. The warnings and threats continue for months, escalating each time. As the threats intensify, so do our war preparations. We, again, duct tape an X-shape on our windows and stock groceries, water, and gasoline. Winter is approaching, and we have learned from the previous war that resources will be scarce.

* * *

"Hear now My words: if there is a prophet among you, I, the Lord, make Myself known to him in a vision; I speak to him in a dream." Numbers 12:6

BAGHDAD - 1990

Since the invasion of Kuwait, the citizens of Iraq have been living in turmoil, surrounded by uncertainty. Anxiety is looming, and fear is palpable. Despite threats issued by America and the panic that batters our minds, Iraq continues to move forward with life. Businesses operate, and schools resume as scheduled.

One month after school begins, a pink dot suddenly appears on my arm while in class. I gently run my fingers across it to ease its itching. *It's a mosquito bite*, I tell myself. Before long, there are pink dots across my body. *Mosquitoes must like me today*, I keep telling myself, not realizing what is happening. Shortly after my walk home, I change and help Mom set up our little dining area. Like most people, we rarely use our small dining table in the kitchen. Instead, our dining happens on a thick, clear tarp in the family room. We spread the tarp on the floor, place the food, plates, and silverware on it, and dine. We use small cushions for support. Once finished, we collect everything, wipe the tarp, fold it, and place it in the kitchen until the next meal. This custom takes place even when family and friends visit.

As I sit on the floor next to Mom, she notices my ongoing itching. "What's wrong?" she asks. "Why do you keep itching your arm?"

I shrug my shoulders as I roll my sleeve up. "Mosquito bites," I reply.

"Those are not mosquito bites, honey; those are chickenpox." She explains chickenpox to me, followed by, "You will spend the next week with your aunt and grandparents, so your sisters don't get it."

Quickly, Mom quarantines me while she packs a small suitcase for my week at her parents' house. With limited medication and vaccinations, being exposed to and getting certain illnesses is inevitable. Within minutes, Mom is on the phone with Babi Matti, and an hour later, he is at the front door, ready to take me with him. With my pink spots slowly spreading, I walk alongside Babi Matti, head down, heartbroken, listening to him tell me I will be okay. His words sound muffled as my snot and sniffles mask his voice. I am in disbelief that Mom would send me off when I need her the most. My aunt and grandmother are not my mother. No one can provide the relief she can.

My aunt does her best to entertain and keep my mind off the itching, especially for the first three days. The week moves slowly as we play board games like Chutes and Ladders, Four in a Row, and building blocks. We watch cartoons whenever possible, which isn't often, as they only air for an hour in the afternoon. It is challenging to keep from scratching. My one desire is to scratch my body to get any sort of relief, but I am reminded that itching will lead to scars, and I don't want those. Instead, I gently rub the spots by running my hands over them to ease the itching sensation. Being sick without my mom is just as painful, but I understand her tough decision; she must be with my sisters. This doesn't stop me from missing her, however.

My grandmother continues cooking my favorite meals and attempts to ease my heartbreak the best she can. Once the week concludes and my healing begins, I can finally come home. I can hardly sleep from the excitement of seeing my family. My welcome, however, is bittersweet as I walk through the front door and find Sona with pink spots covering her body. My mother's efforts to keep my sisters healthy failed.

Experiencing separation from my mother for a week was extremely challenging, yet it was my duty to comply as the oldest child. I could have pleaded to recuperate at home, but that would not have been beneficial for Mom. Being the firstborn involves much responsibility and pressure. I didn't ask for either, but I make the most of it—my "eldest daughter" responsibilities weigh heavy on my shoulders. The perfection my parents expect of me extends beyond my education and into the house chores and caring for my sisters. At seven years old, I clean the house thoroughly and learn how to cook meals alone. I use a small stool to increase my height to reach the stove. Failing to meet Mom's requirements or falling short of what is expected of me leads to occasional discipline or harsh conversations with Mom.

Pursuing perfection is difficult for anyone, especially a child my age. And sometimes, I fall short of the "good daughter" bar set before me. Nonetheless, I am a quick learner. Every so often, I tread the thin line between good and not-so-good. My aunt and her three children are here to visit. As I watch my cousins run around, I say the F word in Assyrian in a quick outburst. Before I know it, and before I even finish saying the word, the back of Mom's hand slaps my mouth. I am caught off guard, trembling, and embarrassed because it happened in front of everyone. Cursing is not tolerated in my house—a lesson I learn quickly. Thirty minutes later, I look in the mirror, and the outline of her hand is still imprinted on my mouth, lips, and chin. She did not yell or say anything else in that instance, but the humiliation of the smack was enough to shape me quickly. I don't dare curse again. Just the thought of doing so spreads fear through my body and angst of her hand appearing.

When disciplining me, Mom follows the same routine as her parents and most other parents in our community. Whenever I do something that earns me a correction, my mother will say, "Get me a sandal so I can beat you with it." This is not a joke. When she tells me to retrieve a sandal, I must bring one that will meet her expectations. I can deliver nothing too small and flimsy, nor do I want one that is too heavy or thick. The best and most tolerable option for me is Mom's sandals. Those sandals, mainly made of rubber, hurt when they make contact. It is humiliating to fetch my instrument of punishment and then take the punishment itself, but I take comfort in knowing that all my cousins and friends experience the same disciplinary measures. I don't like the humiliation associated with the beatings, so I do everything in my power to prevent them.

Being on my best behavior at all times is overwhelming. Occasionally, I venture into my mischievous self, where my curiosity peaks and often leads to more trouble, especially on an afternoon when Babi Matti comes to visit. He brings a thermometer for our house. Upon walking in, he places it on the coffee table and follows my parents into the family room. I run to the coffee table, curious to see what he has brought. I have never seen a thermometer before, nor do I know what one is used for. As I play with it, I notice every time I rub the small red ball at the bottom of the thermometer, the red liquid rises through the glass tube. If I let go, the liquid drops back down. I watch the red liquid move up and down for several minutes before my curious personality takes over. My determination stops at nothing in discovering the content of the red substance. I break the little red ball and ask my one-year-old sister, Rodina, to taste it. Instantly, she is screaming in excruciating pain. At the sound of her screams, my parents rush in. Mom picks up Rodina and immediately walks her to the bathroom to rinse her mouth out. Still shrieking in pain, Rodina places her tongue on Mom's shoulder, hoping for relief. The little liquid on her tongue is so strong it stings Mom's shoulder through her shirt.

Fortunately, she washes the liquid off and calms Rodina. Quickly, I learn the red substance is a hazardous chemical called Mercury. My parents and Babi Matti explain the severity of what I did and why Rodina was in so much distress.

My childhood is still fantastic. Despite all my challenges, I learn to make the best of every situation. I also continue to learn to be grateful in all circumstances. No matter how difficult I think my life is, someone always has it worse. The firstborn expectations I experience are similar to most. However, I have it much easier for many reasons. One, in particular, is watching young girls in my neighborhood and school be married off as early as twelve and sometimes, even younger. One morning, I am playing with my friend outside, and the next day, there is an announcement that my friend will soon celebrate her arranged marriage to a much older man. Young girls are often married shortly after they begin their menstrual cycle. This tradition with teen girls is more common in the Muslim culture than with Assyrians, although a few subcultures within the Assyrian community follow similar practices. The menstrual cycle is thought to transition girls into young women, preparing them for a family. At this time, a girl's father begins searching for a suitor who can care for her. These men are usually much older, well-established, and sometimes have other wives at home. Muslim men are allowed to have up to four wives simultaneously. Many girls are married off before reaching high school. Getting married and bearing children is considered an honor, a "duty" bestowed upon women.

Similarly, boys in their middle school years are thought to be on the cusp of manhood. They are often drafted to join the military, forcing them to drop out of school before high school. Others quit school and start working to help care for their families.

Watching kids my age disappear to responsibilities much heavier than mine teaches me to appreciate everything I have and the circumstances I am blessed with.

* * *

"The Lord is good, a stronghold in the day of trouble; and He knows those who trust in Him." Nahum 1:7

BAGHDAD - 1990

Despite living in a third-world country, education is crucial for many families, particularly the Assyrians. Obtaining a college degree is one of the highest achievements an individual can attain in a beaten and battered society. Doing so brings joy and pride to the family, especially the parents, as well as helps to secure a better job. As a result, schools operate regardless of the circumstances of the country. Even the invasion and the threats of the upcoming war don't stop schools from continuing. It is rarely paused unless a missile directly impacts it.

On a beautiful October morning, as I wait for my teacher to arrive, the student beside me speaks the name Uncle Saddam. Anger fills my chest at the sound of his name, the name that has inflicted so much pain and suffering and so much tyranny. My mental filter turns off as I proclaim my death sentence, "I wish Saddam were half the president George Bush is." Utter silence falls onto the classroom with thick tension. Fear stabs at my heart as I watch my classmates and teacher slowly back away from me. Stunned and appalled at my foolishness, they stare at me. Glancing around the room, I notice the sheer terror on every face, prompting me to come to my senses. *Why couldn't I have remained silent and kept my opinion to myself?* Standing alone and trembling, I stare at everyone, astounded by my reckless comment and behavior. Realizing what I have done, at this moment, I know there is no going back. I have sealed my fate; I begin to resign myself to the fact that I will die today. I beg God to deliver and save me from what's to come. Overwhelmed with anxiety, I know I have brought my worst nightmare to pass as I sit at my desk waiting for my punishment. *Would it be a beating from the principal or the school officials? Are the police on their way? This has to be my last day alive.*

I look at the clock; each tick is a step closer to my punishment. I can't concentrate; the teacher's voice is a muffled sound in the background. I'm not learning; nothing seems to penetrate through my fear and into my brain. Thoughts of torture and death consume my mind. When females are involved, the probability of rape is high. I was taught this as early as six years old to prepare me for the possibility if ever captured. This is an added fear that females across the country agonize over. Death is a welcome concept if I can skip the horrific suffering that precedes it.

The final school bell rings, and nothing transpires. I take a deep breath of relief and walk home, hopeful the storm has passed, and I can relax. I cautiously consume a midday meal with my family in silence, too afraid to tell my parents of my foolish behavior. Though I am trembling on the inside, I maintain a stable appearance on the outside. I proceed by completing my homework and then step outside to play. None of my friends dare to mention my comment, surprised to see me still alive. Mom calls my name at dusk and asks me to help her with dinner. The evening proceeds like any other, just as I have been praying for. However, dinner is interrupted by the doorbell. Anxiety hovers over me, and fear fills my chest like wet cement as I wait to see who is on the other side of the door. *My life is coming to an end within minutes.*

Dad opens the door, and he is faced with several government officials. Among them is an agent of General Security, the highest government agency, who happens to be one of our neighbors and a good friend of my dad's.

"How can I help you?" he asks, oblivious of my incident at school.

"Are you aware of what occurred at Ramina's school this morning? It is obvious you're not teaching your daughter manners and the proper method of addressing the president," the Agent accuses. Trembling, I stand in the next room and listen to the conversation, praying for God's mercy to pour over me in this instance and spare my life. I don't want to die yet; I'm not ready.

"It's lucky for you and your family that you are my friend. We will allow this incident to slide this time, but if this happens again, you and your family will pay the price by execution," our neighbor warns.

"Understood," my father replies as he apologizes profusely and continuously thanks the Agent for his mercy.

As I hear the front door close, I approach the front room. I am slightly relieved, but then I see the look of sheer terror on my father's face. He breathes deeply before giving in to his rising anger.

Cautiously, I approach him. "Who was at the door, Dad?" I ask, fully aware of who it was but attempting to gauge how much trouble I am in.

My father, gasping for air, has lost his color as if he's seen a ghost. His dark eyes lock with mine, and with a stern voice, he exclaims, "The next time you open your mouth at school, I will kill you before they do."

Threatening to kill me doesn't mean that he is literally going to act on it. This is a threat that many parents use as a disciplinary tool. But I learned my lesson today. I am fortunate to escape what could have been grievous to my family. God's mercy allows me to see another day. Many are not as lucky and have lost their lives for their honesty. No individual dares to stand up to the government or question their policies or actions. As civilians, we constantly fear someone is listening to our conversations, so we ensure we never speak ill of the president or his government. Freedom of speech is a concept that is unheard of.

* * *

"In the world you will have tribulation; but be of good cheer,
I have overcome the world." John 16:33

BAGHDAD - 1991

Four months have passed since the invasion of Kuwait in early August. Anguish and frustration spread across the country as the citizens continue to prepare their homes. So much is unknown. The city of Baghdad is still rebuilding from the last war, and now, more destruction may be headed our way. *How much more devastation can a small country endure?*

With Christmas fast approaching, my family intends to celebrate, carrying on with our traditions as usual. Although fear's stronghold has gripped everyone's heart and mind, one thing Iraqi citizens do well is pick up the pieces and push through. All the while, the news of a potential war continues to play in the background. We have developed a love-hate relationship with the news anchors. In part, we appreciate the updates, while at the same time, we resent the ongoing uncertainty and the doom and gloom outlook.

Christmas passes by, and before we know it, New Year's Eve is here. Although New Year's Eve celebrations tend to be elaborate with Assyrian parties hosted at various banquet halls, ball gowns, and gourmet dinners, the celebration is smaller this year. The uncertainty of the threats escalating to a full war leaves everyone on lock down in their homes. One thing my family knows for certain, we should not stay in Baghdad as the verbal threats from America continue. Considering Baghdad is the capital, it is safe to assume it will be the first target. As my family gathers for the subtle celebration of another year, a decision is reached. On January 15, my family will escape from Baghdad and travel to Diana.

Preparations begin immediately. Babi Matti reserves a large bus to transport the family. Although my parents have a vehicle, none of the other family members do. It is our first and only car, a white 1970 Volkswagen Beetle, old and rustic with a vintage look. We cannot take it as it will not survive our long drive nor be comfortable for our family of five. The Beetle is mainly used to assist with groceries, as carrying everything is always a workout. Bringing the Beetle home led to yet another family celebration of being the first to own a car. Everyone took turns inside the car; those who knew how to drive drove it around the neighborhood. As I stood next to the vehicle, excited for all the adventures I would have in it, my oldest cousin stormed out of the house with a live chicken in his hands. He snapped the chicken's neck and poured the blood on the ground. He then asked Dad to dip his palms in the blood and stamp the car's hood to bless and protect the vehicle. The unfortunate chicken was sacrificed for an old vehicle that would not be driven as often as everyone anticipated since life took an unexpected turn. The Beetle will stay behind, along with a few men, to oversee the houses and ensure no break-ins happen.

Near midnight on January 15, twenty-two family members, including me, board the white and blue bus, leaving Babi Matti, my dad, and four uncles behind. We converted our shower room into a shelter for Dad and one of the uncles. This room is 2.5 by 2.5 meters (8 by 8 feet) with a drain, a showerhead, and two faucets on the left wall. Its location in the center of the house provides protection from each corner. We laid foam mattresses, sheets, pillows, and blankets on the floor. The men will spend their time in this little room while missiles fly over the city. Surrendering Dad and our other family members to the unknown, leaving them behind, and not knowing when and if we will see them again is terrifying. I tightly hug Dad as I say my goodbyes before boarding the bus.

Between people, luggage, and bedding, the bus is packed to the brim. We begin our trip to Diana, an Assyrian village in the northern part of Iraq, in the Kurdish territory; this destination was chosen because we have family ties there. Diana is also called Soran by the Kurdish population that resides with the Assyrians. After eight long hours with a few bathroom breaks, we finally arrive at the village where we intend to wait out the danger in Baghdad. The bus stops in front of Khatoony's home, an elderly woman living with her disabled twenty-year-old son, Fraydune. The small house is constructed of mud bricks. Across the street is a home and a church my maternal great-grandparents built. Both were passed down to Babi Matti and his family. But since he doesn't live in Diana, he has entrusted Khatoony with the keys as she maintains both in our absence.

It is early in the morning, and unbeknownst to Khatoony, we have arrived. My grandmother, Younia, greets the mother and son and retrieves the keys to the house and the church. With so many family members, we are able to unload the bus rather quickly, unpacking the thin mattresses, pillows, and blankets first to set up the sleeping arrangements between the house and the church. With all of the luggage, food supplies, and people, both the church and the house are left with very little space to move around.

My maternal great-grandparents were born and raised in Diana. They built this home when Babi Matti was a young boy. Through the years, they built the Mar Gewargis (Saint George) Church next to their home. The building has a rustic structure with brown, stucco siding that gives the illusion of mud. Two wooden doors swing open to a sizable room with a smooth, concrete floor. To the right is a large altar with a smaller one on each side. A purple curtain separates all three altars from the rest of the room. This tradition is carried on from the early Old Testament when the curtain separated the holy of holies. Only priests can enter the curtained space. Near the front door, there is an oak table with an Assyrian Bible and a large metal cross. When entering the church, people touch the cross, kiss the hand that touched it, and then make the cross sign on their chest, per tradition.

The church rests on 4,000 square meters (1 acre) of land and is gated all around. In the front of the church is a large, sturdy, white mulberry tree. My cousins waste no time creating a swing. They tie the ends of a thick water hose to one of the largest branches, and place a blanket on the curved bottom part to create a seat. The blanket is beneficial, preventing our thighs and bottoms from getting sore. As children usually do, we take turns pushing each other and finding a way to make the most of our situation. To the left of the church courtyard is a well. It has a rope tied to a bucket handle, which we use to retrieve water. Thankfully, the well has a wooden cover to prevent us from falling in. I have no desire to be near the well, especially when the lid is lifted. Given my fear of water and inability to swim, I am terrified of falling in and not being able to get out. It doesn't help that whenever the ladies are around it, they yell at the nearby children to stand back, or they will die in the well. Most of the children have a fear of wells instilled in them at a very early age.

The backside of the church has an open concrete slab as well, and a part of it holds my great-grandparents' graves. Each of these above-ground graves is covered with concrete. A plant has grown beside each grave that drapes over it. Since the two built the church, it was their honor to be buried there.

As for the house, it is another mud brick home. It has two bedrooms, one family room, a large open court, a small shower room, and a small sheltered cooking area. The 1 by 1 meter (3 by 3 feet) concrete brick restroom happens to be an outhouse, positioned between the church and the house, so both can share it. The toilet is primitive, comprised of a small hole in the ground that holds everyone's bodily waste. Two metal shingles lay on top, serving as a roof, and a black curtain is hung in place of a door. Stepping outside to use the bathroom at night is terrifying since it has no electricity and no street lights nearby. If the need arises to use the restroom at night, we use a gasoline lamp to light our path; we also go in pairs so one person can guard the curtain door and hold the lamp while the other takes care of business. Recruiting someone to accompany me to the bathroom is always a challenge. It takes effort and bravery to go out at night, surrounded by darkness, while listening to wolves howl from a distance. I am amazed no one in my family has fallen into the repugnant hole. It's a miracle, really.

This is not my first trip to my favorite place. I have spent many summers in Diana. Life here is simple, yet so rich and full. The houses are made of mud and are covered by metal shingles. Neighbors, at times, sit on the roof and visit. When it rains and the roof begins to leak, more hay must be spread on the roof and then pressed into the mud using a large cement cylinder roller with a large metal shaft. We push the heavy cylinder, pressing the hay into the mud while maintaining distance from the edges to prevent falling. To access the roof, we climb a wooden ladder that is not strapped to the house or anything, for that matter. The ladder is loosely leaned against the wall and can easily be moved if necessary. During hot summer nights, the villagers carry their bedding up their wooden ladders and sleep on their roofs. Waking up in the middle of the night to use the restroom during summer is a challenge as I have to wake Mom to help me descend the ladder, escort me to the bathroom, and ascend up, all the while holding me and the gasoline lamp. She does this with no hesitation or fear.

Diana also has two of my structurally favorite churches, Saint Mariam and Saint Joseph. The two churches sit side by side on a small hill overlooking the village, a 3 kilometer (2 mile) hike from the Mar Gewargis Church. These churches are tiny, measuring just 1.5 by 2.5 meters (5 by 8 feet), and the ceiling is only 1.2 meters (4 feet) tall. Most people have to crouch to enter. Diana's Assyrian residents take turns cleaning these small churches with pride. Serving the Lord by providing services that help the churches is considered a privilege. Many visit these churches and light candles in honor of the saints and anyone else they desire to light a candle for. Two of the outside walls are covered with wax and are considered our "make-a-wish" walls. After praying inside, we step outside, find a small river rock, and slide it up against the waxed wall. If the rock sticks to the wall and remains up, our wish will come true, but if the rock falls, our wish will not come true.

Although the churches are always open, church services are never held here due to their size and distance from the village. Despite this, everyone treats them with the utmost respect. While in the proximity of these buildings, we always whisper, yet we refrain from any horse play. The atmosphere of the churches is peaceful, and the space provides solitude to whomever visits. The Assyrian culture has a unique outlook on anything faith-based. The Bible, the cross, the priest, and the church building are sacred and holy, and it's an honor to be in their presence. Bibles and crosses are never placed on the ground or casually carried around. They are held with dignity and high regard. It is a unique trait that many other cultures lack.

The citizens of this little village are very hospitable. They care for each other and attend to each other's needs. Electricity is limited here, so most spend their evenings huddled around a candle or lamp, drinking tea, and sharing myths and legends. One of the common topics that is discussed during these evenings is Mar Gewargis (Saint George). Assyrians who reside in Diana believe in Mar Gewargis, as do most Assyrians worldwide. He was a Roman soldier born to a Roman father and a Greek mother who were both Christians in the eleventh century. Mar Gewargis was repeatedly tortured, lacerated, and eventually beheaded by the Romans for refusing to renounce his faith and refusing to offer a sacrifice to the Roman gods. The Assyrians often speak of the grace and protection he provides them, along with his heroic acts.

Legend has it a dragon had built a nest at a spring of water in Silene, which is in Libya. The dragon prevented the people from retrieving water. At first, the people offered sheep, and the dragon would temporarily leave the nest. But when they ran out of sheep, they decided to provide young girls instead, which served the same purpose. The girls were chosen by drawing straws until one day, the princess's straw was drawn. Before she was sacrificed, Mar Gewargis came along on a white horse, defeated the dragon, and spared the princess's life and the lives of all future girls who would have been sacrificed. Images of this act have been painted throughout history, and to this day, many Assyrian homes display one, if not more, of these paintings. Assyrians worldwide celebrate him by holding a feast called Dukhrana'd Mar Gewargis. A special church service is offered as well as communion, followed by a banquet where a lamb is sacrificed in his honor. Everyone celebrates together by feasting on the sacrifice. Stories of hearing a horse riding outside the church or in their neighborhood and believing it to be Mar Gewargis looking over them and protecting them are not uncommon in Diana.

"But the hour is coming, and now is, when the true worshipers will worship the Father in spirit and truth; for the Father is seeking such to worship Him. God is Spirit, and those who worship Him must worship in spirit and truth."
John 4:23-24

BAGHDAD - 1991

I t has been forty-eight hours since we left our homes in Baghdad. Nana Marna is extremely troubled about Dad and Uncle David as they remain behind. Her anxiety is so high, it seems to rub off onto the rest of us. She has a small radio, tiny enough to fit in her pocket, that is always in her hands. She places it down only to cook and clean, but it is continuously running even then. Daunting news of the war is played at all hours of the day. We can't seem to escape the bleak news. The radio has become our lullaby, except this lullaby is unlike any other. Instead of soothing music, it provides heart palpitations, and instead of serenity, it provides utter mental chaos. Yet, somehow, Nana Marna finds comfort in knowing every detail of the city where her two sons are. The dreaded news everyone has been praying against reaches through the waves of Nana Marna's little radio. It is January 17, and the strikes against Baghdad have officially begun. Although the strikes are truly against Saddam and his Regime, Baghdad and its citizens are paying the price. With the irreversible emotional, mental, physical, and financial damage along with the inevitable casualties, it is a heavy price to pay. People are still mourning their losses from the previous war as they

121

prepare for the potential loss of the Gulf War. Each night, the radio sounds the sirens, and though I'm not in Baghdad, their resounding blare crawls into my mind and finds its way into my nightmares again. The direct impact of the sirens is distant, but the effects on me mentally and emotionally are imminent. As the daily details of the strikes and the war are released, Mom glances at me with a look of disbelief. My predictions of the war and what I had witnessed in my dream slowly unfold, leaving us with more questions than answers. *How is this possible? How did I know?*

A month has passed but so quickly. With each passing second comes the news of the extensive damage Baghdad is enduring and the news of the increasing number of casualties. Such an ambiguous word—casualty. A person's entire life is summarized in one word. Casualty. Their purpose is reduced to a number. A number that will forever be associated with Hussein's evil regime.

February 15, I hear a knock on the church gate. I peek around the fence. "It's Dad!" I yell. Everyone rushes from the church and finds my father, Uncle David, and another uncle standing in the church courtyard under the mulberry tree. In shock, Nana Marna lunges to her feet and stumbles forward, pushing past everyone with open arms, ready to embrace her sons. The three traveled to Diana to ease our minds and hearts. It has been a long month not knowing if they are alive. Relief and gratitude wash over us as we embrace them.

My father and uncles tell us of the damage Baghdad has incurred. "It is safe to return and start rebuilding. The war is subsiding, and there's less bombing each night." Dad tells us.

We are determined to put the pieces of our lives back together again. With everyone in agreement, my family rents another white and blue bus. We pack our belongings, return the church keys to Khatoony, and begin our descent back to Baghdad with another grueling eight-hour trip.

We have low expectations of what we will find on the other side. We have heard the news, and the previous war has imprinted pictures of the devastation that may await us from this war. As we near the city, indications of the darkness roaming around are clear. Evidence of the evil that was responsible for so much destruction is seen at every turn, with lumps of concrete crumbled near partially demolished buildings. I can see inside some of these properties, primarily offices, and they are covered in black from the explosions.

On February 28, President Bush announces a ceasefire. It's time to pick up the pieces. By necessity, the citizens of Iraq are resilient and determined. Returning to Baghdad means resuming life as usual, at least to the best of our abilities. Everyone is returning to school and work as long as these places have not been turned to rubble. The businesses that survived the attacks continue to operate. Our sense of normalcy is returning, except for the structural damages, the many lives lost, and what feels like permanent emotional damage.

"The Lord also will be a refuge for the oppressed, a refuge in times of trouble." Psalm 9:9

BAGHDAD - 1991

Dad is pacing in the living room, trying to comprehend the rationale behind Mom's unreasonable and alarming suggestion.

"This is absurd. We can't continue living like this," Mom states, weary of the endless wars and turmoil in Iraq, not to mention the ongoing terror inflicted by Saddam's regime.

"Well, what option do we have?" Dad asks.

"Look around; everyone is leaving. I think we should too," she counters.

"Do you have any idea how much work that takes? And what if we get caught?"

To suggest escaping Iraq is equivalent to volunteering to die. At eight years old, listening to my parents argue, I know our chances of dying a brutal death are high if we attempt to escape, but I also know staying could lead to the same outcome. With a dictatorship that has inflicted so much pain and suffering upon everyone, it is unlikely they will let their citizens go easily. If apprehended, the probability of not only death but a savage one is almost guaranteed. After several weeks, many endless conversations, and much convincing on my mother's part, my parents finally agree that we should flee from Iraq. With many citizens fleeing to Jordan and Turkey during the war, my parents decide that Jordan is the best viable option for us due to its convenient location near Baghdad. We gather with the rest of the family and share the news. Finding everyone else with a similar thought process and desire to escape is bolstering.

Mom, being the brave woman she is, has volunteered to be the first to investigate the environment and the situation in Jordan. A week later, Dad purchases her bus ticket. Before I know it, she has a small duffle bag in hand, and I'm preparing to say goodbye. Trembling inside while maintaining a brave face, I hug my mother tightly, interlacing my fingers around her back. I don't want to let go, but the sooner I let her go, the sooner she can return. I have to keep my emotions in check. I cannot fall apart; doing so will only add to my father's sorrow and cause my little sisters to worry more. But I can't help but think, *What if Hussein's people ambush her bus? What will happen to her if she's caught? Will she find hope in Jordan?* So many questions and no answers. Even though the turmoil is growing inside me, I press on by keeping my mind in check and pushing aside any fearful thoughts. I only have faith to believe she will return safely.

She has been gone for a week now, and it has been one of the longest weeks of my existence. I have been anxiously awaiting her return as I continue to care for my sister, Sona, who is five, and my sister, Rodina, who is two. Luckily, it is late June, and I don't have school. Early in the morning, I wake up with an extra spring in my step. Mom is coming home today. The anticipation of seeing her is too strong to contain as I rush through feeding and dressing my sisters to be at the bus stop before she arrives. To my relief, we make it on time.

Waiting at the station, I see the bus nearing before coming to a complete stop. I can't see her. I stand on my toes, extending my height a bit more, praying for a glimpse of her. And there she is. I smile as her eyes meet mine. A massive sense of relief washes over me. My heart is nearly bursting, yearning to hug her. I have to restrain myself from powering through everyone to reach her. Mom is home and safe.

The next day, the family gathers in our home to hear Mom's findings in Jordan. It does not take long for a unanimous decision to be reached. We are moving. In a blink, our furniture is listed for sale, and the landlord has been notified we will not be extending our lease past July.

Emotions are high as day after day, I watch my belongings, labeled with a price tag, slowly walk out the door to their new homes. The couch I spent so much time on watching *The Muppet Show* and the Christmas tree we proudly displayed each year are the first to go. Soon, my toys and everything else I own are gone too. Everything that represents me and my life is being traded for a small amount of money. No dinar can compensate for the sentimental value of these items. My memories are stepping out the door, and there is nothing I can do or say to change it.

However, none of these belongings compare to what I will soon lose. My Halla, the blanket that has given me so much comfort throughout the years, will not accompany me to Jordan. "You have to leave it behind," Mom says, "It is time to grow up."

I understand why I have to give up Halla, but it doesn't make it easier. Heartbroken, I pass it on to someone I cherish and respect very much—my third-grade teacher, Jameelah. She is my favorite teacher who spends a lot of time with my family. Upon finding out I am moving, she has come to the house to say goodbye. I walk toward her. With hands shaking and tears streaming down my face, I extend my Halla to her. Sorrowfully, I explain the significance of the blanket. Her face lights up as I hand it to her, followed by a compassionate and empathetic smile.

* * *

"He heals the brokenhearted and binds up their wounds."
Psalm 147:3

BAGHDAD - 1991

It is two weeks before our departure to Jordan. I wake up to noises in my bedroom. As I roll over and rub my eyes to clear my blurry vision, I see Mom rummaging through my drawers, selecting various pieces of clothes, and tossing them into the duffle bag she's holding. "What are you doing?" I ask, struggling to make sense of her actions.

"I'm taking you and your sisters to the hospital to have your tonsils removed."

I fling myself forward and scramble to my feet. "Where are we going? Did you just say hospital? Does that mean surgery?"

Her eyes lock with mine, and in a stoic voice, she says, "Yes." She seems distant, cold almost. She is on a mission, and there is no stopping her.

"I don't want to have surgery, Mom!" I cry out, begging her to change her mind, but she continues packing my sisters' clothes as if she can't hear me. Feeling nauseous and scared, I continue to cry out to Mom until she finally snaps.

"You and your sisters need to have your tonsils removed before we leave for Jordan. I need to ensure you don't get sick there."

Though I understand Mom's concern, it doesn't ease my worry. *I do not want to be operated on. How can I help Mom see this? How can I change her mind? Her determination is scaring me.*

Lost in tormenting thoughts, I assist Mom with my sisters to prepare them for this unplanned adventure we are embarking on. I begin praying and imploring God to stop this from happening, but nothing changes in Mom's attitude or demeanor. Nothing, that is, until the doorbell rings. I run to the door hoping for a rescuer, and that is just what I get when I swing the door open. It's our neighbor friend, Farida.

Farida spends many mornings visiting with Mom while they enjoy tea and pastries. She can sense the energy within my house with one look at my frantic face and the packed bag near the front door. The atmosphere has shifted from the typical cheerful greetings she is accustomed to.

"Why is there a bag by the door?" she inquires.

"I'm taking the girls to the hospital to have their tonsils removed before we leave for Jordan. I don't want them to get ill while in another country." Mom says this as if it is the most ordinary thing in the world.

Shocked and confused, Farida reaches for Mom's arm and stops her. "You can't possibly think putting your girls under the knife is wise before your trip?"

Standing in my bedroom, within hearing distance from where Farida and Mom are, I eavesdrop on their conversation as I earnestly pray for a change of mind. Minutes pass as Farida continues to urge Mom to abort her plan and leave her girls as they are. Farida is slowly able to bring Mom back to her senses by tapping into her logic, and in doing so, Mom's change of heart immediately takes effect. Mom quickly realizes the unnecessary pressure she is inflicting upon herself and us for something she can't control. "Never mind, Ramina, we are going to hold off and see what happens," she announces, unaware I have been closely listening to their conversation. Immediately, a wave of relief washes over me. My prayers have been answered. An hour ago, I felt as if Mom was standing on the edge of a cliff, ready to jump with my sisters and me tied to her waist, and now, we've metaphorically moved away from the cliff's edge, and Mom is thinking more clearly again.

* * *

"I will praise You, for You have answered me, and have become my salvation." Psalm 118:21

JORDAN - 1991

The house is empty, fully depleted of everything we once owned. Seven bedrooms, once so lively, are now vacant with nothing but an echo to accompany each word spoken. The walls of our large house, now barren, hold nothing but memories. At nine years old, everything I own is packed into a small suitcase, resting next to my family's luggage and large bags that hold pillows, blankets, and thin mattresses.

July 14, 1991 is a day we have been anticipating, yet dreading all at the same time. This is the day we begin our new journey to a foreign land. Passports and tickets in hand, we travel to the bus station. After loading our luggage into the storage compartment, we patiently wait for our turn to board. One step at a time, we find a seat and quietly sit back. Confusion and pain cloud my mind and heart as I reflect on the painful goodbyes. A knot of emotion forms in my chest and fights its way up to my throat as I process the last moments with my family and friends, knowing I may never see them again.

Grief-stricken, we rest on the bus en route to a country we know very little about. We have limited knowledge of life and the culture there.

We have one commonality with Jordan, the Arabic language. Thankfully, understanding and communicating are still doable despite the accent and dialect differences.

The bus ride to Amman, Jordan's capital, is thirteen hours long with only a few stops. Most of the landscape we drive through is desolate. As I sit next to the window, my view is dreary with endless dry land, a few tumbleweeds here and there, and heat waves rising from the hot ground. Everyone is discouraged and overwhelmed by the fear of the unknown. The road seems long, with no end in sight, no games to play, and no entertainment. I am mostly alone with my thoughts, except for the occasional short conversation with my parents or cousins.

Staring out the window into the dry distance, I realize I have two options: weep and mourn what I left behind or embrace this change and accept my new reality.

Upon arriving in Amman, Jordan, the bus stops at the end of the block beside the house Mom arranged for us to move into. It is a small busy neighborhood that is slightly rundown, but I am reassured that there are many other Iraqi immigrants here. Located alongside the busy main street, with several bus stops and grocery markets, the area is ideal as everything is easily accessible.

My family members travel to Jordan in two waves. The first consists of my immediate family, Mom's three sisters, their spouses and children, and my grandparents. Tired, sad, and discouraged, we carry our luggage and belongings and walk down the street to the third house on the right facing an open dirt field. We step through the rusted, tall, and skinny gates and face the large, square, open court covered in concrete. There are three bedrooms on one side of the open space and one on the other next to the kitchen, bathroom, and shower room.

Each aunt and her spouse and children move into one room, while my grandparents and youngest aunt take the fourth room. The bedrooms have a concrete floor where we spread a thin rug and lay out our bedding—no bed frames or headboards, just foam mattresses, blankets, pillows, and a few sheets.

Living in one house with eighteen people is chaotic, especially when eight of those individuals are children between the ages of two and fifteen. We take turns sharing the kitchen, bathroom, and shower room to control the chaos. Like our previous home, this house also does not have a water heater. Instead, we boil water in a large pot on the stove and mix it with cold water to reach a comfortable temperature to shower with. With only one stove, we are lucky enough to shower once every three days.

Most of the adult family members have found labor jobs while the rest of us stay home and tend to our domestic duties. Everyone carries their weight to support each other and survive. Having recently turned nine, I quickly assume the caretaker role for my small family. I feed and dress my sisters, clean our room, wash the dishes, and cook lunch and dinner so when my parents arrive tired, they have nothing to concern themselves with except rest. Once a week, I wash my family's laundry, rinse it, and then hang it to dry on ropes using clothespins. Not having a washing machine, this activity leaves my arms, shoulders, and wrinkled hands aching for hours after.

A family of five living in one small bedroom is rather confined. Our bedding takes up most of the floor space at night. During the day, however, to create a livable space, I stack all the bedding against the wall, building a tall mountain. I then cover it with a large blanket and gently tuck the blanket edges under the pile. Tidying up our beds requires finesse as everything must be folded neatly and packed in one of the room's corners. I tear the mountain down at bedtime each night and lay everything on the ground. Our Middle Eastern mattresses have no cushion to them or much support. They are made of a simple foam that can be rolled or folded with the rest of the bedding. It is nothing but a 12 centimeter (5 inch) foam wrapped in a custom-made sheet cover, like a duvet, that can be taken off and washed. Box springs do not exist. Our version of a box spring is the concrete floor that supports our mattresses.

On a good note, life in Jordan is not all chores and duties. My neighborhood is primarily surrounded by dirt, and the unpaved street leading to the main road is mostly dirt and rocks. Through exploring, we have discovered that a small grocery shop at the end of our block sells popsicles. They are red, strawberry-flavored, and shaped like a hand—palm, fingers, and all. The popsicle is giant and worth my Dinar. I'm in love with these sugary treats. I find myself begging my parents and grandparents for coins to satisfy my craving. This is my time to disconnect from my chores and reality and enjoy the sweet taste of strawberry before it melts and runs down my arm.

Though my daily tasks are daunting and exhausting most days, I keep my focus on what matters most—supporting my family.

"If one member suffers, all the members suffer with it; or if one member is honored, all the members rejoice with it."
1 Corinthians 12:26

JORDAN - 1991

I t is August, and we have lived in Jordan for a month. We feel lost in a sea of uncertainty, learning to adapt to our new norm. The school has resumed for the Jordanian children. Early each morning, shortly after my parents leave for work and before my sisters wake up, I rush to sit outside the large metal doors. I slump on a small rock and observe the neighborhood kids departing for school. I watch them walk to the bus stop wearing school uniforms similar to ours in Iraq and backpacks tightly strapped onto their shoulders. Oh, how I envy them, wishing I could continue my education. I also envy their friendships as I watch them walk in groups, talking and laughing. Every morning I am reminded of what has been taken away from me. My jealousy can quickly turn into anger and hatred if I allow it, but I can't. That's not who I am.

Despite Jordan being an Arab country that is also primarily Muslim with a similar belief system and lifestyle to that of Iraq, the Iraqi people are treated as outcasts—rejects. Iraq's involvement in the past two wars has caused the surrounding countries to grow bitter toward my country and its citizens.

Regardless of our new environment and living situation, my parents and family members insist that my cousins' and my education continue. Enrolling Iraqi children into the school system is a painstaking process but worth the effort. We are fully aware of the reality that this is a short-term step, as our stay in Jordan is temporary. Nevertheless, I'm elated to embark on a new adventure, attend school in a foreign country, and further my education.

My youngest aunt and grandparents agree to care for my sisters while I'm in school and my parents are at work. It is encouraging that my cousins and I are placed in the third grade together, although none of us are in the third grade, and our ages vary. We are told this is the only classroom with the capacity to accommodate us. I don't care as long as we attend school and are together. I am equally excited and anxious about this next step. I want to prove to myself and those around me that I am more than a "reject" from Iraq. Yet, I can't help but listen to the whispers of fear and doubt, reminding me that I am just an unwanted immigrant.

I wake up early in the morning, prepare breakfast, and pack a small bag for lunch. I quickly call my cousins, and we rush to the bus stop. Immediately, all eyes are on us; we don't have a uniform, and our casual attire stands out. Although Jordanian children wear uniforms, we don't have to. Since we are immigrants, our presence is considered temporary, nothing but an inconvenient gust of wind passing through. The rejection extends beyond adults as the children have also been encouraged to alienate us. We follow the neighborhood children from a distance, close enough to hear them conversing but not close enough to feel like we are a part of the group. The bus rides are similar. We are with them, but we are not of them.

Attending classes with the Jordanian children is excruciating. The teacher's bitterness toward us is obvious whenever she addresses the four of us. Her tone is different. Often, she ignores us when we raise our hands. Whenever her eyes meet mine, there's a sternness to her glare that tries to pierce through me, making me uncomfortable. The school refuses to give us textbooks. Instead, we must listen intently to each teacher and decipher the material ourselves. During recess, my cousins and I keep to ourselves, watching everyone play from a distance as none of them will interact with "the outcasts."

I enjoyed learning in Iraq, despite the strictness of the school. But now, for the first time, I hate going to school. I hate the very thought of it. Even though I participate in class when given the opportunity, the school system does not acknowledge my presence. My attendance record is not mandatory, nor do they keep track of my grades. There is no report card to take home to share with Babi Matti and no certificate at the end of the school year. It is disheartening as I have always thrived in school. This, too, is another obstacle I have to embrace and find my way through. But I know that if I want to succeed in life, I must further my education, and nothing will stand in my way.

Another month passes before the second wave of my family arrives in mid-September. My paternal grandparents and aunt are en route. This leaves Uncle David and his family behind in Baghdad. Our current home does not have the capacity to add three additional people, forcing my parents to search for another rental for the eight of us. Hoping for a house within walking distance, we desire to remain close to the family, but our efforts are to no avail as there are no options nearby. The nearest home is a two-level duplex that is a twenty-minute bus ride from the rest of my family. With this move, I leave behind Babi Matti and my cousins. My sisters and I no longer have our closest friends to play with. The duplex is split with the landlord. We rent the lower level, which consists of a two-bedroom house with a very small living room. My parents continue working while Nana Marna and my aunt care for my sisters and me. This is a great relief that eases my workload, giving me more time to play.

One of my new favorite pastimes is bossing geese around. We have a small yard next to the front door that is separated from the patio by a short, brick ledge. The yard hosts eight white geese owned by the landlords. They are beautiful, obnoxious, often loud, and sometimes friendly. I name the biggest goose, Mortin, after the main character from a cartoon I watched in Iraq. I command them to line up, and magically, they listen and obey. Baba Sawa often sits on the patio and laughs as he watches me work my magic. My aunt calls it bossiness—I would like to think of it as my leadership skills developing at the age of nine.

With my aunt and grandmother easing my household responsibilities, I ask my parents to enroll me in school again in this new location, hoping the change in cities yields different results. I quickly realize I am mistaken. The same awful treatment continues. Attendance means nothing. Attending school, only to be mistreated for the sake of education, doesn't seem to be worth it. However, I continue to endure it, but this time alone, as my cousins are no longer with me. My motivation has drastically decreased; I only attend school when convenient. Needless to say, I miss many school days. It is heartbreaking to admit that my desire for school has fully diminished. It doesn't take long for my cousins to quit their schooling either, feeling defeated by the unfair treatment.

Human rights isn't even a concept in Iraq. Every Iraqi citizen understands that there are no inherent rights given to people under tyranny. But now, I am sad to live in Jordan, where I am alienated from others simply because of my country of origin, and I get to sit back and watch everyone else move freely and enjoy their life. My skin tone and looks are very similar to the kids around me; however, my accent differs, as each Middle Eastern country has a unique dialect. I don't think it's fair that I'm ostracized for such a small difference, for something I cannot control. No child should feel alone and excluded for their race or ethnicity. It is sad and confusing for me.

* * *

"But those who wait on the Lord, shall renew their strength;
they shall mount up with wings like eagles, they shall run and
not be weary, they shall walk and not faint." Isaiah 40:31

JORDAN - 1991

Thursday, October 10, 1991, is a day unlike any other. I am in bed by 9 p.m. in the room I share with my parents and sisters. My sisters are asleep, and my parents are watching TV with my aunt and grandparents in the living room. I lay on my thin mattress facing the wall, attempting to sleep, when a magnificent bright light shines. I turn to see the source, but it is blinding. The room is brighter than the sun. Suddenly, Jesus appears in the midst of the light as if He is glowing. I rub my eyes to adjust my vision, assuming I am imagining what's transpiring in front of me. Yet, nothing changes. I stare in awe. Jesus is standing in front of me. I don't dare tear my eyes away from His beauty. Though I have never seen Him before, deep down, every fiber of my being somehow recognizes Him.

I'm startled by what's transpiring before my eyes, but I can't help but feel peace—complete and utter peace. Looking into His beautiful, brown eyes, my eyes are opened to a glory beyond comprehension or words.

He serenely lifts His hand and points His index finger at me. I can't help but notice the holes in His hands. My eyes slowly gaze at His feet only to find them pierced as well. "Rise; in two days is the resurrection." He softly speaks.

"What do you mean by—" I plead.

He disappears. Confused, I search around the room. He is gone. Darkness takes over the room again; only the faint light from the moon's reflection remains. All is as it was before. I look to my left, astonished that my sisters are still sound asleep.

Sitting on the floor, facing the now ordinary and dull wall that was so bright seconds ago, my heart races as adrenaline rushes through my veins. I am in awe, absorbing what just happened, trying to make sense of His words. *What could He possibly mean?* My head spins. *"In two days is the resurrection."* His words continue to echo in my mind. *If only I had a few more minutes with Him. I have so many questions. Resurrection. How can that be?* I know it's a powerful word, yet I do not know its meaning in this context.

The idea of resurrection in two days inflicts fear in my young, nine-year-old mind. I fear it because, in my perception, it is associated with the end of the world and judgment day. My confusion persists. *Why would Jesus choose me? I don't understand what's happening to me. First, the Gulf War dream, and now this.* In this instance, I realize my Bible knowledge is minimal, and my understanding of God and His different methods of communication is limited. I need to learn more. I need to discern what is happening.

I force myself to stand up. I need to tell Mom. As I walk into the living room, everyone stares in my direction, surprised to see me still awake.

"Are you okay, Honey?" Mom asks.

"Yes, I need to talk to you. Something just happened. I just saw Jesus standing next to my bed."

Her eyes briefly scan the room before her gaze returns to me. "What do you mean you saw Jesus? What did He tell you?"

I tell her every detail, from His beauty to His pierced hands and feet to His words that continue to ring in my ears.

Mom takes it all in stride. She learned long ago that my visions are not to be taken lightly. She inquires further, "What do you think He meant by resurrection? What do you think you need to do?"

"I think I need to read the Bible," I say with a sense of urgency. Asking for a Bible is not a common request, especially by a child. It is not customary for me to voluntarily read the Bible instead of attending church and having the priest read and interpret it.

"Okay. Tomorrow, I will find you a Bible," Mom replies. Offering to purchase a Bible for a child is not common for Assyrian parents, yet I have been blessed with a mother who does not conform to societal norms but instead, makes choices based on what's best for her family. Mom's willingness to find me a Bible is a welcomed gesture—a beautiful one, really.

True to her word, Mom rushes to the store shortly after breakfast and finds The Action Bible. It is an extensive children's Bible with images, similar to a comic book. Minutes after receiving it, I am in my room, sitting on the floor, reading my new Bible. Starting with Genesis, I intend to read through to Revelation in two days.

Like many Assyrian families, we attend the Orthodox Church of the East but do not customarily read the Bible. I remember hearing the stories while growing up, but until today, I have never picked up a Bible. My only mission for the next two days is to read it, cover to cover; I desire nothing else. With so much to take in, the task feels a bit daunting, but I am determined, and nothing can stop me.

As Saturday slowly approaches, there is a mixture of emotions brewing within me. In one way, I am excited, but in the other, I am anxious and scared. I did not finish reading the entire Bible in two days, even though I turned down watching television with my family and playing outside with my sisters. I allowed no distractions, only taking breaks for meals and the bathroom. I anxiously await the end of Saturday to see what will come to pass.

Nothing.

I don't know what I expected, but "nothing" was not part of it. Sunday morning brings disappointment and relief.

"Okay, God, you said two days, and I patiently waited, but nothing happened. I will wait two weeks." I reason aloud, just to be sure He heard me.

I continue reading my Bible, absorbing as much as my tiny brain can hold and experiencing stories I've never heard before. I read about Moses and his powerful encounters with God, Samuel and his leadership, David and his heroic take down of Goliath with a simple rock, Esther and her bravery, Peter and his simple yet honest personality, and Paul and his boldness for Christ. These stories give me hope and the encouragement I need to press on despite my circumstances.

However, disappointment hovers as two weeks pass and—NOTHING.

Nothing transpires. My bedtime prayer is short and to the point. "Lord, I don't understand what's happening. You said two days, and here I am at the two-week mark with no changes. As you know, I am not the most patient person, but I will wait two months. Amen." To my surprise and disappointment, the two-month mark is just as dull as the other days. Nothing happens. Everything is the same.

"This is it, Jesus; I'm giving you two years. I want to know what's happening. Why did you say two days and then leave me in silence?"

I continue to read my Bible. As I near the book of Revelation, I am reminded by family members of the magnitude of this book—a book that encompasses the end of the world. The responses and remarks of others who have read it have been strong enough to build a terror in me. I've endured enough turmoil in my life up to this point that I would like to avoid more. So I skip it, flip back to Genesis, and start reading again while holding out hope that October 10, 1993, will be an extraordinary day.

* * *

"I wait for the Lord, my soul waits, and in His word I do hope." Psalm 130:5

JORDAN - 1991

I n a moment, fear and panic jolt me out of a deep sleep. *Something is wrong. Something terrible is going to happen today.* As I utter the words, "Babi Matti." Sweat beads across my face and chest. Trembling, I push myself to the edge of my mattress. Confused, I attempt to make sense of the awful dream I experienced just moments ago. Daylight gently peers through the window. I gaze around the room. My sisters are still soundly asleep as I watch their chests slowly rise and fall, I envy their deep, restful sleep.

I should tell Mom about my dream. Wait. What if she isn't as understanding with this one as she was with the other ones? What if this dream comes true, and she blames me or, worse, hates me? What bearing will this dream have on my family? The questions keep coming, one after another, and I don't have an answer for any of them.

I haven't felt fear like this before; this is a whole new level. Anxiety attempts to stifle me, but I muster the courage to head toward Mom. I need to tell her the truth. I hear dishes and silverware clanging. She must be in the kitchen preparing breakfast. It's almost time for her to leave for work. Mom has found a job at a sewing factory a few blocks from our house in Amman. The factory is close enough that I can visit her and work as her little assistant. Her work environment is so vibrant with so many types of fabrics, buttons, beads, and even zippers, but the work itself is often dull and monotonous as the workers endure countless laborious hours on the job. Several times a week, I cook lunch and take it to Mom's work. We share a meal while she shows me her latest project. I enjoy this limited time with Mom; it makes me feel grown up. But today, I need to convince her to stay home.

"Good morning, Mom."

She faces me and smiles, "Good morning, Khayee." Meaning "my life," it is a term of endearment Mom often uses for me, along with most of my family members.

"I need to tell you something," I utter, trembling with nervousness. "I just woke up from a bad dream."

"What was the dream?"

"I don't think you want to know. You're not going to like it."

"What makes you think that? Just tell me," she implores. Mom has always been gracious and attentive regarding my dreams and visions. She listens earnestly and asks questions to help me piece together my thoughts. I take a deep breath and recite my dream to Mom.

"I was standing at the bottom of a hill that had a large cross planted on top. As I walked around the hill and began climbing, I noticed Babi Matti standing at the top of the hill holding his own cross. I rushed to him, hoping to reach him, but it was no use. The faster I walked, the further away he got from me. I began running, sprinting, but the distance continued to grow. In that instance—" I pause and glance at her face, trying to read her body language, but nothing. She is focused on my dream.

"Then what?" She beckons.

"I don't think Babi Matti will live through today, Mom," I whisper as I choke on my tears.

Mom, listening patiently, musters the courage to calm me down as she wraps her arms around me and holds me close to her chest. She has been extremely patient and understanding with my dreams and visions up to now. But this—this is new. This impacts her directly. It affects her hero, her favorite person besides Dad and us girls.

"I just told you, I don't think he will survive today. Something bad is going to happen to him," I reiterate, in case she didn't hear me.

"Honey, that's ridiculous. He's young and healthy. Nothing bad is going to happen, I promise." She tries her best to assure me of this as she rushes me to get dressed, brush my teeth, and prepare for the day ahead.

She gives me a faint nod as she strides out the front door, over the concrete patio, and past the metal gate. I hear the clink. She's gone. The hours slowly pass by. My sisters and I are playing with the geese on the patio when we hear an urgent knock on the gate. With each knock, my heart pounds. I rush to the gate, pull the handle, and swing the metal door wide open, only to find my oldest cousin at the doorstep, frantic and out of breath.

At the sound of the gate, my dad, aunt, and grandparents rush to the patio. "Who is it?"

"Is Auntie Mado home?" Mado, short for Madlen, is the nickname Mom inherited at an early age.

"No, she left for work a few hours ago. Is everything okay?" Dad asks.

"Babi Matti is in the hospital and asking for Auntie Mado," my cousin explains.

This is it. I can feel my heart hammering against my chest; with each passing beat, my world crumbles as my dream plays through my mind. My legs feel weak, almost numb. *I can't lose Babi Matti.* As Mom said earlier, he is healthy; he seemed healthy to everyone. Yet, *why would he need to go to the hospital if he's healthy?*

Immediately, Dad and Nana Marna run out of the house and head to Mom's work. They tell her the news and rush her to the hospital. Frantic and afraid, she hurries through the hospital hallway, her short heels clacking against the tile floor as she looks for her family. She sees her sister in tears, pacing outside one of the rooms from a distance. In that instant, Mom *knew.* Deep down, she knew hours before but pushed those thoughts to the back of her mind, trying not to give in to them. But now, it is too late. As she nears the room, eyes brimming with tears, she can hear the grievous mourning; everyone is gathered around Babi Matti's cold and pale body. He is gone.

He passed minutes before her arrival.

Mom and Babi Matti always had a unique bond. They were obviously father-daughter, but they were also best friends. Whenever he was stressed or navigating life's challenges, he always found comfort in sharing his heart with Mom. With a glance, they knew what the other was thinking. Today, at fifty-six years old, he has journeyed to the other side from a heart attack. Two days ago, he had complained of chest pain all morning, so Mom escorted him to the local hospital. The two spent hours in the waiting room as his symptoms progressed, but in the end, he was released and sent home.

"Unfortunately, you need to come back another day," the nurse had told them. "As you can see, the waiting room is full, and we cannot accommodate everyone."

"But my father—you have to help us. He's been having chest pain all morning, which could be serious. Please, I beg of you, just have a doctor take a look!" My mother pleaded.

"I'm sorry, you will need to come back another time. Two days would be ideal as the schedule is at capacity."

Two days were too long for Babi Matti, and his heart gave out.

With life's stresses, wars, and other hardships, most people in Iraq don't live very long. Life expectancy is below fifty-five years old. Living past the mid-fifties is a luxury and is considered old age. Although it seems premature, Babi Matti passed within his life expectancy, just like most Iraqi men.

"And God will wipe away every tear from their eyes; there shall be no more death, nor sorrow, nor crying. There shall be no more pain, for the former things have passed away."
Revelation 21:4

JORDAN - 1991

Anxiously waiting for news, I pace in my living room. Suddenly, the landlords above shout from their balcony, "Telephone! You have a phone call." We don't have a phone, but our landlords are gracious enough to allow local calls to be made when necessary. My aunt rushes up the stairs, and within minutes, she slowly stumbles down, her face wet with tears. One look into her eyes, and I know he is gone.

I drop to my knees and cover my face with my hands as a terrible groan escapes from my throat. *This cannot be. He can't be gone. This has to be a nightmare. My dream did not turn into reality today.*

And yet, it is real. I feel the anguish. My heart breaks. Tears flood my eyes, and I weep. All of the hardships I've endured in my young life do not compare to what I feel right now. The pain in my chest is fierce and overwhelming. Feeling powerless and in despair, nothing seems to ease the hurt. The more I cry, the harder I want to cry. The man who took pride in my simple report cards, took me on my first date, and motivated me to achieve and excel is no longer here.

Loneliness and depression set in as I begin to accept the reality that my biggest cheerleader has been stripped away from me. Anger at the world and its injustices grow inside of me. He is gone, and I didn't even get to say goodbye. If only I could hug him again, kiss him on the cheek, and tell him I love him one last time. But I can't. He is gone. There is nothing I can do to bring him back, not even for a moment, to tell him how much I love him.

Memories of Babi Matti flood my mind, each moment we shared plays back like a movie. I especially cherish my final date with him in the spring of 1991 when I came home with my third-grade report card. Had I known that was my last date, I would have extended it for as long as possible. I would have given him a bigger, longer hug than I did that day. The special moments and memories we built together were priceless. In the immediacy of his passing, I know life will never be the same.

Babi Matti lived a life full of compassion, always setting the example of loving others. Losing him in a foreign country builds up resentment in all of us. We have already lost so much; losing the family patriarch in a stranger's land feels unbearable. Living in Jordan as refugees means our stay is temporary, and our fate is uncertain. Though our departure is unknown, we trust that it will eventually come. Knowing our departure is imminent increases the pain in our already grief-stricken hearts. Soon, we will have to leave Babi Matti behind. His body will remain in Jordan, where visiting will be nearly impossible once we depart.

In the Assyrian culture, a great deal of time and effort is invested in funerals. After Babi Matti's passing, family members, relatives, friends, and neighbors continue to visit our home to share their condolences. At this time, so many Assyrians have fled Iraq and live in Jordan near us. As the mourning family, it is our duty and honor to host everyone and provide mourners with tea and pastries, and sometimes, even a meal. It has been three days since he passed, and we have a church service planned for the funeral followed by the burial. The Assyrian community living near will escort us as a way of showing support and will join us afterward in our home to continue grieving with our family.

The Roman Orthodox Church we occasionally attend has agreed to host Babi Matti's memorial service. The service is a blur—a few scriptures are chanted followed by the priest mumbling. My mind is foggy, and I can't seem to clear it enough to absorb my reality. Looking around the church, I see many heads bowed and tears streaming. There is so much gloom all around, the adults and children alike dressed in black. We slowly escort the casket outside the church and drive to the cemetery. A few generous church members volunteer and drive my large family. Like a strong wind sweeping through the desert, a wave of emotions strikes me as I watch his coffin, holding the remains of my grandfather, being placed in its fixed position.

Being in a foreign country, my family wants to protect his grave at all costs. We want to provide him with a beautiful and comfortable space that ensures the safety and protection of his physical body. This is a significant expense that we do not have the financial means to achieve without the assistance of my aunt, who has been living in America since the early 1980s. She provides the necessary money to build the most elaborate gravesite possible. His coffin is placed above ground, with three steps leading up to it. The steps and the coffin are covered in white marble, and a black metal cage with a lock secures the grave. Because we are temporary refugees in Jordan with no assurance of being able to return, reinforcing his gravesite brings us all a small measure of peace and control. We know the soul matters most, but this is a significant step in our healing process.

On the seventh day, everyone revisits our home, and the church also raises a special prayer for my Babi Matti. On the fortieth day, the church lifts another prayer for him, followed by a small memorial hosted at the church's reception hall. In Iraq, this continues at the one-year mark as well, where the church performs its routine prayer for the deceased, followed by a final reception that is much smaller. These ongoing remembrances provide much-needed love and support for my mourning family and allow us to take our time grieving.

As is customary, my immediate family dresses in black or navy for the first forty days of mourning to display our grief and honor my grandfather. We can slowly introduce other colors after the forty-day mark, but most grieving mothers and spouses will remain in black and navy clothing for an entire year, if not longer. During the mourning season—sometimes for up to a year—immediate family members and relatives will not attend any parties, will not listen to loud music where others can hear them, and will not be seen outside the home participating in any celebration. These actions are seen as a sign of disrespect to the deceased. This is a long, drawn-out ordeal, but it's also one of healing in which family members are always consoled and tended to; they do not face grief and mourning alone. It is a comfort to experience the most challenging time of someone's life surrounded by family, friends, and love.

Grandma Younia remains strong, like always. Already having had a rough life, she endures this struggle and grieves her significant loss in a foreign land. She is resilient and thanks God for having her family by her side while she mourns. My grandmother knows she has to find a way to move forward, to hold on to the hope that the pain will lessen, but she still spends many long, sorrowful days shedding tears.

Babi Matti's loss has given Mom additional clarity that there is more to my dreams than any of us understand. Though she has been supportive before, now she truly embraces them and does what she can to help me decipher them. She never makes me feel stupid or crazy when I share my dreams with her, nor does she blame me for her father's death, which significantly relieves me. Mom reassures me that what I have is a gift, not a curse. Though I have never met anyone who has experienced anything like this, her encouragement helps me accept this ability and not let it scare me. Somehow, I understand God has chosen to reveal things to me for a reason. I know He has a purpose for me, but I don't know what or why. I just embrace it and move forward.

* * *

"Blessed are those who mourn, for they shall be comforted."
Matthew 5:4

JORDAN - 1991

Jordan. What can I say about it? It's a beautiful proverbial land, rich in history and culture. Yet, I struggle to fully embrace the experience of it. I'm consumed by the stresses of life as my family and I attempt to adjust mentally, emotionally, and financially. But, through it all, we focus on the positives, remembering that every morning is a new beginning, a new possibility. For one thing, we are no longer living in Iraq's demise. For another, we have access to embassies—any and all embassies. Shortly after the Gulf War began, many of the embassies in Iraq were either shut down or destroyed by missiles, especially the American one.

Leaving Iraq in a legal manner requires the government's permission, which is unobtainable unless the government benefits from it. This leads to all unauthorized travel to be considered illegal. It takes a leap of faith to escape the wars and Iraq altogether. It demands courage. Even though we departed for Jordan with passports and bus tickets in hand, we defied the government. Our rebellion is righteous, however, because living in Jordan opens doors to embassies, which gives us hope for finding refuge elsewhere.

Seeking refuge in another country requires energy, hard work, patience, and perseverance. Refugees must submit completed applications to the United Nations (UN) for review. The UN has exclusive information on how many refugees any given country will accept each year, and the opportunities are limited. Once an application is submitted, it is ranked by the UN or the embassies. The ranking is primarily based on how many relatives, if any, the applicants have in the particular country in which they seek refuge. For example, if an individual applies to Denmark with a son or daughter living there, their application will receive a higher ranking, increasing their chances of getting into Denmark. If the applicant has siblings there, their application will be ranked a bit lower, and so on.

Once the embassy officials review an application, which can take up to thirty days, the approved applicants' names will be listed on a large sheet of paper and taped to the outside wall of the UN building. Being listed on that wall is terrific news as it means the family is approved to move forward to step two. Since we do not have a phone, which is common, we must take a twenty-minute ride by bus or taxi every two to three days to review the list for our names. Arranging transportation and staying optimistic is arduous.

I can't help but stay positive and be hopeful an embassy will accept our application and select my family. If we are lucky enough to have our names appear on the wall, the next step will be to notify the UN officials and schedule an interview.

To be interviewed is a privilege; it means someone sees us and knows we exist. From what we have heard and seen from other families, the interview process can take two to eight hours. At first, the entire family is interviewed together. Then, family members are separated for a second interview to ensure their stories align and they have no ties to the Iraqi government. The officials will also confirm the verbal information shared during the interviews with the written statements submitted on the application. Every so often, children seventeen years and younger are also interviewed. Grueling is one way to describe it. Emotions shift like the speed and turns of a roller coaster. The pressure is intense; one wrong move, statement, or gesture can lead to immediate rejection. There is no room for mistakes.

After the initial interview, we must return to that wall and see if we have advanced to the next step. If our names are listed, then our family moves forward yet again. If our names don't appear after several trips to the wall, we ask UN officials to search the system for our status. Most times, requesting an official to search the system means our application has indeed been declined, which means we must start the process again. It is an exhausting and strenuous process that seems to intentionally wear down those who dare to take it on, leaving only the most resilient still standing.

We live in a constant state of wait-and-see, which gives birth to resentment and occasionally, despair. The invitation is ever-present to pick up rejection and abandonment.

In the event of a miracle and we advance to the third step, which is another interview, we must make the same trip to the wall to read of our fate. If our names appear on the wall, it alludes to our family's acceptance into the country we applied for.

It has been seven months since we moved to Jordan, and my family's names have never progressed beyond step one. We watch neighbors and distant relatives pass through without impediment. It is always easy to envy someone else's success; how can we not? People who moved to Jordan after us have been advancing through the process faster, despite them following the same process we do. The challenge comes in being supportive and encouraging when others succeed, and we don't. That's where the true test lies.

My family has endured the application process for several countries, including the United States, Canada, Australia, Sweden, Finland, Germany, Denmark, and France. We meticulously followed the process for each of these countries, and each one denied our application. Some of the embassies we applied to several times, yet each time, we received the dreaded rejection. Despite Mom having a brother and a sister who live in the United States, our request for asylum is turned down every time. We also applied directly to the United Nations, hoping they could aid us in seeking refuge, but the outcome has been the same. Nothing. Silence. We have nowhere to go.

Jordan provides refugees with a visa that allows them to live here, but it has an expiration date. The visa can be renewed. However, the process is just as grueling. Our visa is nearing its expiration date, and we must acquire legal assistance to renew it, which is costly. If we are found and captured with an expired visa, deportation to Iraq is immediate. We don't have the ample funds required to renew our visa, and to make matters worse, my parents will lose their job upon the expiration date. The alternative will be to find generous Jordanian citizens willing to pay immigrants cash under the table in exchange for labor. The trick is finding merciful Jordanians we can trust. Refugees who choose this route live in hiding to avoid deportation and imprisonment.

As days turn into weeks and weeks into months, we experience nothing but rejection from country after country. A young family with three small daughters, limited options and resources, no place to call home, and nowhere to go, we find ourselves lost in a sea of uncertainty, never able to silence the whispers of fear that chase our every thought and step. It makes me wonder if a safe place even exists or if anyone values our lives or wants us. *Humanity* is a word I thought I understood, but my family has yet to experience the feeling behind the meaning. Our lives do not reflect our understanding of the word, "humanity." After all, we feel much less than humans. We have no rights, no voice, and receive no respect. As our visa's expiration date is fast approaching, it feels as if our expiration date as people is soon to follow. All our efforts to extend the date have failed.

Since Hussein disapproved of the Iraqi citizens fleeing, deportation back to Iraq will lead to automatic torture and execution at the hands of his regime. At nine, the terror of rape and torture clouds my mind. I can't help but think of the numerous revolting stories I've heard throughout my childhood of the women violated and tortured at the hands of the regime. Even for young girls, their age is not enough to deter the nefarious actions of these men. If we want to stay alive, we need to act fast.

* * *

"The Lord, He is the One who goes before you. He will be with you, He will not leave you nor forsake you; do not fear nor be dismayed." Deuteronomy 31:8

TURKEY - 1992

We are at a crossroads. With our visa on the verge of expiration and the Jordanian government on the prowl, hunting down immigrants with expired documents, our hope of survival is diminishing. We have limited options. We know one thing for sure, we are on the brink of overstaying our welcome in Jordan, especially given our source of income will soon cease with the visa. If captured, we face immediate deportation. We need an escape plan. Seeking refuge in Jordan has led to endless rejection. If luck is on our side, moving to another country that is closer could lead to better opportunities and an extended life.

With little to no other options, my parents decide to move us to Turkey, a country that has become a shelter for many Iraqi refugees, similar to Jordan.

Turkey is a beautiful country steeped in history, delicious food, and a unique language. Turkey shares its border with northern Iraq. Although it is a Muslim country, the primary language is Turkish rather than Arabic. Unfortunately, Turks and Arabs share a mostly hateful relationship.

After the Gulf War, many Iraqis illegally escaped to Turkey, some on foot, others via car or bus. Many people lost their lives during the escape due to the long, exhausting trek through the mountains that lasted ten to fifteen days and the added difficulties of transporting children and running out of food and water. Others lost their lives when the Turkish border guards captured them. Some of the lucky survivors share horrific stories of their journeys and how they stumbled upon dead bodies along the way. As people died, their bodies were left behind out of necessity. I have learned that survival takes heart, strength, and emotional detachment. Anything less often leads to death. Thankfully, moving directly from Jordan to Turkey is safer than the trip our fellow Iraqis have experienced hiking through the mountains on foot.

Those who can withstand the relentless mountains and successfully seek refuge in Turkey are placed in refugee camps and granted visas. This visa comes with an expiration date as well. Considering we have exhausted all alternative options in Jordan, moving to Turkey seems the most viable choice.

In March of 1992, Dad flies to Turkey first, to seek refuge and find a safe place for us to live. Shortly after his move, we purchase our plane tickets to Istanbul. My youngest aunt will join us with her husband.

Separating from and saying goodbye to my friends and distant relatives in Iraq was extremely difficult; however, leaving behind my immediate family in Jordan is even more painful. They have chosen to remain in Jordan, facing the unknown regardless of the circumstances. It is a heartbreaking experience to hug and kiss my aunts and uncles, but especially my cousins, whom I have grown so close to, knowing this might be the last time I will see them.

I visit Babi Matti's gravesite to say goodbye, and to make matters worse, I also have to say goodbye to Baba Sawa, leaving behind both my grandfathers, whom I adore and love oh-so-deeply. A small part of me was left in Baghdad when we fled Iraq, but an even more significant part is staying behind in Jordan. Even though I have only spent eight months in Amman, I'm leaving a piece of my heart here. This is the beginning of a life lesson. I am quickly learning how to emotionally detach from objects and people in order to survive. I fully understand why we're moving to Turkey. My parents are put in a tough position as they decide our family's next steps. Though there is no one right or wrong approach, each path comes with the promise of hardship and many unknowns.

Moving to Turkey will present me with several new opportunities. Living in a new country will allow me to explore a new culture. At least, that's what I tell myself as we transit to the airport. Never having been on an airplane before, I am shocked at their massive size. The concept of lifting so much weight through the air and traveling long distances is beyond what my little brain can fathom. I scan the ticket in hand and find my seat. As I reach to buckle my seatbelt, bittersweet emotions wash over me. This is it. The moment we've been waiting for. There's no turning back now. It's hard to believe that we had our weekly Sunday gatherings just a year ago, and today, we are all dispersing to various foreign countries with little hope of reconnecting anytime soon.

Latching my belt, I lean back and settle into my cushioned seat. I hear a loud voice through the speakers, but I'm unable to absorb a single word. I'm overwhelmed by thoughts racing and emotions stirring. *I can't cry right now. I have to stay composed. I need to be brave for my family.*

My emotions slowly dissipate, and adrenaline kicks in as the airplane lifts off the ground. I gaze out the window and watch the surrounding landscape shrink as we rise into the clouds. After a smooth hour and twenty-five-minute flight, the pilot requests that all passengers buckle their seat belts and prepare for landing. Lost in my thoughts and emotions, I realize I never even unbuckled mine. Adrenaline strikes again as the airplane slows and hovers above the ground. The wheels make contact with the runway, and the force jolts us forward toward the seat in front of us. "Welcome to Turkey," the pilot announces.

* * *

"Be strong and of good courage; do not be afraid, nor be dismayed, for the Lord your God is with you wherever you go." Joshua 1:9

TURKEY - 1992

The city of Istanbul is expansive and stunning. A historical city with tall architecture uniquely placed within, its beauty reflects the cultural influences inherited from many empires that once ruled here. The culture seems more modern and upscale than what we have experienced. Istanbul provides us with one of the most challenging steps we have taken so far. The Turkish people don't speak Arabic, which eliminates our primary method of communication. Not only are we outcasts seeking mercy, but we are outcasts with no practical means of expressing our needs or understanding this new culture through conversation. However, I view this challenge with optimism and see it as a valuable opportunity to learn a new language, Turkish.

Dad greets us at the airport. We take a taxi to the small apartment he leased. It doesn't take long to notice this apartment is in poor condition. It is located on the fourth floor, which is also the top floor of the building. With no elevator in sight, we must climb ninety-nine stairs to reach the top. The ninety-ninth step leads to an expansive hallway which ends with a small kitchen. To the right of the stairs is a toilet room, shower room, and a small bedroom. To the left of the stairs are two small rooms conjoined together, separated by a partial wall. Both sides share the kitchen, toilet, and shower room. My aunt and her husband will occupy the tiny space on the right side while we inhabit the one on the left.

Stepping through the threshold of the door, I can't help but notice the peeling plaster and holes in the walls. The first room holds all our furnishings: a single chair and a small TV that Dad had found. The second will hold our bedding. We quickly unpack our things, which doesn't take us more than a few minutes since we don't have much.

Each room has a small window that opens wide with no fence or screen to prevent falls. Large buildings made of brick and concrete hover over our little street. Limited light peers through each day as the adjacent tall building blocks the sun. Though the buildings are tall and sturdy on the outside, they are neglected and weak on the inside. I often open the window to stare into the street and watch our neighbor hang her family's laundry on a rope between our two apartment buildings. Every apartment within these structures is connected to the adjacent apartment building via the laundry ropes. Tenants in the apartments take turns using these ropes while developing superficial friendships as conversations take place through the windows while hanging clothes.

We have been here for fourteen days, and today, there is a soccer game. I can't understand the commentators' words, yet it is almost soothing. The background noise takes me back to all the soccer games I watched with my extended family, gathered around our small television, cheering. Soon, reality sets in, quickly followed by loneliness. In these moments, I find myself sitting on the windowsill, staring into the distance with occasional interruptions of neighbors chattering. I look down at the cracked, concrete street and see people moving around freely, without a care in the world. *Are they free? What makes them happy? What frustrates them? Would they change anything about their lives if given the opportunity?* I know my passions and desires and exactly which parts of my life I would adjust if I ever stumble upon a genie who can grant me three wishes. All my wishes would be spent on changing my circumstances and wishing for a normal childhood. Whatever "normal" means, I want it. I desire it. But no one seems to know how to find "normal" anymore, as everything in our world has been turned upside down.

There is very little for my sisters and me to do here. No toys, no friends, just the three of us, connecting and bonding through the gift of imagination. The only friendships we form in Turkey are with the local pigeons. A small number of them stop on our windowsill every few days, so we feed them what little bread we can spare. This increases their visits and improves our pastime.

As refugees confined in a small, dingy apartment, we have to get creative when it comes to our entertainment. Despite the language barrier, Turkish cartoons provide a short reprieve in the limited time they air. Not having any toys, Mom taps into her crafty mind and designs three dolls using popsicle sticks. She ties two sticks together in the shape of a plus sign, wraps them with foam and fabric, draws faces on them, and voila, we have dollies extraordinaire. We spend hours each day playing with them—my first and only doll. Growing up with three male cousins, I spent most of my time playing with Hot Wheels, Transformers, and marbles instead of dolls. If I wasn't playing with beads or jump-roping with friends, I was playing with my cousins and their male friends.

I loved collecting the little cars and racing them on the street when I lived in Baghdad. I also loved watching *Tom and Jerry* and the Middle Eastern version of *Transformers*, trying my best not to miss even one episode of those shows. I remember how my cousins and I would huddle in the living room, glued to the TV as those cartoons played, and how we'd run right back outside the moment the episodes finished. Reminiscing about our adventures together makes me miss them even more. It also reminds me why dolls have never been my choice of toy. They bring back the memory of when I was invited to a playdate in the second grade.

One of my classmates, who lived a block away from me, asked several girls to meet at her house. I rushed to her place, assuming we would spend time outside playing jump rope, beads, or even hide-and-seek. I was wrong. Each girl arrived with a doll in hand; I was the only one who didn't come with one—because I didn't own one. I did not know it was a requirement for the playdate. If I had, I would have avoided it altogether and dodged spending the afternoon sitting on the bed, feeling excluded while watching the girls play on the floor. That was an uncomfortable experience. I could not wait to go home, be in my environment, and play with friends who shared my interests. I never attended another playdate that didn't include my cousins again. However, today, I don't have the option of playing with either. It's just me and my sisters now, and we need to make the most of our situation, even in a strange land.

I decide to name my doll Nina.

"Do not be conformed to this world, but be transformed by the renewing of your mind, that you may prove what is that good and acceptable and perfect will of God." Romans 12:2

TURKEY - 1992

Merhaba: hello. Teşekkürler Ederim: thank you. Ne Kadar: how much?

I ask my parents to find me an Arabic-Turkish dictionary so I can teach myself the native language. Watching my parents struggle is heartbreaking; hence, I take it upon myself to expand my vocabulary. This is the first exposure I've had to the Turkish language, which is so unique and distinct from Arabic or Assyrian. It is not an easy language, but I am always up for a challenge. It keeps me occupied. Within a day of exploring the dictionary and documenting which words I need to know, I begin forming sentences and practicing them at the small shops below our apartment building. My dictionary has become my companion; I don't travel without it. Grocery shopping is a fun and adventurous outing now because I can practice conversing in Turkish. The downside of grocery shopping is carrying our groceries ninety-nine steps of stairs—exhausting.

Downtown Istanbul is a fifteen-minute walk from our apartment. Most evenings, we stroll through the dingy streets to reach magnificent beauty. It is hard to believe the difference between the city's two parts. Mainstreet is large, wide, and open, with many expensive and fancy shops that feel out of reach for our empty wallets. We're only rich enough to window shop.

The open court on the street has large benches spread throughout with unlimited pigeons that stroll around searching for food. My sisters and I look forward to visiting Mainstreet as we get to spend more time with the pigeons and self-enacting.

Lounging on the benches can be challenging at times, especially when hungry. Food carts are spread throughout downtown, and each cart smells more inviting than the previous. Most provide sandwiches, with a few sweets carts scattered throughout. When my parents can afford it, they buy us one of my all-time favorite sandwiches, a gyro with warm, fresh, French bread stuffed with meat marinated in special spices, peppers, and onions. This doesn't happen often as our finances are limited with my parents unable to work due to our immigration status. We rely on the money my parents saved while working in Jordan and the financial provisions we receive from our extended family living in Australia and America. Despite not always being able to get a treat, these short trips ease our loneliness and give us a glimpse of hope; knowing our visa days are numbered brings additional stress and anxiety to our family.

At home, my chores continue, and caring for my sisters remains the same, even with both parents currently unemployed. Early one morning, Sona asks for an egg, sunny side up. Happy to oblige her, I approach our 1 meter tall (3 feet) gasoline stove. I pour oil into a pan and place it on the burner. As I wait for the oil to reach the right temperature before I crack the egg, Sona accidentally touches the panhandle, tipping it over, and dumping the hot oil onto my right foot.

I scream in agony. Pain shoots through my foot and leg, almost reaching my heart. I'm nine years old and have never experienced this much physical pain before. Tears stream down my cheeks as I gasp for air. My uncle, standing nearby, is the first to run to me. He witnessed the pan drop in slow motion but wasn't close enough to intercept it. He quickly sweeps me in his arms, puts me in the bathroom sink, and runs cold water over my throbbing foot. I sit on the sink, trembling and crying. Mom and Aunt rush over at the sound of my screams. They stand by me, attempting to console me. Mom tries to rub my back gently, but I don't want her or anyone else touching me; everything hurts. The cold water is the only remedy I want right now. Mom allows me to sit in the sink with the water running for twenty minutes. The excruciating, throbbing pain resumes each time I move my foot away.

Not having the means for a doctor's visit, Mom resorts to the home remedy almost every household uses to help with burns—placing toothpaste or tomato paste on the burn. My family primarily uses toothpaste. Mom takes the tube, dries my foot, and rubs the minty paste over the affected area. On the floor, holding my toothpaste-covered foot, praying for relief, I hear Mom and Aunt discuss what to do.

Later today, there will be a farmer's market that sells groceries at low costs. With our limited budget, this is an ideal option for us to put food on the table. Feeling responsible for the well-being of my family, as I often do, I can't be the reason we don't go. The neighborhood and building are unsafe, which makes me unable to stay home alone, and my family needs as many hands as possible to carry the grocery bags and make it up all of the stairs. Wincing, I find my way up. "We're going. I will be fine." I lather more toothpaste over the affected area, noticing the growing blisters forming on my foot. I put on my summer sandals with two elastic straps that cross over my feet. Limping, I walk to the market, shop, and walk back. Though I have to resist whimpering with each step, the toothpaste seems to take the edge off and make walking tolerable.

* * *

"We also glory in tribulations, knowing that tribulation produces perseverance, and perseverance, character; and character, hope." Romans 5:3-4

TURKEY - 1992

The clock is ticking on our three-month Turkish visa. It is time to assess our options again. Staying in Turkey with an expired visa will lead to deportation, but not before a trip to the torture chamber. While strolling through downtown Istanbul and shopping in the local markets, we encounter several Iraqi refugees. Like us, they have escaped from Iraq and hope to immigrate to any country that will accept them. During one of our rendezvous, one of them mentions a camp that is assisting refugees by renewing or offering new visas. With no other options, this is a path worth considering. Living as refugees, desperate for a place to call home, we are always in search of hope.

My parents, aunt, and her husband discuss the possibility of this camp, evaluating every scenario that comes to mind. Finally, it is decided this camp is worth exploring. My aunt and uncle would be the first to go, seeking information. It takes them several days to connect with a few distant cousins who live in the camp and to acquire the necessary information and validity of this camp. Within a week of their departure from our rundown apartment, my aunt calls and suggests we join them. "You need to pack and come here. Moving to the camp will increase your chance for a new visa."

"That's great. I will speak to James when he comes home and let you know."

Minutes after Dad enters the room, Mom shares the news of the camp and the possibility of a new visa. We pack our few belongings and prepare to join them. A day later, we are on a bus traveling to more uncertainty.

The camp only accepts illegal immigrants in need of visas. My family, however, traveled to Turkey legally, using a passport. Fearing being caught with our passports in hand, my parents boldly decide to leave our most important documents with a family friend, leaving us with our soon-to-be-expiring visas and Iraqi identification cards only. This is a temporary and brief trip, just long enough to renew our visas and travel back to Istanbul to begin the application process with the United Nations and the embassies.

We join the camp with my aunt, her husband, and other relatives. Upon arrival, we are assigned a small, two-bedroom, one-bath apartment, which we share with another family of five. The apartment is lightly furnished, and the camp provides limited weekly groceries. We are eager for this prospect as we feel a second chance on the horizon, a chance to renew our visa, and hopefully begin our application process with the embassies again. Yet, we are also apprehensive. The distress of living as a refugee in a foreign country with young children is exhausting. The possibility of deportation is terrorizing. But we must go on, holding onto the hope of a miracle.

The camp consists of several apartment complexes, a store, and a park. Sona and I quickly befriend a few children, spending most of our time at the playground. The park is not ornate by any means. It has two swings and a metal slide that has rusted through the years. At nine years old, I almost forgot what being a child running through a park with friends feels like. I can't recall the last time Sona and I were on a slide.

During one of our outings, Sona begins to climb the ladder attached to the slide. In a rush to reach the top, she loses her footing. From the corner of my eye, I see her foot slip as her balance falters, and she begins to fall backward. I quickly rush over and catch her, but not before my left ring finger comes in contact with one of the rusted pieces of metal bulging out of the ladder. The metal stabs my finger, cutting the inside from the middle knuckle to the top one. Unaware of the cut, I swiftly grab Sona's arm, preventing her from hitting the ground. Only after I ensure she is unharmed do I feel a warm liquid dripping from my finger and onto my leg. I lift my hand to find a grisly cut with flesh partially peeking out. My heart pounds as I fear the severity of the cut, and the sight of blood makes me nauseous. I quickly push the protruding flesh back in and pinch my skin. I rush home, looking for medical supplies. Nothing. No bandaids. No gauze. Absolutely nothing. I resolve to find the next best thing—tape. My finger is throbbing as I rinse it with water. I cover the cut with toilet paper and then use the tape to wrap it around my finger.

"Don't tell Mom and Dad...please. I don't want to worry them," I urge my six-year-old sister, Sona. Understanding my family's circumstances and my parent's lack of means for medical treatment, I must keep this from them. I spend the next two days in pain. My finger pulsates, and all the while, I make sure my parents don't notice the random tape around my cut.

"We just received a letter from the camp officials," Dad states as he steps into the apartment, holding a white envelope in hand.

"What does the letter say?" Mom asks.

"It is requesting our presence tomorrow at the dining hall in the camp's center." He continues, "The letter also states all newcomers must be present with every family member. And bring any documentation available to review our visas."

The excitement of this news quickly masks my pain. This is something my family and I have been praying for. The following day, our eagerness and anticipation increases as we impatiently wait for 4 p.m. Dad grabs the yellow manila envelope filled with our identification cards and documents at 3 p.m., and we begin our descent toward the military-type warehouse. We intend to arrive early to secure our place in line closer to the front.

As we enter the large doors to the warehouse, we discover that we are among the first to arrive. The warehouse is a tall building with a wide open concrete slab, big enough to house an airplane. In reality, it looks like a hangar surrounded by sturdy metal walls. With each passing minute, our excitement grows; this will allow us another opportunity to reach out to the United Nations and other embassies in hopes of success this time. We are desperate to settle in whatever country is willing to welcome us and look at us like human beings instead of rejects.

It is now 4 p.m., and the families that received the same note have arrived at the warehouse, totaling about five hundred people. Turkish government officials slowly walk in and sit on the opposite side of the long tables that face us. They have numerous papers and applications sectioned on each table, along with pens. But nothing is happening. The officials converse and seem busy, but we can't understand a word as they speak Turkish. I try to lean in and listen but cannot grasp any part of their conversation. Eventually, they reach for our envelope and begin reviewing it. Or so we think.

Focused on the Turkish official staring at our documents, I hear footsteps marching in unison toward the building, and the sound gets louder and louder with each passing second. I turn my gaze to the entrance only to see armed soldiers blocking it. They have surrounded the location on all fronts. We are trapped from every corner. Machine guns lift and point in our direction. The building is enclosed with armed men as if they are hunting dangerous criminals. Too stunned by the scene unfolding before us, our hope quickly turns to gut-sinking dread. I shift my gaze to the open area behind the soldiers and notice a line of large buses driving toward the warehouse. Immediately, the realization and probability of deportation hovers over us like a dark cloud.

In disbelief, I stand in the middle of the chaos. I hear everyone around me sobbing. Frightened children cling to their parents, fearing what is next. In tears, parents tightly hold onto their families, begging for compassion. Screams and wailing fill the air at the sight of the large buses now lined up behind the soldiers. I feel my parents' quivering arms tightly wrap around my sisters and me as we stand before them, facing the guns.

Fear overtakes me, and every part of my body trembles. I know what will transpire soon. While I hear everyone's cries, I remain silent. Not a single tear forms.

My focus is on something else.

The enormous warehouse doors are wide open. As I look beyond the chaos, beyond the buses and the heavily armed soldiers, I see an opportunity. I close my eyes and imagine myself running through everything and crossing to the other side unscathed. *If I can get beyond all of this, I can stay behind and hide and maybe save my family.* I'm not sure how a nine-year-old can accomplish such a victory, but I am determined to do something as I face certain death otherwise.

With very little thought, I act on my imagination. I take off running. Fearing my legs will give out from underneath me, I focus on my goal as I pass a few soldiers. *Phew, one significant obstacle down.* Then I pass the buses. *Another one down.* My heart is racing, and my knees shake as I run as fast as my short legs can manage, ignoring the desperate cries from my parents calling me back. *I am almost there; I just need to run a little faster.* Everything is moving around me as if in slow motion. *I can do thi-*

My escape comes to a screeching halt when a soldier reaches out and captures me, his grip tight on my arm. Without a word, he picks me up and walks me to my parents. To my surprise, he drops me at their feet. Alive.

I am alive.

Relieved, my parents wrap their arms around me even tighter this time, in disbelief at what I did. The soldier could have easily shot me right then. Though I am a child, he has full permission to do so, but he spares my life instead. For that, I am grateful.

Standing in the warehouse, trapped, my terror rises, and I finally break down and cry as I wait with my parents, sisters, and so many others. Our fate is sealed—deportation.

The cries of pleading for an alternative supersede all other sounds. It is overwhelming. Nothing works. No one is listening. No one cares.

"Oynat (Move)!" One of the soldiers shouts.

"Hadi gidelim, acele et (Let's go, hurry up)!" another soldier screams.

Like sheep headed for slaughter, we are escorted to the buses, one person at a time. We walk between the tips of the machine guns. Some are aimed high at taller individuals, while others are aimed low at women and children. If we protest, death. If we participate and accept deportation, death. Caught between worlds, to give in to either is suicide, but what choice do we have?

Downhearted, we step onto the bus and take a seat. We are left alone with our thoughts, fears, and assumptions. Each bus is heavily armed, with two soldiers sitting in the front and two in the back to ensure no one escapes. And so we begin our new, yet familiar, journey back to the motherland.

I have grown accustomed to being treated as less than human, sometimes even less than animals. There is no difference. Unhappy endings are becoming the norm. My days lived in fear outnumber my days lived in happiness.

I slump in my seat, still stunned at the events unfolding. After the wailing and crying subsides, the passengers sit quietly on the bus, awaiting their fate. Pain, anger, and frustration manifest within me. I'm devoid of hope, drained of life, cast into the sea, drowning. As I gaze out the window, my finger begins to pulsate. The adrenaline had masked my pain, but that only lasted so long. Instantly, I realize I have no means to clean and tend to my finger. However, considering our situation, my injured finger seems minuscule and insignificant.

The bus ride is eighteen hours long with a few bathroom breaks. There are no restrooms along the way, just open fields. Going to the bathroom in the open, with hundreds of people, surrounded by soldiers, is humiliating—dehumanizing.

The soldiers provide us with water, French bread, and tomatoes as our meals, which we quietly consume. With each bite, we swallow our pain and the bland, dry food.

Eyelids heavy from exhaustion, I rest in my chair, lean my head against the window, and fall asleep. Morning light casts a bright hue through the window. I open my eyes, amazed at the reality that I could fall asleep at such a time as this. I wake up hoping everything that transpired the night before was nothing but a nightmare. One look around me dashes that hope. This is my new reality. We are on our way back to Iraq.

Since we were instructed to come to the warehouse with only our paperwork, we are left with nothing. With the rushed chaos of being quickly herded onto the buses, we weren't allowed to retrieve our few belongings from the apartment, forcing us to leave everything behind. The clothes on our backs and the yellow manila envelope are all we own now. I watch my life slowly diminish to almost nothing. I have a physical body, clothes, and my identification card. Anything else would be a luxury.

My life has been nothing but constant change. I feel as if I am incessantly forced to relinquish anything with value. Adjusting to always giving things up has led to developing a sense that everything I own is nothing but a material object that will depart one day. In this instant, I feel myself embarking on a new journey, a journey of turning off emotional attachments. After all, I am quickly learning that having an attachment to anything will lead to disappointment, loss, and heartbreak.

My finger throbs again. I peel the tape back and notice the cut is not healing. Part of the flesh is looming again. I push it back in and wrap it with that same tape. This is getting harder as the tape is now dirty and hardly sticking. Despite this, I still keep my cut a secret from my parents. I trust in time, it will heal; that is, if death doesn't reach me first. In that case, it won't be a problem.

My attention is pulled back to the road when the buses come to a complete stop. The soldiers point their guns at us yet again, forcing us to exit. As we set foot on the dry, hot dirt in the middle of nowhere, we see the dreaded sign: "Iraq-Turkey" at the border. Once the buses are emptied, the soldiers line up behind us with guns aimed at our backs, forcing us to walk to the other side of the sign.

We are standing in the face of a new change unlike any other. This change puts our lives in the hands of Hussein's regime, with execution being our likely destination.

Tired, hot, and hungry, we march into Iraq's territory. Everyone walks with their head down, overwhelmed by fear, shame, and rejection. Turkey never planned to renew our visa; they planned to gather as many Iraqi refugees into one location and deport them. Mission accomplished.

July heat in Iraq shows no mercy, with temperatures ranging from 30° to 40° C (90° to 115° F). We feel the heat waves rising around us as we slowly shuffle forward. Once everyone crosses, the soldiers board the buses and leave. We watch the dust settle and the road clear as we absorb our reality.

I can't help but feel a dreadful sense of abandonment and fear. My heart is in my throat as I stand on the dry and barren land, waiting for the Iraqi soldiers to appear. *Will they arrive with a thirst for blood? Will our death be quick with a simple gunshot, execution style? Or, will there be more?*

I try to ground my mind, focusing on this moment, focusing on the fact that I am still alive. But I fail. I am about to turn ten years old at the end of this month, and yet, all I can focus on is the torture awaiting me. With dread, we wait in the heat. We wait for the soldiers. We wait for something or someone.

But, nothing. Nothing happens. No one comes.

Now what? As far as my eyes can see, we are surrounded by desolate land; there are no structures—just dirt.

With the sun beating down on us and our confusion growing at the lack of a terrifying welcome at the Iraqi border, we come to the conclusion that there is nothing to do except pick a direction and walk. One by one, we begin walking, drawing courage from within. With every step, solace begins to swarm the fear we feel. With every step, we wait for the sound of boots. We wait for the sound of gunshots, but once again, we are met with nothing.

Only after walking 3 kilometers (2 miles) do my eyes finally spot a building in the distance. As I wonder if I'm imagining it, the murmurs from the people around me confirm it's not an illusion. I find myself once again scared of what we will find.

As we near the small town, we see a sign designating it as the town of Zakho. At the edge of the city stands a white building in what seems to be the middle of nowhere. As we approach it, we are struck by confusion at the banner.

United Nations.

How is this possible? They don't exist in Iraq.

I am hesitant to let my hopes up, and yet I can't help but feel a little bit of relief at seeing the giant banner. Between the fact that we are not greeted by Iraqi soldiers holding us at gunpoint at the border and the words *United Nations,* I am overwhelmed by the turn of events. My heart begins to fill with peace as I slowly accept the possibility that we might be safe.

With no other option, my uncle walks up to the building and thumps on the door. After several knocks, a gentleman answers; shockingly, that gentleman is a relative of my uncle's. Astonished at the sight, he takes a few minutes to understand our situation. After he is brought up to speed, we quickly learn that the UN is unable to assist. We had hoped he and the UN team could send us back to Turkey to give us another chance at seeking asylum in other countries, but unfortunately, that task is outside their capability.

Although the United Nations is unable to assist us in leaving Iraq again, their presence brings absolution. Their presence is the reason why I and everyone else did not get slaughtered by Saddam's regime. Their presence is the reason why we can experience a deep exhalation, something we have lacked in the past twenty-four hours. Though we still face the unknown as we stand in front of the UN building, in the meantime, we have the opportunity to live, a moment to take another breath and plot our next step.

We had assumed we were walking to our execution and that death awaited us on this side of the border. Little did we know that God had another plan for us, faithfully watching over us all along—even before we learned to recognize it.

* * *

"The Lord your God in your midst, the Mighty One, will save; He will rejoice over you with gladness, He will quiet you with His love, He will rejoice over you with singing."
Zephaniah 3:17

IRAQ - 1992

The Gulf War caused Iraq to split into two parts: the northern, controlled by the United Nations, and the southern, controlled by Hussein and his government. Mercifully, Turkey borders the northern side of Iraq, which means we have been deported into the UN's territory instead of Hussein's. Learning of this change brings instant relief as we experience vindication from an unwarranted death sentence.

My uncle quickly reacquaints with his family member. Even though the UN can't help us, his relative is generous enough to open his house to my family for a few days until we can assess our situation and our new reality. During our short stay in his home, we must develop a plan, identify our next steps, and start a life in northern Iraq. The problem is we don't know much about this region, have no money, and have no family to help us. The obstacles continue to rise, creating a seemingly insurmountable situation. We've lived most of our lives in Baghdad; what little family we have in Iraq reside in Diana, a five-hour drive from our new location.

News of our deportation travels fast throughout Zakho and the surrounding cities. Mom's distant cousin, Ashur, lives in a city nearby called Duhok. He is informed that our family is one of the many deported and stranded in Zakho. He immediately inquires about our location and contacts us, graciously opening his home. One of the many beautiful qualities of the Assyrian culture, no matter the distance of a relative, everyone is always treated like family, and Ashur is no different. He is a distant cousin, but that does not prevent him from driving an hour to pick us up and bring us to his home. Meanwhile, my aunt and her husband decide to stay behind. They want to attempt Turkey once more, hoping for a different outcome. Living in Iraq is not an option for them, and they have the funds to leave, seeing as it's only the two of them.

Since legal travel is banned, any form of transportation between Iraq and the surrounding countries requires smugglers. As for us, we have nothing. Paying smugglers to escape Iraq for a family of five can cost thousands of US dollars, which we do not have. I, again, have to say goodbye to more of my family members, not knowing if I will ever see them again. The pain of farewell never eases, no matter how many times I have done so. I hug them tightly before entering Ashur's car, waving until I can no longer see them.

Ashur has offered for us to move in with him, his wife, and five young children; we are beyond grateful for their invitation. We arrive at Ashur's house and are welcomed with a large feast his wife, Linda, has prepared. We consume the delicious meal and are finally able to rest. What a wild few days it has been. Assuming we were headed toward our death, we are a bit shocked to find ourselves safe and well-fed in the company of family.

After settling in, the reality that we have no spare articles of clothing sinks in. The Turkish officials did not allow us to pack our belongings before deportation. Linda, being the generous and amazing woman she is, sifts through her children's clothing and finds the most gender-neutral articles for my sisters and me. They have four boys similar to our age and one infant girl. I happily wear the boys' pajamas and crash in bed, exhausted and thankful. I'm also relieved to finally clean my wounded finger and find sanitary supplies to treat it. With each passing day, the cut shrinks, eventually leaving me with a small scar.

Our first week back has been emotional, filled with sorrow and mourning. After everything we have endured, we are back to square one. Facing the unknown has become part of our daily routine, but being around the people, language, and lifestyle familiar to us in Iraq is a pleasant relief. Not to mention, the joy that comes with knowing that Hussein is not in control of this territory, leaves us safe for the time being.

Twelve of us live in Ashur's home, but we manage. Everyone contributes, helping with chores and doing what is necessary. My family slowly finds peace as we accept our new chapter of life.

With the UN in control, UNICEF, the Red Cross, and many missionary organizations have come to Iraq to provide support. They roam throughout the north in their white SUVs with the organization flags waving high and proud. Some of the organizations offer food and medicine, while others provide Bibles along with their aid supplies.

Many of these organizations rent fully-furnished houses throughout the cities of Duhok and Arbel for their staff. Most homes have around-the-clock security services, with one or two guards on duty. The guards are armed and screen everyone who comes through. Ashur is one of these security guards and works the night shift for a Red Cross house on the same street as his home. He cannot work tonight, so Dad volunteers and asks if I want to join him. Excitedly, I agree. The two of us spend the night watching movies, eating copious amounts of food, and enjoying more television channels than we are used to. The house is upscale, with multiple levels, marble floors and countertops, and seated toilets instead of the hole in the ground I am accustomed to. We are living luxuriously for one night. Considering my tenth birthday is in two weeks and knowing my parents cannot celebrate in the same way we did in Baghdad, I happily consider this quality time an early birthday present.

"Be kindly affectionate to one another with brotherly love, in honor giving preference to one another." Romans 12:10

DUHOK - 1992

The front yard of Ashur's house is lined with red, triangular bricks with the pointy tips facing upwards. One afternoon, my sister Rodina, who is three years old, is sitting in a stroller at the top of the two steps between the house and the yard. While Sona and I are playing with the rest of the kids, our moms are sipping tea. Rodina begins to rock herself in her stroller by shifting her body weight from side to side. She's quickly amused by her self-made game, so she rocks harder and faster, and her laughter increases. Her belly laugh is contagious, but in a moment, it turns into a scream, followed by a long pause, and tears. I look in her direction and notice Rodina has fallen out of her tipped over stroller and landed in the yard. Mom reaches Rodina first and pulls her up, only to find blood streaming down her face. At first glance, it looks terrifying, and we presume the edge of one of the bricks has punctured her eye. At Mom's frantic instructions, we quickly retrieve the outside hose and turn on the faucet. As Mom and Linda clean her face, we are relieved to find her eye is safe but dismayed that the brick's corner has pierced her eyebrow. To make matters worse, Rodina proceeds to pass out. Mom's face turns white as she feverishly works to treat the gaping wound near Rodina's eye. She quickly cuts a small chunk of a leather belt and, with trembling hands, covers the opening with the leather. Not having the funds to take Rodina to the hospital or seek medical treatment, Mom is helpless and has to improvise. Rodina comes to after several minutes and is in agonizing pain. In the aftermath of the incident, Rodina experiences massive headaches, discomfort, and grogginess, but we are left to manage these symptoms without the assistance of medicine.

Our days at Ashur's house begin to blend. Each day is like the one before. We are mourning our life's circumstances, feeling guilty about Rodina's injury, and at a loss of how to move forward with little direction. Dad is struggling to find a job as we attempt to start over, rebuilding our lives from nothing.

Twenty days have passed since we moved in with Ashur's family. Bitterness has crept into our hearts and minds, especially in the last year. It is hard not to pick up resentment after everything my family has endured. Turkey's deportation rooted that bitterness even deeper within us. With the never-ending rejection, always being on the run, and continual worrying, the stress has built up and is beginning to manifest on my parents' faces. There is now a mask of sadness, a mask I have never seen before as they used to be cheerful people. Sighs of anxiety are constantly released. They are arguing more than usual. Life seems like an abyss, pulling us closer and closer to the edge with no hope. Watching my parents struggle daily but press on regardless of the circumstances, is both heartbreaking and admirable. Recently, I've noticed the impact of the stress reaching further than just their mental health. Mom's physical body displays the battle scars of war as well. She's begun experiencing short headaches that overtime, have increased in intensity and have morphed into migraines. The nerves in her left shoulder have stiffened, forming a solid knot that refuses to release. As if all our struggles have bonded, they pinch her nerves together, limiting her mobility in her left arm. I try to massage it to no avail. Nothing brings her relief.

Sometimes, I find Mom pressing the palms of her hands against her temples, running her fingers through her hair, and even gripping her hair tightly enough to induce pain. Other times, I find her tapping her forehead against the wall, hoping for relief. How many times has she comforted me when I've needed her? Cleaned my wounds? Kept my fear at bay when I had my dreams and visions? Now, she is in agonizing pain, groaning in misery, yet pushing through to care for her girls, and there is nothing I can do to help.

Despite the physical and mental pain my parents brave daily, Dad desperately needs to find a job and support our family. After several rejections, he finds one as a clerk at a nearby liquor store. His limited salary will be enough to move out of Ashur's house. Although we have enjoyed living with his family and are incredibly grateful for their hospitality, we are excited to live independently and have a fresh start.

My parents find a house that has four bedrooms, one bathroom, and a 1 by 1.5 meter (3 by 5 feet) patio that is covered with metal shingles and converted into a kitchen. The makeshift kitchen on the patio is equipped with a tiny sink, a two-burner stove, and a short wooden shelf that holds a few plates and cups, all donated to us. Only one room is available for rent, as that's all my father's salary can afford. The rest of the house is vacant but not accessible. We move into this room rather quickly. Everything is gray—the floor, ceiling, and walls. This room is small, but it is our living room, dining room, bedroom, and shower room for my sisters and I. Despite having a separate shower room we can access, it is cold and dark. Stepping into it feels much like stepping into a dungeon. No lights and no windows. A candle is used to light the room when my parents shower. As for us girls, Mom boils water in a large pot on the stove and mixes it with cold water. My sisters and I sit in a circular plastic bucket. While Dad pours water over us, Mom lathers and rinses.

We use the UN's blue tarp, given to us when we first arrived, as a barrier between the five foam mattresses we have managed to gather and the cold concrete floor. We also have eight blankets and five pillows to keep us cozy. At night, we place the mattresses next to each other to sleep. In the morning, we line them against three of the four walls and use them as a seating area, opening up the center of the room to eat, hang out, and play.

Dad's small income is enough to cover our rent, but we have little to spare on everything else. We live each day in the shadows of the unknown. Almost daily, our evenings are capped with a prayer for provision for the following day. We simply do not have enough food to survive, and we never know where our next meal will come from. Yet, somehow, we never starve. There have been many instances when we don't have enough to eat, and random generous neighbors bring us their leftovers. It never fails; each time my parents mention we don't have sufficient food for the family, in a matter of hours, there is someone at the door holding a pot. God continues to provide. We begin our journey of living by faith and trusting God will take care of us. He continues to give even when we don't recognize His work.

Every so often, Mom burns our food unintentionally and doesn't have the means to cook another meal, so she recites the old wives' tale most Assyrian moms tell their children when they burn food; "If you eat it, you will find money." This is a crazy myth passed down for generations to encourage kids to eat charred food with no complaints. Magically, we always find money on the same day, whether it's a coin or a dinar. This encourages us never to complain when the bottom of the rice pot crisps a little or if the egg is cooked a bit longer than it should have been. We trust we will find the money.

In the Middle East, most people live as a community, spending time with each other almost daily, visiting friends and family, celebrating events at church, and building ongoing relationships. No one lives a secluded and private life. For us, family or not, everyone is friendly and present. Living in such a tight community, people talk, rumors spread, and our story circulates. We stand out—our accent is different, we look different, and we behave differently from the people of Duhok. Everyone who hears our story shows us compassion by bringing us food and supplies.

A month after moving to our own place, a new panic slips in when I wake up early in the morning feeling very ill. I am extremely lethargic, have a fever, lack an appetite, and the whites of my eyes have turned yellow. Not having any financial means, my parents attempt to treat my illness at home with no luck, and soon, my sisters become ill. After three days, in desperation, my parents are left with no choice but to take us to the doctor. Dad has only fifty dinars in his wallet, and it costs fifteen dinars per child to visit the doctor, leaving my parents with five for the remainder of the week. It is another leap of faith moment as we all travel to the doctor's office on foot. Upon arriving, the receptionist charges forty-five dinars for the visit, then escorts us to the doctor's office. Jaundice, he concludes.

Before dismissing us, he asks what city we are from as he recognizes our accent, which is obviously different than the dialects in Duhok. He quickly surmises we're not local. An Assyrian family who happens to have the same accent as he does causes him to sense there's a back-story. With three ill girls, my parents explain our challenging journey so far. Soon, the three adults are exchanging stories.

As they conclude the visit, the doctor says, "Please excuse me for a moment." He slowly stands and moves toward the front desk. After being gone for a few minutes, leaving my parents waiting in silence, he walks back into the room with forty-five dinars in hand and gives it to my father. He then gives my parents medicine and a treatment plan at no additional cost. With tears in their eyes, they humbly thank him. Our trip home is full of relief and bliss. God provides, yet again.

Medicated, we finally experience relief. Restful sleep is welcome tonight.

Early the following day, there is a faint knock on the metal front door, and, to our surprise, we are greeted by the doctor at the doorstep, smiling. "Do you have space? I brought a few things."

"Sure," Mom replies, curious as to what he means. He begins unloading his SUV, which is full of food and supplies. He brought us one-hundred-pound bags filled with rice, sugar, flour, and many fruits and vegetables. We stand at the door in awe, jaws nearly hitting the ground. Our mouths are watering; it has been years since we indulged in a red apple or a banana. Now, I am staring into a large bag of both.

The doctor gives Mom five hundred dinars in addition to everything he just bestowed upon us. He has blessed us in such a way that his good deeds will never be forgotten. It is Christmas at our house today with five, happy, beaming people in our little room.

* * *

"And my God shall supply all your need according to His riches in glory by Christ Jesus." Philippians 4:19

DUHOK - 1992

After living in Duhok for several months, it is time to resume my education. A year has passed since I lived in Baghdad, where I completed third grade. School in Jordan was torturous, which led me to have a love-hate relationship with education. I am embarking on a new yet familiar challenge—school in Duhok. Being gone for a year, I missed fourth grade entirely, and considering education is of such value to my family, I must resume at all costs.

My education is one of Mom's top priorities and something she takes great pride in. When we were in Baghdad, she loved boasting of my grades and success in school to family and friends.

She finds the nearest elementary school and acquires the necessary information for me to return to school in August. Mom doesn't take long to find out I must test out of fourth grade. Since I missed that entire school year, I must study every subject independently and pass each test to advance. This is not a small feat, but dedicating time and effort to this is critical as it will determine my grade. I want to be in fifth grade along with everyone else my age. I have no desire to be the oldest in my class if I'm forced to take fourth grade instead or worse, if I fail.

Mom borrows the necessary textbooks for Math, Science, History, Arabic, and Geography from the school and quickly creates a rigorous study schedule. I have one month to take the tests. My determination takes over as I buckle down, focus, and apply myself. This is a substantial amount of information to absorb in one month, but I'm up for the challenge. As the days pass, playtime diminishes, and my every waking moment is spent expanding my knowledge, and sleepless nights become frequent. I am grateful for my mother, who is by my side, enduring all this with me. She is my support system, my teacher, and my cheerleader.

While I review one subject, Mom takes the time to create flashcards for another one. She cuts the paper in half and writes bullet points for me to study. She also quizzes me every few days to ensure the material is being retained.

The month seems endless yet short all at the same time. It has been grueling. As my studying intensifies, so does my anxiety, restlessness, and stress level. With each sunrise, I'm reminded the tests are fast approaching, and each day feels more and more daunting.

Finally, the dreaded yet much-anticipated test day is here. Mom and I leave early in the morning to be the first to arrive. During our walk to the school district office, we review the material, scanning the flashcards one final time.

We turn the corner, and I see the gray, concrete building. With each step, my heart thumps louder. Anxiety takes over. Though I am breathing heavily, my lungs are not getting enough air. With every breath, doubt increases. *I didn't study enough. I could have done better. It's not fair that I had to learn an entire year's worth of lessons in one month.*

We stride down the long and empty hallway, our footsteps clacking against the tiled floor. We are directed to the testing room, where I check in. I freeze in the doorway.

Move. I'm trying, but nothing is happening. My legs seem heavy. The second I walk in, it's over. I can't back out.

Move.

I feel stuck until Mom nudges my arm. "We need to go in; it's time." She tells me.

I see a long table with administration staff seated, facing the main door. Twelve paces forward and—

"Name?" one woman asks.

Stuttering, with a quiver in my voice, I say, "Ramina Babani."

"Take a seat," she replies with a blank look. She shows no expression, not even a hint of a smile.

"Thank you," I tell her nervously before walking away.

Mom and I find a seat near the middle of the room. I do not want to be at the front, near the staff. My anxiety is high enough; I don't need them to add to it.

We patiently wait as I scan through the flashcards yet again. *One last time*, I tell myself. Palms sweating, legs trembling, I feel a heavy weight against my chest that intensifies with each passing minute.

"Mom, I don't think I studied enough," I say in a panicked tone.

"You studied plenty, and you worked very hard to be here. You've got this."

"What if I fail and don't remember anything I've studied."

Fear and doubt rear their ugly heads this morning, interfering with my confidence and peace. I have always excelled in school—failing

195

has never been an option. I have been through enough already, and failing this test would elevate my defeat to a new level, almost making me feel as if I am moving backward. Although I love education and school work, tests have never been my greatest strength. They only serve to heighten my anxiety. And here I am, facing the most important tests of my life, which will determine my educational fate for the coming years.

"Ramina Babani, please come to the front."

My move from sitting to standing feels slow. I walk toward the woman who called my name, shaking, nervous, and sweating but determined to conquer the tests. The administrator confirms my personal information. She reviews the file Mom had previously completed, explaining why I hadn't attended school the past year and why I am here today requesting the tests. She pauses. Though it's only a few seconds, it feels like hours as I stand before her. Finally, with a stoic expression, she reaches to the corner of the table with her right hand, finds a yellow form, completes the blank fields in silence, and gives it to me. Then she proceeds to say, "Congratulations, you can start fifth grade with everyone else; we are not going to test you."

What? I am stunned. *Could this be happening? I don't have to take the tests?* I pull myself together, find my voice in my parched throat, and thank the administrator. Speedily, I walk toward Mom, praying this woman does not change her mind.

"We need to get out of here right now," I whisper.

"What happened? What about the tests?" Mom asks, puzzled.

"I will explain everything once we go outside. I want to make sure she doesn't reconsider. Hurry up, let's go!"

Mom looks confused as she rushes outside, trying to keep pace with my speed. I face the field across the school and scream, "I don't have to take the tests!"

I catch my breath, inhaling relief and exhaling fear and anxiety. I look at Mom and explain what happened. Our walk home seems bittersweet. A mixture of emotions begin to overwhelm me again. I should be thrilled and relieved, yet a part of me is bitter. Bitter at how much time and effort I invested into studying. Bitter about the stress I have had to endure. I gave up a month of my summer. Why didn't they inform us of this when we personally delivered the application?

I decide that I am going to ignore the bitter part of this experience and focus on the bright side—I learned the fourth-grade material in one month. The thought of attending school with the rest of my age group supersedes everything else.

* * *

"Do all things without complaining and disputing, that you
may become blameless and harmless, children of God."
Philippians 2:14-15

DUHOK - 1992

My new school is made of concrete and has a large open square in the middle with classrooms all around it. A door in the front of the building allows access for faculty and an entry in the back for the students. Both are locked and chained shortly after the first bell rings. We have nowhere to go except our assigned classrooms. Skipping a class is unacceptable and results in severe consequences. Three-hundred-plus girls from all walks of life and all socioeconomic levels are brought together in this concrete prison.

None of this matters because from the minute I step through those large metal doors until the final bell of the day, I have one goal— improve my education. Assyrian parents take pride in their children's education. Living in a poverty-stricken country, my parents have little to be delighted with. This only pushes my drive to excel in school and give them a reason to be proud, something they desperately want.

A new school year means a new beginning. A chance to better myself. A chance to make friends. But little do I know that starting school here will come with a major challenges. Although the structure of the classes, seating assignments, textbooks, and the intensity of the education system is the same as in Baghdad, the language that dominates most of these classes isn't. On my first day of school, I learn that my classes are mainly taught in Kurdish, the primary language in the North and a language I do not know.

The northern part of Iraq is also called Kurdistan, and most who live within this region are called Kurds, an Islamic group that coexists with the minority Assyrians and a small group of Arabs. The majority of the people in Kurdistan know how to speak Arabic but don't practice it often, choosing to speak Kurdish instead. Even though the textbooks are in Arabic (except for the English textbook), the teachers conduct classes in Kurdish. The only exception is if the teacher is Assyrian, in which case, they teach in Arabic.

Growing up in the South and being Assyrian, my home language is Assyrian. I had to learn Arabic to attend school in Baghdad. Now, living in the North, I need to expand my vocabulary and add Kurdish to my list of languages in order to attend school and hopefully excel academically.

I quickly fall into a pattern where I have to learn the lesson in Kurdish, go home and memorize the required pages in Arabic, then come back to school and recite them to the teacher in Arabic while she conducts the class in Kurdish. Recitation has to be verbatim; missing a word or two can result in punishment. It is incredibly confusing, but I work through it. At age ten, I begin teaching myself Kurdish. I start by asking my parents for an Arabic-Kurdish dictionary. I also implore my classmates to speak Kurdish outside the classroom, forcing me to dive deeper and learn the language quicker. I want an education so badly that I am determined to overcome any challenges to obtain it. As I learn my fourth language, I am encouraged to find familiar words. The Kurdish language contains words drawn from Arabic and Turkish. With each complete sentence I can formulate and each lesson I can comprehend without my dictionary, I feel a sense of joy that motivates me to keep going.

Just as in Baghdad, I quickly realize teachers within this region have as much authority to use whatever force necessary to discipline their students. They believe punishing students pushes them to try harder and learn more in school. Weirdly, this method is effective. My geography teacher has a stick as her sidekick, much like most teachers, except hers is unlike any I have ever seen. It is a 1 meter (3 feet) long, rounded stick with a thin sheet of metal wrapped all the way around it. This stick accompanies her to all her classes, including mine, where I watch her bring girls to tears. Attending school unprepared is my worst nightmare. While the pain can be unbearable, I can bear it. It is the humiliation in front of my peers and teachers I detest. This only pushes me to try harder. However, a few students cannot excel in the school system, no matter how hard they try or how many times they are beaten. Eventually, these students quit school. The girls mostly stay home or are married off at an early age, while the boys either find a job or join the military.

In addition to the language barrier, education in Kurdistan has two other challenges. The first is electricity or the lack thereof. Unfortunately, electricity is supplied from Baghdad, meaning Hussein has complete control. Since he dislikes Americans so strongly and losing part of his country to them angers him, he has turned off the electricity to the North. This leads to families needing to improvise their refrigeration methods, using coolers to maintain the freshness of milk and eggs. In some parts of the city, homes with a yard often have a secluded area where dairy products are stored in glass containers and buried in dirt to stay cold. Other families, including mine, use wooden boxes to store fruits and vegetables, separating each layer with hay to prevent the moisture and mold from spreading.

Our classroom windows have no barriers to the outdoor environment. We struggle through winter days and rely on gasoline space heaters to stay warm. Unfortunately, each classroom only has one space heater placed next to the teacher. Since my seating assignment is in the front of the classroom, I am fortunate to feel part of the heat, but the students assigned to the back of the room must find other ways to stay warm. Each classroom has a window that provides enough light to brighten the room without electricity. At home, a candle sits next to my books as I focus on my homework. We also use gasoline-infused lamps from sundown to bedtime.

The second challenge is lice. Yes, LICE. I fear abuse from the teachers, and now I have to endure coming home with lice. Oh, the misery of the constant itching. Kurdistan is known for its high poverty. Many students come from crowded, poverty-stricken homes where living a sanitary life is not much of an option, which leaves them at a much higher risk. Lice is practically an epidemic among girls, especially those with long hair.

Because lice is a common problem in northern Iraq, the vice-principal conducts random hair inspections. Each student is asked to come to the front of the room to have their hair examined. If the student wears a hijab, she must remove it and expose her hair. Per the Islamic religion, she is allowed to do so as long as no men are present.

The inspector will then poke around the hair, parting it using a pencil, the same pencil that was used on the previous student's head. If a student shows any signs of lice, they are sent home. As if standing in front of the classroom and having my hair inspected isn't humiliating enough, the treatment for lice is worse as there is no medication or shampoos to eliminate them. The only tried and true remedy our mothers, grandmothers, and great-grandmothers have is gasoline. Coming home with lice, telling my mother one of my classmates was sent home during the inspection, or even mentioning my desk partner itched her head, I immediately receive the special gasoline treatment.

For the gasoline treatment, I sit outside on the front porch in the scorching sun, where Mom pours gasoline over my head, parts my hair into very small sections, and brushes through them with a fine-toothed comb. If any lice stay behind, she pulls them out and pops them between her thumbnails to ensure they don't escape. If we have family visiting, they participate in the activity to speed up the process.

"Did you hear how loud that one popped? It must have been the mother," Mom exclaims as she listens to each pop, ensuring no survivors.

Having very thick hair prolongs this process for several hours. I must keep my head down, chin almost touching my chest, until they work through every strand. My neck takes a beating as my hair is brushed and pulled. It feels like a cruel and unusual punishment for something I cannot control. My neck is sore from keeping my head down, and my butt and legs are numb from sitting on the tiled floor. In addition to the aching my body feels, the gasoline burns my scalp the entire time, and washing it out takes several shampoo treatments to fully clean my hair and eliminate the terrible odor. Unfortunately, I go through this process several times a year. As a precaution, I stay far away from girls who itch their heads. I want to avoid the gasoline treatment at all costs, but I am not always successful.

"He who keeps instruction is in the way of life, but he who refuses correction goes astray." Proverbs 10:17

DUHOK - 1993

Today is a beautiful day outside, so I ask my parents if we can eat on the balcony, to which they quickly agree. Our house has a second level with two vacant rooms and a small balcony. Since we are the only ones living here, we occasionally eat on the terrace when the weather allows it, enjoying the sunset and the beautiful hills partially surrounding the city. It is a welcome change of scenery from the four walls in our living area.

As we share dinner, we gather around a metal tray holding a bowl of rice, salad, and stew we pour over the rice. I gaze up into the beautiful sky, admiring the blue, red and orange hues of the sunset. I jolt in surprise when a giant black cloud of smoke suddenly taints the sky, and a thunderous sound shakes us and the foundation of our house. Instant flashbacks of Baghdad resurface—the missiles, the explosions, the deafening blasts. We have never experienced one during the day; the attacks always come at night, always at the darkest hour. But this one, we can witness the effects of the explosion directly. Hours later, we discover a large hotel was destroyed by a vehicle parked outside, packed to the brim with explosives.

Unfortunately, this isn't anything new. It is well known that Hussein provides his men with explosives and sends them throughout the towns in the North to deploy the bombs at various times and locations. Hence, we are unphased by the explosion as we continue our dinner and discuss Hussein's deeply rooted hatred and anger towards America. He will stop at nothing to destroy any cities they reside in, no matter the cost or the casualties.

Peace and safety are not guaranteed as long as there is hatred and anger.

We may be safe from Saddam to an extent by living in Duhok, but that can change in a split second. The unpredictable explosives being set off remind us of this over and over again. Is it *time to escape again?*

Moving to Iran crosses my parents' minds as Dad's uncle, Sargon, lives in Tehran, Iran. We are hopeful living near family will ease the bitterness of life and its challenges. More importantly, moving to Iran will give us another opportunity to reach different embassies.

After considerable deliberation, my parents decide that we are going to escape to Iran. Dad will trek the grueling journey first, and we will follow once we receive his message that things are in order. Dad packs and leaves for Iran within days while the rest of us stay behind.

Mom relies heavily on me to succeed with this new arrangement. I'm eleven and need to step up and be her support system since she has no one else. During the day, we have things in order, a routine, and a schedule to follow. When darkness falls, the whispers of doubt and fear creep in. Four females living alone, two of whom are under ten, is a bit scary, especially at night when our protector is gone. But I push past the anxiety and am grateful when the morning comes each day.

A week has passed since Dad's departure. While walking to school early in the morning, I feel an object stab my right foot. It punctures my heel, and pain spreads through my foot. I lean against the neighbor's house to take my boot off, only to find a piece of glass has cut my heel. I'm unsure where the glass came from; I don't recall anything breaking near my boots. I wipe my heel with a tissue, put my boot back on, and finish my walk to school, pushing the discomfort aside. I am already stressed out enough with the school as is; I don't need any distractions deterring my attention from the teacher and the lesson.

Limping home, I clean my heel and continue to help Mom. With each step, my pain heightens. I notice the cut on my heel changing, and not for the better. *Infection.* The thought scares me, but not enough to tell Mom. I don't want to increase her stress level. I clean it again the best I can and carry on with my day. Two days pass, and I notice the pain continues to expand, as does my cut. A large yellow blister now surrounds the cut, covering most of my heel. Despite my self-treatment, the wound is worsening.

During dinner, as we consume our last piece of bread, Mom reminds me of our task early the next morning. To purchase fresh bread, we must walk to the little bakery in our neighborhood and stand in line with the rest of the women. The bakery opens at 4 a.m., and it is best to come early as the line extends quickly and lasts for hours.

I feel like I have just fallen asleep when there is a gentle grip on my shoulder and a slight shake, "Wake up." Dazed, I roll over. My eyelids are heavy, refusing to open. "Wake up. I need you to go with me to the bakery. We won't be long. Hurry up."

I drag myself off my mattress and onto the ground, crawling to my jacket and boots on the floor near the door. Turning my head so Mom can't see my expression, I wince as I slip my right foot into my boot. We lock the door and walk, leaving my sleeping sisters behind. The cold mid-November air wakes me instantly. Unable to walk fluidly, I begin to limp again. I try to hide it from Mom, but it's too obvious. I am a fool for thinking I can keep this from her much longer.

"What's wrong?"

"Nothing." I pause, debating on whether I should tell her. "Well, I cut my heel, and it hurts. I think it's infected."

Confusion covers her face. "Why didn't you tell me?"

"I was afraid to. I didn't want to stress you more than you already are." I feel relief for telling her, yet I also feel guilty for doing so.

"I will take a look once we get home. Just don't keep anything from me again, okay?"

"I won't," I lie, knowing that if I can relieve my parents of a burden, I will.

We stand in line for an hour before receiving our freshly baked and warm bag of bread. The aroma is strong; my mouth is watering. I resist devouring the bread as I freely limp my way home. When we return, Mom immediately roasts half an onion, places the fragrant chunk on my heel, and wraps it with an ace bandage. She does this onion trick for a few nights, and by the third night, the infection begins to diminish, and the pain slowly disappears. We are both very relieved that this helped cure my infected cut, as home remedies are all we have. Living close to the poverty level is frightening, especially when one is sick and in need of medical attention. Having to tell my parents I am injured elevates their stress. I cannot bear the thought of adding more stress onto them, especially Mom. It is my job as the oldest to protect not only my sisters but also my parents. In less than a week, my foot is completely healed.

* * *

"But God is faithful, who will not allow you to be tempted beyond what you are able, but with the temptation will also make the way of escape, that you may be able to bear it."
1 Corinthians 10:13

IRAN - 1993

A firm knock on the front door startles us. We are not expecting visitors at this hour. "It's 10 p.m. Who could it be?" Mom asks as she steps towards the front door. Slowly and nervously, she reaches for the handle and pulls the metal door towards her. We are greeted by a tall and dark gentleman holding a picture of Dad.

"Hi, Madlen. I'm Sargon, your husband's uncle. He has sent me to escort you and your girls to Iran."

"Welcome, come in," Mom gestures, happy to hear the correspondence from Dad. It has been two weeks since he left.

Mom prepares him dinner and gives him Dad's mattress, but not before she pulls it aside, away from the rest of us.

"James is doing well and is ready for you to join him. Everything is in place for your family," he reports.

Sargon then urges Mom to pack for an immediate departure. It doesn't take long to do so. We place the few articles of clothing in a bag and shuttle everything else to Ashur's house. A day later, we are on a bus traveling to Diana, which is at the base of the mountains we must traverse through to reconnect with Dad. I am relieved to hear Dad arrived in Tehran, Iran, safely, and I am elated to know I will be seeing him soon. I have to admit, I am saddened to be traveling again, leaving what I have adapted to and beginning a new journey, another journey into the unknown. Knowing we will spend time in Diana eases my heartbreak as I am eager to see my extended family and my favorite village.

After a three-hour drive, we surprise my mother's family with our presence at the door. Her aunt stands at the gate, stunned to see us. The last time we encountered each other was during the Gulf War. She quickly ushers us in and prepares a meal. In the meantime, one of the younger cousins rushes to share the news of our arrival with the rest of the family. It takes no time for us to reacquaint ourselves with everyone. While Mom and Sargon make the necessary preparations to travel, my sisters and I quickly connect with the children.

It is incredibly comforting to be in the presence of family as Mom's two aunts, her cousins, and their families all live on the same street. *I love this little village so much. I wish I lived here. Life is simple. Living near my extended family brings a level of comfort I have not experienced since Baghdad.* To my disappointment, Mom and Sargon inform us that we will leave in two days.

Our last night in Diana passes quickly, and we wake up early to another departure day. Another trip into the unknown, with so much uncertainty. Tears cloud our eyes as we say our goodbyes and climb into a vehicle to begin our journey to the border. One of Mom's cousins accompanies us to ensure our safe departure. Upon reaching the border, Sargon announces, "This is as far as we can travel by vehicle. The remainder of the journey will be on horseback."

I've never seen a horse before, and now I must ride one. My anxious thoughts are interrupted by Sargon. "We only need two horses," he tells the smuggler in charge of escorting people in and out of the country.

"Two horses?" Mom exclaims, "What about my girls?"

"Two of them will ride in the saddle pouches of my horse, and the third will ride in the pouch of your horse," Sargon tells Mom.

"You want to do what? You want my daughters to sit in saddle pouches for seven to eight hours? That's absurd." Mom's frustration begins to turn to anger.

Before Sargon responds, I hear one of the men strapping and preparing the horses shout out instructions, "Make sure you keep a tight hold of your horse and stay on the identified path. The trail is extremely narrow; only one horse can pass through at a time." He then elaborates on the potential dangers of stepping off course. "Both sides of the trail are covered with landmines. One wrong step and the bombs will be triggered."

One look at Mom and I can sense the overwhelming stress and fear she's hit with. The idea of possibly being blown to pieces, having her girls ride in pouches, and being smuggled from one country to another with risk of being caught and executed, is terrifying. "This is all too much," she whispers.

I can't help but think, *Can this get any worse?* Just when I think it can't, it does as I watch Sargon step near Mom and give her four large pieces of cloth. "Put these on."

"What are these?"

"Hijab," he says matter-of-factly.

A hijab is the veil, or headscarf, that most Muslim women wear. In Iran, it is the law for all women to dress in this way, regardless of their faith. Women must cover their hair and bodies from head to toe with loose clothing. They are not to show any skin except for their face and hands. Those who violate the law are given a warning. Failure to comply and continuing to violate this law leads to lashings, imprisonment, or in extreme cases, death by stoning. The overpowering thought of us dressed the same as Islamic girls, against our wishes, potentially for the rest of our lives, is a troubling reality we are unprepared for.

As I see her face turning red, frustration rising within her, I know this moment will break Mom.

"Nope, no way! We will not move to Iran. This is a mistake," Mom tells Sargon.

"Seriously? I came all the way here, and you're not going?" he yells at Mom.

"We are not going. Please send my husband back."

Sargon vehemently argues with Mom to change her mind but is unsuccessful. He angrily climbs on one of the horses and begins his trek back to Iran. I am amazed at Dad's bravery in trekking this same path and facing this landmine to seek a better solution for our family.

I am also overjoyed to hear Mom's words but cannot understand what led to the change of heart. "Why did you change your mind?" I ask her.

"I don't know," she replies. "I heard this gentle voice asking me what I was doing, urging me that this is not what is planned for me," she explains, still confused. She ushers us to her cousin's car, who, fortunately for us, waited to ensure we departed safely before leaving. Relieved at the turn of events, we run to him and jump into the car.

We head back to Diana, where we will stay until Dad returns one week later.

* * *

"But the Lord is faithful, who will establish you and guard you from the evil one." 2 Thessalonians 3:3

DUHOK - 1993

U pon returning to Duhok, we are relieved to find our little room vacant. We move our bags into the tiny room and travel to Ashur's house to retrieve our foam mattresses and kitchen utensils.

This relief, unfortunately, is short-lived as it doesn't change our circumstances. Though Iran seemed ideal from a distance, when we neared its border, Mother was able to discern the warning signs that slowly presented themselves. It doesn't help that our attempts to escape to several countries, begging for mercy and hoping someone will pity us, have led to nothing but rejection. Being back in Iraq again, in the same small room, and returning to our familiar routine, separated from friends and family, and living on the edge of poverty and homelessness does not lift our spirits. We can't help but feel defeated. Again, we have failed.

Is this it . . . for the rest of our lives?

Not seeing a glimpse of hope, no matter which avenue our family takes, causes us to feel like we've hit rock bottom. It is a stressful time for all of us but especially for my parents. Though Dad was able to resume his job at the liquor store, his low income is only sufficient to provide a roof over our heads and the bare essentials such as rice and flour. Everything else is considered a luxury that we cannot afford. As we rebuild our lives again, I cannot ignore the tension rising between my parents as the frustrations of life continue to mount. Resuming our life in Duhok means resuming the daily uncertainty over the provisions for our next meal as my parents take turns refusing to eat to ensure the rest of us don't starve. *How much more can my family endure? How much more suffering can my parents embrace?*

Our days of feeling hopeless begin to blend. Dad's sighs of anxiety seem to increase in frequency and sound. He is desperate to distract his restless mind from our situation. "I need to take a walk," he states as he approaches the gate. His walk leads him to the local library, where he connects with one of the Assyrian church deacons he has met several times. In desperation and looking for a diversion, he searches the books to find anything to calm his racing mind. The deacon, aware of my family's circumstances, recommends Dad read the Bible. My family, much like every Assyrian household, usually has a Bible. Ours was left behind in Turkey when deportation was inflicted upon us. As I mentioned earlier, it is not customary to read the Bible as most attend church to hear the priest speak God's word rather than read it for themselves. Dad hesitantly reaches for the Bible and agrees to read it.

Upon Dad's return, it takes a few moments to notice the thick book in his hand. Once Mom recognizes the book, she is furious at the sight of the Bible. She harbors anger towards God for everything our family has endured—for a very long journey full of unanswered prayers.

Mom seizes the Bible from his hand and angrily throws it across the room. My gaze tracks the Bible as it lands on the ground. Hesitantly, Mom's head turns toward it and finds it open to Acts, chapter seventeen. Her gaze is drawn to verses twenty-six through twenty-eight. She briefly pauses before she reads the passage aloud:

"And He has made from one blood every nation of men to dwell on all the face of the earth, and has determined their pre-appointed times and the boundaries of their dwellings, so that they should seek the Lord, in the hope that they might grope for Him and find Him, though He is not far from each one of us; for in Him we live and move and have our being, as also some of your own poets have said, 'For we are also His offspring.'"

Seemingly intrigued, Dad proclaims, "This is why God brought us here, so we can seek Him."

Mom ignores him, too angry to be impressed, and disregards his astonishment at the verses.

Dad is taken captive by this encounter and begins reading and meditating more and more each day. In doing so, he begins to view our reality as part of a larger plan that we can't fully see yet. Mom is not convinced by any means, but having so many strangers show us mercy by bringing us food and supplies is beginning to soften her heart. In our desperation, strangers who are familiar with our story feel the urge to bring us food. They are led to do something outside the norm to lend a helping hand. It's as if God is tugging on their hearts, sending them with hands full of food, enough to fulfill our exact needs. Mom seems at a loss by the provision.

Mom's heart slowly softens. Watching Dad continue to grow spiritually encourages her to find an evangelical church in the city. It is a large house turned into a church. My family is greeted warmly and welcomed to this unfamiliar environment. We are delighted to meet so many people. The connections we instantly develop encourage us to attend the Bible studies conducted by Yousif, the pastor. Mom's disposition about God is beginning to shift.

The sun is sinking on this beautiful October evening when Mom and I approach the church for another Bible study. Minutes after stepping into the courtyard, Mom and I are separated. Suddenly, I find myself in one room and Mom in another. Today's study seems different, more like a conference. Though a wall separates the two large rooms, they both open to a common room facing the same pulpit. A gentleman named Assad, who is blind, is escorted to the keyboard located in the left corner of the room. "Please open your hymn books to page twenty-seven," Assad instructs.

He begins playing the keys, and everyone starts singing. I join in, singing along, never having heard this song before, but I catch on quickly. After three songs, a tall man steps to the podium, prays, and introduces the guest speaker, Victor Hashweh, an evangelist from Jordan. Victor begins speaking, and I find myself enthralled. His words are so powerful, full of hope. He is presenting me with a new hope I have never experienced before nor am familiar with. That is, putting my hope in God. I've spent my life wishing for a better existence, but nothing came of it. Yet today, I feel encouraged and eager to learn more about it. He proceeds to share the message of Christ, the hope we have in Him. His sacrifice for my salvation. Again, this is a concept I am unfamiliar with. Jesus knows me. He knew me before I existed. He sees me through and through and finds me with no shame. He loves me unconditionally. My mind is captured by every word Victor speaks. Peace washes over me as I reflect on my life, even with all of the pain and suffering. Suddenly, I can see Christ in all of it as well. His faithfulness weaved through every situation I have experienced. In an instant, I find courage in my journey.

Victor concludes his sermon with an altar call, where the congregation is invited to accept Christ into our hearts and lives. This is an opportunity to respond to the message of the gospel Victor just delivered. He begins praying and asks the church to repeat after him if prompted by the Holy Spirit. Altar calls are not a common practice within the Assyrian churches. I thought I was a Christian my entire life, just like all the Assyrians who consider themselves Christians, not realizing I was missing this. Having never experienced this before, I follow Victor's instructions. I close my eyes and take the extended invitation to accept Christ into my heart and life.

Tears streaming down my face, I pray with intention, yearning for something or someone. I joyfully welcome Christ as my Lord and Savior at the age of eleven and begin learning about Christ's love, a love so warm and welcoming.

I rush out of the room after the gathering comes to an end, searching for Mom, excited to share my experience. Unbeknownst to me, Mom had the same experience in the next room. As our eyes meet, tears stream down our cheeks. We both feel overjoyed and overwhelmed by the unfamiliar emotions of gratitude and peace.

I also notice something odd—Mom embraces me using both arms. It has been too long since she could do so. After years of struggling with stress and anxiety, Mom had lost feeling in her left arm to the point that it became almost paralyzed. For the last year, she has had a minimal range of motion and could not extend, raise, or lift anything with that arm.

Yet, she fully embraced me using both arms.

"What happened? How are you moving your arm so freely?" I ask in astonishment.

Amid her tears, she says, "I don't know. As I was praying, I felt someone put a block of ice over my head, and as the prayer continued, the ice slowly moved through my body and healed me. Even my migraine is gone! And somehow, I know it's not coming back," she confidently states with a smile I haven't seen.

Neither of us can comprehend the emotions we are experiencing. The magnitude of what took place is monumental. We both recognize the difference between our old and new selves— tonight, something within us has changed. We are blissfully overwhelmed by peace. Our circumstances have not changed, yet our perspective has. Our mindset has shifted. Love has suddenly taken up residence. Loving our enemies is the message of Christ. My enemy is Saddam and his ruthless men, and today, I no longer hate them. I cannot comprehend this love as I no longer desire ill for him and his men. It feels as though we've been born again and given a brand-new start, a second chance. This is the second birth I read about in my Action Bible back in Jordan. I now understand what Jesus describes in the Book of John, chapter three. In the story, Nicodemus, one of the religious rulers of his time, called a Pharisee, visited Jesus one night, acknowledging a miracle Jesus had done and proclaiming that God was with Him.

Jesus replies, "Most assuredly, I say to you, unless one is born again, he cannot see the kingdom of God."'

"How can someone be born when he is old?" Nicodemus asks. "Surely they cannot enter their mother's womb a second time to be born."

Jesus answers, "Most assuredly, I say to you, unless one is born of water and the Spirit, he cannot enter the kingdom of God. That which is born of the flesh is flesh, and that which is born of the Spirit is spirit."

Today, Mom and I stand in a church, among strangers, crying and experiencing what Jesus calls the second birth.

Though it takes a while, we finally compose ourselves and begin our thirty-minute walk home. As we discuss the experience, I come to a halt, struck by a realization.

Mom stops when she notices I am no longer matching her pace. "What's wrong?"

"Today is October 10, 1993," I state.

"Yes," she confirms, though I can tell that she is still confused.

"Mom, it's October 10!" I repeat, ecstatic.

I can see her struggling to understand my emphasis on this particular date.

I cannot contain my revelation any longer. "It has been two years, Mom! *Exactly* two years to the day since I had my encounter with Jesus, where He told me that the resurrection would happen in two days!" I explain this in a rush, too excited at the connection.

I watch Mom's face turn to one of surprise as she processes that information. "This is what He was talking about. This exact day." Mom says in amazement.

"Yes! I still can't believe it." I have been waiting for the Lord to fulfill His promise, and two years later, He does not disappoint.

October 10 is our second birthday, and the day Christ fulfilled His promise. My gratitude for Him increases exponentially, and His peace flows through me like a river.

Mom and I waste no time diving into our new Bibles the church provided, eager to read and absorb it all. We have a newfound hope. Our domestic conditions have not improved. We continue to live in the tiny room. Dad's earnings are below what our family needs to thrive. Yet, somehow, we see it all with a new lens. Fear has lost its grip on us. Fear tries to come knocking at times, but it cannot take away what has already been freely given to us, our salvation and our Heavenly kingdom. Since our mindset shifted on October 10, we begin to find joy in the little things. We begin to find joy in our humble dwelling. Though small, it's a safe shelter. Though poor on earth, we learn in the book of Matthew that we are rich in Heaven.

Our joy has become permanent, rooted deep down, instead of the temporary happiness that comes only from positive circumstances. We can finally reflect and find God at every step of our journey. We see His faithfulness in our protection and safety up to now. Only God's mighty power could split Iraq into two parts, and Turkey deport us to the Northern border where the UN resides. Only God's grace could provoke our neighbors to bring us food. Only God could lead us to a generous doctor who showed us love when we needed it. Only God could speak to Mom and remind her that Iran was not part of His plan for us. We can also see what Satan meant for evil, God has turned for good. He has seen us through so much. His faithfulness is our courage, and no matter what we face, we know He is on our side, just as He has been all along. With this new frame of mind, we are energized and hopeful to see what God has in store for us next.

We continue attending Bible studies hosted at that same church. This is a foreign concept. Never before have we participated in a meeting where we sing songs, discuss a specific chapter from the Bible, and close the session with a prayer. I also join Sunday School classes on Friday mornings since the school system operates Saturday through Thursday. Attending these Bible studies has encouraged us to meet more people and allows us to escape our room and breathe a bit more. Instantly, we have built a community of brothers and sisters in Christ.

In addition to the church community, we begin breaking out of our shells a bit more. Through Christ's power, the cloud of depression that has hovered over us for the past two years has dissipated. The shame and embarrassment we experienced were nothing but Satan, the enemy, attempting to oppress us. With our new perspective, we can see that God doesn't see us as failures, and there's no shame in our story.

One of the neighbors we meet is the Assyrian church's deacon (referred to as Shamasha in Assyrian, a title of respect). He and his wife and eight children, four boys, and four girls, live at the end of our street. He has a spare bedroom on the second floor, which overlooks the main road on a large, open intersection. The room is used to store wool-making tools. Many Assyrian households in this region provide for their families by turning wool into thread and selling it to factories to turn it into fabric. It is a unique trade that requires skill.

During one of our visits to their house, Mom jokingly asks, "Shamasha, what will it take to give me your spare room?"

"Nothing. You can move in right now," he says with no hesitation.

He immediately calls his children and commands them to vacate the space and move everything to the storage room on the roof. Within an hour, the children empty the room, clean it, and help us relocate. Just like that, we move into a large house with an actual kitchen that has a sink and a complete stove. We are finally able to cook in a warm, covered room. Not to mention, we now have the luxury of taking a shower in an actual shower room instead of the bedroom, sitting in a circular bucket.

Above all, we have company—human contact outside of our family. As a bonus, the second youngest child is my age, and the youngest is Sona's age, so we have children to interact and play with. They introduce us to the neighborhood children, and instantaneously, our circle of friends expands even further, and life begins to feel almost normal again.

* * *

"Therefore, if anyone is in Christ, he is a new creation; old things have passed away; behold, all things have become new." 2 Corinthians 5:17

DUHOK - 1993

"**C**ome to Me, all you who labor and are heavy laden, and I will give you rest. Take My yoke upon you and learn from Me, for I am gentle and lowly in heart, and you will find rest for your souls. For My yoke is easy and My burden is light." Matthew 11:28-30.

Fully surrendering to Christ, laying our burdens, struggles, and fears at His feet has lightened our load. A heavy weight has been lifted. Acknowledging Him in all we do and seeking His wisdom in every decision brings peace. We no longer fear the unknown because we trust He will provide and protect us. The more we learn to trust Him, the more we see His faithfulness as He answers our prayers, which only makes us want to trust Him more. As our trust increases, our faith does too. The more we trust, the more we want to trust. The deeper we root ourselves in the Bible, the hungrier we grow for the Word. In every step, there He is, leading us. In our despair and loneliness, He provides us with a church community and a large family to dwell with. In our need for increased financial provision, He opens an unexpected door.

Behind that door is a missionary organization called World In Need (WIN), operated by a Lebanese man named Tofiq and his co-worker, Andrew, who is from France. This is one of the many missionary organizations bringing aid to Northern Iraq during Hussein's absence. The two men provide medicine to those in need while sharing the gospel. People of all ages come to WIN with their prescriptions and walk away with medication and a Bible. Tofiq has become friends with Gilbert, who owns the bookstore next to the liquor store where Dad works. Gilbert and Dad have built a relationship through the months as well with the many books Dad has borrowed. Reading is another favorite hobby of his.

"I need someone Who can cook and clean for WIN," Tofiq tells Gilbert during one of his store visits. Immediately, Gilbert thinks of Mom as he's aware of the financial breakthrough this opportunity could bring for our family.

While I help Mom set the dining area on the floor, one of Shamasha's sons runs upstairs and announces, "You have guests downstairs." Mom glances at Dad as if he's expecting visitors. He shrugs his shoulders and raises his hands in confusion. "I'm not anticipating anyone," he says.

Dad strides down the stairs and finds Gilbert and Tofiq at the door. Unannounced visits are standard in the Assyrian culture. No notice is necessary for the visits. Dad invites them in and leads them upstairs to our humble abode. As is customary, we invite them to dine with us. However, we have limited food, barely enough for my family of five. The embarrassment of our simple dinner of plain rice causes Mom stress. But, we take a leap of faith and serve the rice on a tin foil plate placed in the center of the meal tarp as I pass around silver spoons and cups of water. Dad prays over our meal, requesting nourishment and satisfaction. We begin to consume, seven of us, yet somehow, everyone is full, and there is rice remaining on the plate. A miraculous experience, to say the least. We are grateful for and relieved by the provision.

Tofiq turns his attention to Mom. "Andrew and I need someone to cook, clean, do laundry, and maintain the house for WIN. Is this something you are willing to do?" he asks, offering her a job.

Mom gazes at Tofiq in shock at his forward request only minutes after meeting him. "Yes, of course. My family can use the additional income. When would you like me to start?"

"Tomorrow morning? 8:30?"

I notice Mom's slight hesitation before she says, "I will be there."

Morning comes relatively quickly, and Mom stays home, too embarrassed to work as a maid. This is a new mindset and a reality she is not prepared to accept. Then again, she takes one look at my sisters and me and feels instant guilt, realizing how wonderful it would be to have financial stability.

It has been three hours since Mom was expected to report for work. I watch her in turmoil, alternating between doubting the job and its humiliation and doubting her decision not to work. She begins to do the one thing she's learned to do best since October 10—pray. Seeking God's wisdom and guidance seems appropriate right now. Before she concludes her prayer with "Amen," Tofiq is at the door.

"You didn't come to work today," he queries, looking puzzled.

"I'm sorry...something came up, but I will be there tomorrow," she replies sheepishly. She can't seem to bring herself to tell him the truth. His arrival was the sign she needed to take this step.

Early the following day, Mom is up and ready for work. I stay behind with my sisters while Dad walks her to WIN. Upon arrival, they are greeted with tea and pastries, followed by a tour and an overview of the tasks to be completed. WIN offers Mom five hundred dinars per month, which is a high salary considering our rent is only seventy-five dinars. While Mom works, Dad continues to join her, building a friendship with Tofiq and Andrew. Three weeks later, Dad, too, is recruited to join the team. His new job consists of maintaining the house, learning how to share the gospel, and progressing in understanding the Word of God.

My family continues to grow and prosper—personally, spiritually, and financially. My parents are generating enough income to supply our needs and wants. Additionally, Tofiq and Andrew train Dad to become a pastor and continue encouraging our family's spiritual growth. When WIN announces the new Bible study classes and the Sunday School program, both my parents volunteer to teach alongside Tofiq and Andrew.

WIN hosts missionaries from around the world. One of the missionaries we meet is Mahir, a pastor from Egypt. His light brown skin resembles mine, yet he seems so different. His nationality and his dialect remind me that we are not the same. They also remind me that he can leave Iraq, and I can't. Though I have found peace in my reality, I can't help but wish that I could see what is out there for me. I dream of adventures outside the Middle Eastern borders.

When Mahir preaches, his sermons are simple, yet his words carry power. He reminds me of Victor. After our first Bible study concludes, he brings a large leather case to the room. Curiosity grabs a hold of me as I watch, with anticipation, his every move. He lifts the lid, and I catch a glimpse of a velvet-like, red material lining the case's interior. Next, I notice him pulling out the unusual instrument with black and white keys laid out in a circular pattern. The keys look like buttons. He notices my excitement as I watch him play it during worship. I'm intrigued with the instrument and rush to discuss its uniqueness shortly after. I spend the rest of my time at WIN learning the ins and outs of this instrument, never having seen one like this before. "When I leave, this will be yours," he tells me. Beaming with gratitude, I rush to hug and thank him. I am thrilled. It doesn't take long after his departure for me to tinker with it, teaching myself how to play. It has become my new hobby, one that requires my family's patience as I learn.

My family loves music, and my childhood is filled with it. Dad's part-time gig in Baghdad was singing at weddings and playing the keyboard and guitar. His sister sings beautifully and does so whenever the opportunity presents itself. Even Mom sings at family functions. Music is a large part of who we are. Whenever we travel together on a bus, whether going to a picnic or visiting another city, we sing the entire way. It is a form of entertainment but also, a family tradition, and everyone chimes in, whether they can sing well or not. A good voice is not a factor. It's all about having fun.

It turns out I have the music bug, too, as I spend most of my spare time teaching myself how to play the accordion. My confidence increases with each song I learn, and now, I play during the Bible study worship time. Soon, I will accompany the kids during the summertime Sunday School concert hosted in the backyard of WIN. The children will perform Arabic and English Christian songs and recite Bible verses so the parents can attend and experience what their children are learning. This is a new concept for the parents since the school system does not have theater or choir concerts. They do not have an opportunity to watch their children perform in any activity, including sports.

WIN has become a blessing to my family in so many ways. I am grateful for Mom and her courage to overcome the hurdle as she focused on the bigger picture. Her willingness to look past her embarrassment has provided my family with new possibilities.

* * *

Ramina Wilkerson

"Trust in the Lord with all your heart, and lean not on your own understanding; in all your ways acknowledge Him, and He shall direct your paths." Proverbs 3:5-6

DUHOK - 1993

Living with Shamasha's family has provided us with ongoing company and an opportunity to meet new people. Not only is he the deacon at the church, but he is also the city's chiropractor. He was trained by his father, who was trained by his grandfather—all self-taught. People from different parts of town and the neighboring villages come with dislocated body parts to be adjusted, and all are treated at no cost. This is his way of giving back to the community. I have witnessed so many people limp their way into his house in pain, trusting his gentle touch, and within minutes, relief washes over their faces, and they depart in total health. Today, I am one of them. While running outside with my friends, I stumble and twist my ankle. I limp my way to Shamasha, seeking his adjustment, which he does so gracefully, and immediately, I experience relief. But before I rush back outside again, I find my parents to let them know I injured myself. It has been a long time since I have had the boldness to share an injury with my parents. I have always been their protector, someone who carries their burdens instead of adding to them. But since the change, I have witnessed their faith increase and their anxiety decrease, allowing me the space to share with them when something is wrong.

Three months have passed since we moved into Shamasha's house. Our path is full of excitement as we continue to walk in faith and grow in the Spirit. Today, we are greeted with an unexpected visit from a close relative. We are faced with a decision that will alter our circumstances. Najiba and two of her three sons are standing at the door. In shock, Mom embraces them with excitement. The last time we were in each other's company was two years ago when we lived in Jordan. Their family accompanied us to Amman but stayed behind after our departure to Turkey.

Illegally, she is back in Iraq for a short time with a dilemma. Since she, too, left Baghdad without obtaining the government's permission, if caught, she could face an appalling death. Her dire situation left her with no choice but to risk her life and the lives of her sons to come back to Iraq and seek us out to make a life-changing request.

Ninos, her eldest, recently turned eighteen, and according to immigration law, he is an adult and will need to process his application separately from his family. His age is of no concern; the criminal record he has obtained is the hindrance. He made friends with the wrong crowd, which led to legal trouble with the Jordanian government, which led him to jail several times. His criminal record halts his application process with any embassy. Meanwhile, Najiba and her two other children received approval to immigrate to a European country. Though heartbroken at what this means, she has no choice but to break apart her family. Being the sole provider, she needs to reach safety for the sake of her two younger sons before they turn eighteen.

Leaving Ninos in Iraq with family might be a safer alternative than leaving him in Jordan. Leaving him behind in Jordan with strangers could potentially lead to additional problems with the law and possibly more jail time. She trusts my family and trusts that we will love him as if he's one of us. Unable to contact us, her visit is a surprise and her request, a bigger one. This would be an enormous responsibility.

We would have one more mouth to feed.

One more person to agonize over.

One more person to care for.

But we don't reject family. Looking back at how Babi Matti always cared for those in need even when he didn't have the means to do so and how Ashur stepped out of his way to care for us as long as we needed encourages us in our decision. It is our turn to make Babi Matti proud and do right by Ninos and Jesus. We are happy to step in, knowing we will love and support him unconditionally.

Eight of us dwell in the tiny room with mattresses aligned wall to wall for a full week before Najiba and her son depart. The sun has not peeked through the clouds yet when she wakes her younger son, tiptoeing around everyone asleep. Mom is startled awake when she hears the luggage zipper several paces away from her mattress.

"Is everything alright?" Mom asks, fighting to keep her eyes open. "Wait! Are you leaving?"

"Yes, I need to leave before everyone wakes up, especially Ninos."

"How can you leave without saying goodbye? That's insensitive; it will break his heart."

"I can't fathom saying goodbye. It's too hard. It is better this way. My heart can't take it."

Minutes later, the two are outside waiting for a taxi.

Now distraught for Ninos, Mom cannot return to sleep as she grieves for him and the heartbreak he will face when he wakes up and finds his mother and brother gone.

I break out of my deep sleep at the sound of a deep groan. I lift my head off my pillow and find Ninos on the ground, hands covering his face, hiding his tears. I pull beside him and wrap my arm around his muscled body, struck by his distress. I have never witnessed a man cry like this before. Even with everything my family has faced, Dad never cried. And if he did, it was never in our presence. My heart breaks for Ninos as he murmurs and cries, "How can they leave without saying goodbye?"

Ninos moans for the next two hours, "Mom, where are you? Why did you leave me?"

Although he understands his mother's difficult circumstances, it doesn't lessen the pain and rejection of them leaving without a proper goodbye.

Growing up, Ninos faced many challenges. His alcoholic and abusive father favored his younger sons and expected too much from his eldest. During our weekly family gatherings in Baghdad, Ninos' family often hosted dinners. Several times, we found Ninos being physically abused by his father. When that happened, my dad and uncles always jumped in and rescued him from the beatings.

During one of our gatherings, we stepped into the living room; the sight before us was not one I anticipated nor could stomach. Ninos is hanging upside down from the ceiling fan as the fan spins. His father's anger had aroused; as usual, he tormented Ninos. Dad rushes to the wall and finds the fan switch to turn it off. My uncles and dad hold Ninos' unconscious body and slowly lay him down on the ground as they attempt to revive him. On another occasion, we found Ninos hanging upside down from the roof in the middle of July in the scorching, hot sun. Again, Dad and two of my uncles rush to the roof. Two of them held his body while Dad untied the tightrope. I am astonished at how Ninos rarely receives affection from his father. How can any parent inflict such pain upon their child? Occasionally, he moved in with us until things calmed down with his father before returning home. Ninos always thrived more when he lived with my family because he received the affection he yearned for from my parents, and he was part of a family in which everyone was treated equally and lovingly. Although he lived with us before, it was always temporary, and he always had his family to return to. However, this time, it was different. He is left behind, and we are all he has.

* * *

"Defend the poor and fatherless; do justice to the afflicted and needy." Psalm 82:3

DUHOK - 1993

I t is December, four months since Ninos moved in with us. The family is eager to celebrate the second-largest holiday in the Assyrian culture. We have missed joyfully celebrating it for the past few years due to our circumstances and our challenges. But this year, it is different. We have family around us, we have income, and most importantly, we have God, the actual reason to celebrate. Although we miss our large extended family and traditions, we are ready to establish new memories. Even Ninos is eager to celebrate despite his grief for being countries apart from his mother and brothers.

Mom buys new Christmas morning attire for my sisters, Ninos, and me. She also joins forces with Shamasha's wife to make Kileche. A sense of normalcy is returning, along with memories of the celebrations I shared with my family in Baghdad, especially Babi Matti and Baba Sawa. I miss them dearly; it almost hurts to admit it. However, I am excited to set my pain aside and focus on new blessings and memories.

Christmas Eve is celebrated this year with a Bible study and a delicious meal. My sisters, Ninos, and I are then ushered to the pharmacy room, where we sleep on the floor. Traditionally, on Christmas morning, we receive one present from our parents. However, in the past two years, with all the challenges we endured, my parents bypassed this tradition, even though it pained them to deprive us of our gift. To say that we are excited when we wake up on Christmas morning to find a brown bag next to our pillow is an understatement. In each bag, there are three whole chocolate bars and a lollipop. We quickly run to hug our parents in thanks for the unexpected gifts.

We are ecstatic with our treats as chocolate doesn't come by often. Our little pantry rarely contains any chocolate or candy. Having either of those is a luxury that my family cannot afford. However, with our joy of having chocolate comes the fear and sadness of how quickly the bars will be consumed. To prolong our experience, the four of us opted to open one chocolate bar at a time, cutting each bar into four pieces and sharing it. This allows us to enjoy the candy for over a week while extending the feeling of Christmas. With every bite, I allow the chocolate to melt in my mouth, savoring each piece as I don't know when I will experience this again.

"Blessed are you who hunger now, for you shall be filled." Luke 6:21

DUHOK - 1993

"**W**orld In Need is moving out of Iraq this week," Tofiq utters minutes after walking into the house. This is news my parents never wanted nor expected to hear. Instantly, a cloud of doubt and worry hovers over us. WIN has been a refuge for my family. We have grown mentally, emotionally, and spiritually since meeting Andrew and Tofiq. I turn to my parents, who have paled at the news, their breathing shallow as they attempt to process the uncertainty that is to come. We have accomplished so much since working with WIN; now, we're facing another storm.

"What will happen to WIN?" Dad asks.

"The entire operation will be evacuated. Almost immediately," Tofiq continues, "Due to my illness, I can no longer help WIN. I am moving back to Lebanon to seek further medical treatments. As you know, Andrew has been learning Arabic to better connect with the community, and he has decided to stay behind to teach English at the local school."

We have built a strong bond with both men but especially, Tofiq. He was the first to take a leap of faith with my family, the first person to present us with an opportunity that has opened many doors and poured so many blessings over us, and the first to guide us in our spiritual journey. Saying goodbye to Tofiq is extremely painful, especially knowing we will never see him again. The agony of farewells does not lessen regardless of the frequency. Ninos is equally distraught by the news because he, too, has built a unique bond with Tofiq, almost like another father next to Dad. Now, he is losing Tofiq, much like the rest of us. This pain opens old wounds, with his father abandoning him after moving to Jordan.

Two days quickly pass, and the WIN house is empty. Though we witnessed the Holy Spirit shift within the community, an encouraging movement that led many people to Christ, all is stalled now. The ministry is at a standstill. Although WIN left behind all their accumulated books, we don't have the appropriate space to host Bible studies or Sunday School.

Though my parents will lose their jobs simultaneously, one thing makes this storm different from all previous ones—God. We have God to rely on. We have a sovereign Lord we can go to, seeking His presence and His faithfulness. We pray and put our trust in Christ. He has seen us through so much already; we know He will not abandon us now.

As we mourn WIN's departure and the ministry, Mom meets Catherine, an American nurse who has come to Iraq to help those in need. We soon find out she is part of an organization called Horizons International. The two begin serving together in the small, poverty-stricken villages, aiding sick children. During one of their trips, Catherine introduces Mom to Amir, a young man who quickly becomes a friend of the family. His story is all too familiar, indicative of what refugees face in pursuit of survival. In an attempt to escape Iraq, Amir and a few of his friends trekked through the mountains, seeking refuge in Turkey. After countless hours of walking, they reached the Iraq-Turkey border. Unable to continue from exhaustion, they paused for rest and dozed off. While still asleep, the Turkish military found the young men and immediately shot them. One of the soldiers had placed the tip of his gun against Amir's jaw and fired. The bullet burst through his jaw, damaging his mouth and cutting through his tongue, but Amir was still alive. The soldier noticed his shallow breathing, but instead of shooting him again, he dragged his body across the border and left him in the dirt. Bleeding and in unbearable pain and unable to call for help, Amir had thought his death was imminent, but in a rare show of decency, the Iraqi Border Patrol found him and transported him to the nearest hospital. After several failed surgeries, Amir is moved to a nearby village with his family. Iraq lacks the necessary support to aid him, so his move is a gentle way of releasing him to die at home.

Even during Catherine's absence, Mom continues to visit Amir, building a relationship with him as she bandages his wounds and helps him drink his meals. Upon hearing Amir's story and seeing that the treatment he needs is beyond what the hospital in Iraq can provide, Catherine brings his case before Horizons International, a missionary organization from Boulder, Colorado. Through their help, Amir is granted a medical visa and is transported to America at once.

"Now may the Lord of peace Himself give you peace always
in every way. The Lord be with you all."
2 Thessalonians 3:16

DUHOK - 1993

Mom carries great respect for Catherine. The two have built a strong bond as they tend to the wounded and love on the poverty-stricken families.

"There is someone I would like you to meet," Catherine casually shares as she bandages a little girl's arm. "He will be preaching at the Bible study tonight. I think you should accompany me."

"Okay," Mom timidly answers, unsure of Catherine's intentions.

Mom arrives at the Bible study and quietly slips in the back, eager to hear the preacher. Georges Houssney, a Lebanese evangelist and one of the founders of Horizons International, is in Duhok for a short time.

Mom is captivated by the sermon and the preacher. Intently listening to each word, she feels a nudge from the Holy Spirit. "You should speak to Georges about your work with WIN," she hears. The prompting is too strong to ignore, yet she feels unprepared. "I should have pictures and stories of various testimonies before speaking to him," she thinks to herself.

Immediately after stepping into our tiny bedroom, she relays her evening to Dad. In hearing Mom's Holy Spirit prompting, he feels it too. The two begin preparing a presentation, searching for various pictures we captured during the studies and Sunday School. They create a list of testimonies as well. They hope Horizon International will consider continuing WIN's ministry.

Two days later, Mom and Dad attend the same Bible study, which will be led by Georges again. This time, Mom is carrying a slew of pictures in her hand along with her Bible. Once the sermon concludes, my parents rush to introduce themselves to Georges. They waste no time showing him pictures and sharing countless testimonies of lives changed, young and old. Georges remains silent throughout the presentation, which leaves my parents confused. He thanks them for their efforts and steps away. On their trip home, they can't help but feel rejected, yet the Holy Spirit whispers, "Trust."

Three days pass before Georges seeks out my parents. "Your story and the endless testimonies left a strong impression on me. This ministry must continue," he states. "Hearing of all the accomplishments for the Kingdom of God that took place through WIN and your family is remarkable. Horizons can resume operations. I will stay in touch through Catherine in the next few weeks."

At this time, Horizons does not exist in Iraq. Although Catherine is part of the team, she is here as a missionary nurse supported by Horizons. After Georges' departure, we waste no time connecting with Catherine to begin the preparations of expanding Horizons International to Iraq.

The first step is for my parents to find a house with enough space to accommodate my family and the ministry activities. The provisions from Horizons will include a fully furnished house with all the bills and utilities paid, a salary for my parents, and extra funds to hire a team. What an opportunity! We are overjoyed that our prayers have been answered. Jesus came through incredibly.

We find a beautiful, fully furnished two-bedroom home, clean and move-in ready. In addition to the two bedrooms, we have a spacious living room, a small family room, and a large fenced-in yard with an outdoor garage. The garage is an open space that starts at the house's main entrance and ends with two tall metal gates that stand .5 meters (1.5 feet) off the ground. This is convenient for identifying visitors; we know who is knocking simply by looking at their shoes. The garage is tiled, and the roof is replaced by four different grapevines, with each vine producing a different type of grape. As if that wasn't enough, the yard has one large pear tree along with three orange, two lemon, and two lime trees. Our fruit supply is endless, and we savor every bite. It has been years since we've had access to so much fruit, which only makes us more grateful.

We eagerly pack our small bedroom at Shamasha's house, rent a taxi, and shuttle everything to the new house. I cannot contain my excitement as I run through the front door and come across a furnished living room. I am in awe. It has been years since we lived in a fully furnished house with couches, a dining table, and actual bed frames. Unpacking takes little time since we only have clothes, a few pots and pans, and minimal bedding. My parents move into one bedroom, and my sisters, Ninos, and I share the second. Both rooms have one small armoire holding all our belongings and twin beds with mattresses. After living so long without one, sleeping on something other than the floor seems like such a luxury.

Our new home feels like a mansion in comparison to our previous dwellings. My sisters, Ninos, and I love playing in every part of this house—it has been a long time since we have had space to run around and be kids. Our four walls have expanded; we now have a yard to play in, a roof to sleep on during hot summer days, and space to roam around and be individuals.

Every morning, I sit in the open garage space in awe of what God has abundantly blessed us with. As an eleven-year-old who loves to climb, I venture off and climb the pole anchored against the brick wall to reach the grapes. Different types, dangling from the metal poles, call my name. I begin my ascent, and just as I reach for my first grape, I hear my dad shout, "The water is on!" I quickly scramble down, running to the nearest faucet outside.

The water source resides in the South, in Hussein's territory. Due to spitefulness against the Kurds and the Americans residing within the Kurdish region, he only allows water to flow through the North for one hour a day. The hour is unknown, as it changes from day to day. Our solution is to leave all the faucets inside and outside the house open so we can hear the water rushing through.

We leave empty containers, pots, pans, and bowls near the faucets to fill them quickly before our time runs out. This is our daily routine. We have to capture and store enough water to meet all our needs, including bathing. We have a large tank on the roof that will automatically fill up as the water turns on, but the tank is our backup storage in case we consume what we have. This causes us to be very conscious of the amount of water we use, even for daily tasks such as washing our dishes. It takes two people to wash dishes, one soaping and scrubbing, while the other uses a small cup to rinse everything, lightly pouring water over each dish. Having water for an hour a day is a blessing we don't take for granted.

* * *

"Rejoicing in hope, patient in tribulation, continuing
steadfastly in prayer." Romans 12:12

DUHOK - 1993

The second important step my parents are asked to carry out is hiring a team to assist with the ministry. My parents know who they want to recruit. There have been so many individuals who attended WIN Bible studies. The Holy Spirit highlights the specific four, and my parents begin engaging these individuals, three women and one man. They walk to each of their houses and present them with the employment opportunity. All enthusiastically accept. A week later, the team arrives and commences their training, which includes reading the Bible together, meditating on the Word, and growing spiritually.

I do my best to attend all the training when I'm not in school. It is easy to see that we are all hungry for the gospel, the good news of Jesus. Living in the Middle East under the leadership of Saddam Hussein, who demands others to sacrifice their lives for his selfish purposes, is all we have known. Yet now, learning about the God of the universe and His incredible love for us displayed through life, death, burial, and resurrection of His one and only Son, changes everything. It's a love we have never experienced before. The spiritual hunger doesn't stop with our team. The city has it as well. People gravitate to my family, asking questions, searching for answers, and seeking the truth. They are desperately looking for the one thing that has been missing their entire lives. As we continue establishing relationships, our small, casual gatherings quickly morph into Bible studies every morning and most evenings. People attend as often as possible, sometimes daily. Each session begins with a song or two, followed by the study portion, and concludes with another song and prayer. We fellowship after each gathering, and most often, food is involved. I love that we spend quality time with people, getting to know them through their victories and struggles.

The traffic in and out of our house is constant. The constant running back and forth to the front gate to allow access becomes an overwhelming distraction. So Dad attaches a rope to the gate handle and ties it to the top of the gate. Now when people come, they simply have to tug on the rope, pull the handle, and walk right in.

News spreads quickly that Sunday School will resume the upcoming Friday, so when the morning arrives, our front yard is full of children of all ages who have arrived early with their friends in tow. After only two weeks of reviving this program, we have grown larger than we had anticipated with 150 children, to be exact. The house is not large enough to accommodate such a group, but I have learned that if there is a will, there is a way. We separate the children by age group and teach each group in a different part of the house. Some are in the bedrooms, lounging on the beds; others are in the kitchen, both living rooms, the roof, and the stairs leading to the roof. Additionally, we have a group in the open garage area and one in the yard. The house is crowded, and we love it. The team and my parents teach the classes while I assist Mom with the older kids. Some of the parents are beginning to welcome our work as missionaries as they recognize the positive change in their children. Building relationships with the children encourages the parents to seek and learn about the Lord.

Our house is overflowing with people from many corners of the city coming to learn about Jesus. We have found our purpose, and we are living it. We have come a long way since Mom irately threw the Bible one year ago, and the book randomly opened to Acts 17:26-28.

"And He has made from one blood every nation of men to dwell on all the face of the earth, and has determined their pre-appointed times and the boundaries of their dwellings, so that they should seek the Lord, in the hope that they might grope for Him and find Him, though He is not far from each one of us; for in Him we live and move and have our being, as also some of your own poets have said, 'For we are also His offspring."

We finally understand the meaning of these powerful words. Everything we have endured has led to this moment. We seek the Lord, and we reach for Him and find Him. Our journey was not in vain, but to build us up so we can honor Him. We have greater gratitude for Him now than ever before. Faithfully following God's plan for our lives has led to our little house becoming the second evangelical church in Northern Iraq. The first church being the one hosted by our current neighbors, where Mom and I accepted Christ.

Although Catholic and Assyrian churches have physical buildings, evangelical churches have no funding to do so, nor are they allowed by the government. Instead, services are held in our home. Amazingly, the only two evangelical churches share a wall now. To make things even better, the pastor and his wife have three children, two girls and one boy. All three are of similar ages to my sisters and me, and we become instant friends.

One day, while playing with our neighbors, my mom calls out to us to come inside. My smile disappears when I notice her stricken face. "What's wrong?"

"It's Amir. He didn't make it," she tells me before explaining how his body had no strength to continue after numerous surgeries.

I'm heartbroken at the news and struggle to believe it. He was only twenty-one years old. The only wrong he had committed was trying for a better life.

* * *

"Fear not, for I am with you; be not dismayed, for I am your God. I will strengthen you, yes, I will help you, I will uphold you with My righteous right hand." Isaiah 41:10

DUHOK - 1994

While my family and I quickly adjust to our new norm and enjoy our blessings and opportunities, I cannot say the same for Ninos, who has been struggling with abandonment since his mother left. Sadly, this isn't a new feeling for him.

Ninos' life has never been easy. Being rejected by his father since his early years left him desperate to escape his reality. This desperation led to many poor decisions in Jordan, where he was introduced to cocaine and heroin. He quickly developed an addiction, and through it, he found his "happy place"; however, that happy place created many challenges that led him to jail several times. During one of his imprisonments, he was forced to spend weeks in a 1 meter by 1 meter (3 by 3 feet) jail cell that had left him with no option but to spend his time standing, sitting, or squatting as there wasn't enough space to stretch out his long legs or sleep. Despite this experience, Ninos still struggled to stay away from the drugs. And when they weren't enough to ease the emotional pain, Ninos found relief through something else—cutting.

When Najiba brought Ninos to our house to move in with us, she shared a disheartening story of when he was on the run from the government in Jordan. Feeling out of place and looked down upon for the shame he'd brought on the family and the continuous heartache he caused his mother, he began to question his future. His thoughts turned dark as loneliness and fear began to cloud his mind. Slowly, his behavior changed. He became distant and, at times, unresponsive. Unable to see another way, Ninos made a simple yet grave decision: he would end his life. One day, Ninos left the room he shared with his mother and brothers and walked into the kitchen, where he retrieved a knife from the drawer. Without a word, he plunged the knife into his side and slid it across his stomach. From the other room, Najiba saw her son collapse. She rushed into the room to find him bleeding and his organs pouring out of his stomach. She fell to her knees beside him and let out a blood-curdling cry. Her son was in trouble, and she could do nothing. She didn't dare call for an ambulance because, not only was her son in trouble with the local government, he was an Iraqi immigrant with an expired visa. She knew if she called for help, her son would be jailed or deported immediately after treatment. Frantically searching the room, she looked for anything to help her dying son. Her gaze froze as it fell on the iron sitting near a pile of clean laundry. Knowing there was very little else she could do, she rushed to turn it on. Once it was hot enough, she brought it to her son's side. Najiba then pushed her son's intestines back inside his stomach, pinched his skin between her fingers, and used the iron to cauterize the wound and stop the bleeding. Miraculously, Ninos survived, but he endured weeks of agonizing pain as his wound healed. Najiba told us that while her son had fully recovered physically, his mind had not been the same.

Since Ninos moved in with us, our bond continues to grow stronger and stronger. He has become like a brother to me. I have learned to read his expressions and behaviors and how to react to each based on his mood. Though I am only twelve and he is eighteen, I have become his guardian. The reality of being his protector hits home as Ninos continuously paces throughout the house, which is uncommon for him. With his restlessness, I can sense his mind is not where it should be. Lost in anguish, sorrow covers his face. He looks devoid of hope. I refuse to leave his side. I attempt to occupy his mind by engaging him in various conversations and tasks, but it does not distract him.

The sun has set at 7:30 p.m., and darkness slowly fills the streets outside. We have a guest for dinner who happens to be one of the few men Ninos respects and listens to. However, Ninos is very uneasy tonight and seems mentally distracted. He doesn't spend much time interacting with the guest, which is unusual. Closely watching all his cues, I remain nearby at all times. With a low voice and stoic face, he says, "I'm going to shower."

"Ok, I'll wait right here," I tell him. I sit on the couch near the shower room. He steps into the room while I face the wall, anxiously waiting.

Several minutes pass. I listen for the running water, but there is no sound. I approach the door and gently knock, but there is no response. "Ninos, are you okay?" I'm met with silence.

"Ninos!" I yell. Nothing.

My heart is pounding as I pray he didn't sneak a knife into the shower with him. I crouch and peek through the keyhole, squinting, trying to make sense of what's happening. Ninos is on the other side of the door, slowly cutting himself. I see the thin razor retrieved from his shaving kit as he presses it against his skin and slashes. Clenching my fist, I begin pounding on the door. "Ninos, stop!" But he doesn't listen.

"Dad, help!" I shout while begging Ninos to stop, but he ignores my loud cries and urgent knocks.

Thankfully, Dad and our guest respond. The three of us scream at Ninos, but again, we receive no response. Desperate, the two men are able to break the door and physically tackle him as he fights them off. They quickly restrain him, removing the razor from his grip before carrying him to the living room. All the while, he is screaming, cursing, kicking, and protesting. It takes almost an hour before Ninos fully calms down, and the men are able to release him. Through it all, I remain crouched on the cold tile floor beside him, calmly speaking to him as tears stream down my cheeks, praying I can reach him.

When he finally stops fighting, his body becomes limp. The men gently move him to the bedroom and place him on his bed, where he quickly falls asleep from exhaustion.

I am unable to shake the images of the evening from my mind. My body is exhausted, but my mind is running high on adrenaline. I can't sleep. I'm afraid to sleep. *What if Ninos wakes up in the middle of the night and starts cutting again? Who can stop him then?*

I decide staying awake through the night is a safer option. I spend the night by his bedside, watching and caring for him, ensuring he doesn't harm himself further. As he lays on the bed, shirtless, I can't help but notice the varying fresh thin cuts covering his arms, legs, and even his back. *How did he reach his back?*

I spend the night praying over Ninos, feeling helpless and restless myself. The night hours slowly tick by. Fighting my heavy eyelids, I force myself to stay awake. I am relieved when the morning sun peeks through the window, ending the long night.

No one talks about the incident, but Ninos seems more alert and aware since then. We continue to support him, building him up and encouraging him to join various activities through the Assyrian church. Soon after that awful night, he begins courting a young Assyrian girl and becomes more social. I can see his pain easing as time passes, and he gets more involved with the community, giving him a sense of purpose in life and something new to occupy his mind.

* * *

"Yet in all these things we are more than conquerors through Him who loved us." Romans 8:37

DUHOK - 1994

The destruction the Iraq-Iran War and the Gulf War left behind is clearly displayed in the country's infrastructure. However, the impact expands beyond the architecture as war tends to slow down and even block imports. There is a high demand for food and medicine, but the supply is low and, at times, non-existent, especially in poverty-stricken villages. With the United Nations taking control of the North, many foreign organizations have arrived to bring aid. The longevity of these organizations can last anywhere from a few days to years.

Through Horizons, we are introduced to Open Doors, another missionary organization. It is a community of Christians who come together to support persecuted believers in more than sixty countries. This organization delivers the gospel to the most oppressed countries and supports the persecuted. This week, we will host our first team from Open Doors. We have heard of their heroic stories and adventures through Georges, of delivering books to the most challenging countries. We are honored and humbled to be able to host them.

I hear a faint knock on Wednesday evening. *It must not be someone from the church since they are knocking instead of tugging on the rope.* I run to the front and swing the large metal gate open, only to be met by two handsome, blonde gentlemen with blue eyes. "Is James home?" one asks. Lost in his very blue eyes, a feature uncommon here, I pause before finally answering, "Yes." Quickly, I snap out of my awkward staring and call for Dad. "There are two Americans outside looking for you."

"Hello, James...my name is Henry, and this is Joseph; we are from Open Doors and are friends of Horizons International." Immediately, we usher them into our home. After a brief introduction, they freshen up and join us at the dining table in the kitchen. The excitement in our home is high as we have been anticipating their visit. We intently listen to the adventures and stories of Christians worldwide during dinner.

I can't help but notice the long scar that peeks through Henry's slightly unbuttoned dress shirt. "Why do you have the scar?" I ask, looking at Dad, waiting for his translation. Dad is the only one who speaks English well. The rest of us can utter a few words, but not enough to form sentences.

With a gentle smile, he looks in my direction, puts his silverware down, and explains, "Another missionary and I were assigned to smuggle a printer into a European country that does not allow Bible printing. The printer was too large to sneak in with a vehicle, so we had to crawl for miles and drag it behind us until we delivered it to its destination. Once I arrived and my adrenaline faded, I noticed the blood and the big gash on my chest. Seeking medical help, I discovered I needed surgery, leaving me with this scar. But it is worth it because the printer has allowed Christians in that country to print Bibles."

I stare at him in amazement, feeling inspired. Although hearing of other Christians worldwide and their suffering is heartbreaking, knowing we are not alone is encouraging.

Shortly after dinner, Mom serves tea with pastries. As we indulge and continue to listen to their stories, we are astonished at the ways they sneak Bibles into other countries yet inspired by the stories of believers rejoicing in their suffering worldwide.

"Would you be kind enough to help us unload the van?" Joseph asks.

Without hesitation, we all exclaim, "Yes!"

We speed-walk outside, anxiously waiting for them to open the van doors, and when they finally do, we stand in shock.

"The van is empty. Where are the books?" Mom asks in Assyrian.

"I thought you said you needed help unloading. There is nothing here," Dad remarks in English.

Henry laughs, saying, "Hang on, we will show you."

He proceeds to strip the inside walls of the van apart, along with the seats and their cushions. My mouth hangs open in shock as I see book after book appear with each wall removed. There are hundreds of books stockpiled all along the walls and in the seats. What a beautiful sight.

Since spreading Christianity within a Muslim country is forbidden, creativity is a must to proceed through the border checkpoints unnoticed.

Open Doors encourages us, not just through their visits, storytelling, and meal sharing, but also through the books they bring. With their help, we create a small library in our house. We have custom shelves built to store and display the books available for the community to borrow. Most of the books delivered are in Arabic, although a few are in English as well. This ministry broadens our horizons and exposes us to many notable authors, including Billy Graham, D.L. Moody, and Josh McDowell.

Meeting missionaries from different countries and all walks of life gives us so much gratitude. They display such bravery and risk so much to love others and share the gospel that we can't help but be encouraged.

* * *

"I have set you as a light to the Gentiles, that you should be for salvation to the ends of the earth." Acts 13:47

DUHOK - 1994

We are astonished by one missionary who has broken the mold of some of the social norms in Iraq. Irene is a Swedish woman in her seventies who speaks English and lives in Duhok. Age is just a number to her as she lives her best life in a rented one-bedroom apartment. She hosts Bible studies with my parents and helps wherever possible. Seeing a female traveling and living alone in a foreign country is amazing. This is far outside the cultural norm for Iraqi females, as young and old women remain in their fathers' houses until marriage. They become their parents' caretakers if marriage is not in their future. Living alone is not an option for women. In addition to her lifestyle, everyone admires the energy she has at her age. The average life expectancy in Iraq is around fifty years of age. Due to war, depression, and stress, most are considered elderly by age fifty, and people rarely live past sixty. The few that do are considered fortunate. To see someone in their seventies is a rare miracle.

Watching Irene live such an active life, traveling back and forth on foot between her apartment and our house, along with her daily treks through the hills nearby, is a mystery. Since arriving three weeks ago, the neighborhood children have followed her as she marches on her usual walk, excited to be in such close proximity to a foreigner and amazed by her nature. They chant, "Guadalupe! Guadalupe!" as they parade after her.

"Why is everyone shouting, Guadalupe?" she asks, stepping into our house, "Who is Guadalupe?"

With a smile, Dad explains, "Guadalupe is a Spanish show that's been voiced over in Arabic; it airs once a week, and almost the entire city watches it." He continues, "It is one of the weekly highlights, as television shows are minimal."

Since the show is foreign, the neighborhood kids assume Irene knows Guadalupe.

Irene's trip lasts four months before she moves back to Sweden. Though I'm sad to see her go, I'm grateful that I got to witness such a strong and independent woman who has been an incredible motivator and spiritual supporter during her short time with us.

Shortly after Irene's departure, we receive a letter from Horizons International that a new group of missionaries is coming to Duhok. The letter requests us to escort them through the town and help meet any needs, especially with translation. Upon the group's arrival, we find they are three American women. Again, the shock of women traveling alone to another country hits me. It is not a concept we can quickly grow accustomed to.

Michelle, Denise, and Gizelle, three beautiful women, are here to help and serve God and the community. They have a three-week trip planned. They, too, serve during Bible studies, teach Sunday School, and travel to the surrounding villages with Mom to assist in delivering medical aid.

One thing looms more than anything else our neighborhood has seen, which makes it impossible to disregard, no matter how much everyone tries. The three ladies are beautiful, kind, and gentle. However, Michelle and Denise are overweight; Michelle is obese. In Iraq, obesity is almost non-existent. The community is astonished at their sight.

We travel with them to various villages to provide aid and share the gospel. People, young and old, follow us only to stare. It is highly uncomfortable for everyone involved but, especially for the two ladies. The team nominates Dad to have the awkward conversation with the ladies. He explains the sensitivity of the situation to ease the tension and to ensure they are not offended by what is happening. He explains how this is not something people are accustomed to, and they are adjusting to a new concept. Being overweight is a rarity in Iraq; could it be the lack of food, the mountain of stress, or both? Either way, it is not the norm.

The ladies seem very gracious. They understand our culture, and even though the crowd never stops following and pointing, the ladies continue marching on, completing their mission. I am inspired by these women and their travels. Women in my world rarely travel alone from city to city, and at twelve years old, I am witnessing women travel across oceans. Their boldness to defy the odds I am accustomed to encourages me and begins to mold my already daring mind to dream even bigger. To dream outside what I can fathom. Dream of a world wrapped in exploring, traveling, working, and, above all, sharing the gospel.

The missionaries' presence is always a special treat for the children. They are excited to have foreigners come and spend time with them, reading and singing. Although neither speaks the other's language, smiles beam from side to side, and their excitement is palpable.

* * *

"I press toward the goal for the prize of the upward call of
God in Christ Jesus." Philippians 3:14

DUHOK - 1994

Chaos extends throughout Iraq. A country once united, operating in harmony, leading the Middle East in so many facets is now collapsing from within and falling apart at the seams. The division extends beyond the North and the South. Though controlled by the United Nations, the North experiences increased dissension from within, causing turmoil from internal wars led by two political parties residing in Kurdistan: the Democrats and the Republicans. The two have no commonalities beyond the Islamic religion and Kurdish language. Unsurprisingly, the leaders despise one another, their hatred trickling down to the citizens, causing bombardments on each other's territories.

We have lived in the North for nearly three years, primarily in Duhok, charted within the Democratic jurisdiction. In our time here, we have only traveled to the Republican territory twice. The first was our journey to Diana in an attempt to escape to Iran. The second was to visit a friend from Lebanon who works for the United Nations and is stationed in Arbel.

Traveling between the two Kurdish government regions is challenging, as each sector has its own checkpoints. The officials at these borders are harsh and show no leniency, as they are very protective of their territory. Whether traveling in a private vehicle or using public transit, we must stop at each checkpoint for inspection by armed military guards. When traveling by bus, the guards board the bus and walk front to back, studying every single person before exiting. Passengers are expected to comply with whatever pleases the guards. At times, they even search our luggage, looking for the color of the garments packed, ensuring we do not possess the enemy's color. The Democrats' flag is yellow, and the Republicans' is green. Those colors are forbidden in the opposing district.

When stopped at the Democratic checkpoint, the guards search for individuals wearing green. When stopped at the Republican checkpoint, the guards seek yellow items. It is better to avoid both colors when traveling. Objecting to luggage search is considered suspicious behavior and a cause for further investigation. Remaining silent during travels leads to safer travels.

As if enduring the tension caught between Democrats and Republicans is not enough, a third Kurdish party further divides Kurdistan. PKK (Pa-Ka-Ka). These Turkish Kurds live in the mountains between Iraq and Turkey, within the Democratic territory. Their domain is limited to the mountains they reside in, and their identifying color is white. They, too, do not see eye to eye with the other parties. Frequently, the opposing parties randomly shoot and bomb each other. They start at sundown and carry on for several hours. Neither party has a specific target; they fire aimlessly in the dark, instilling fear into the citizens with each blast. The random shooting between the three groups occurs monthly, sometimes more. Warning sirens do not precede these little spats to alert the citizens of the upcoming attack. When the shooting and bombing begin, people run inside and hide in the most sheltered corners of their homes. We stay away from windows to avoid being struck by bullets or shattered glass. As the hours pass, the bombings subside and diminish. We wait ten to fifteen minutes to ensure they are finished before emerging from our hiding and resuming life as usual. Until the next time, that is.

As missionaries who help distribute aid to the city of Duhok and the surrounding villages, we have developed relationships with the United Nations, UNICEF, and the Red Cross. They deliver medicine, food, and other necessities to our home, and we distribute them to the city and the villages since we speak the language and know the poverty-stricken families. Through the interactions with the UN, we have built a relationship with one of their employees, David. He is a man of faith from Lebanon and is stationed in Arbel, a major city in Kurdistan. Every so often, David is needed in Duhok. Though his trips are usually short, he spends his free time at our house, attends Bible studies, and sometimes stays the night.

David is my inspiration to continue growing in my faith. I look forward to his unexpected visits and enjoy spending time with him, learning all I can as he is very knowledgeable concerning the Bible. If I ever have a question about the Bible, I write it down, saving it for his next visit. Shortly after his arrival, I bring my list of questions and start asking and writing down his answers and any verses he shares with me.

Today's visit, David arrives with a large truck and asks for help unloading it. This is unusual as he often drives the white SUV with the UN's logo and flag. Upon rolling the back door up, we see the truck is packed to the brim with large brown bags. The bags are packages of powdered milk—five hundred pounds, to be exact. After several hours of intense work, lifting, and moving, we are able to unpack the entire truck into our family room.

"Please divide this milk and give it out to those in need," he requests, giving us a scale and plastic bags.

"Of course. This is a great ministry opportunity for the city and the surrounding villages," Dad replies as he's optimistic but also anxious about the tremendous work ahead of us.

Immediately, the separation process begins. The Horizons team and my family work tirelessly for several weeks. Every spare moment we have in between school, Bible studies, and Sunday School is used to complete this task. Our living room is covered in powder. Once the milk has been divided into bags, we travel from village to village, distributing it and sharing the news about Jesus along the way.

Not only does the powdered milk help the children and the community, but it also protects my family during one of the PKK and Democratic spats. The large brown bags are stacked against the window, completely blocking it. In need of shelter, we crouch on the ground, leaning against the bags until it is safe to emerge and resume life.

Now, within Kurdistan lives yet another group with a small bit of control: the Assyrians. They, too, have a political organization, a leader, and a small army, yet they avoid engaging in the shootings and bombings that often take place. They live in peace with all the parties involved. While living with us, Ninos found a new purpose by joining the Assyrian military.

Ninos' new commitment has provided him with a task that keeps him busy and occupies his mind from cutting. Most of the duties carried out by the Assyrian military are related to guarding the leader and the rest of the leadership staff, escorting them at all times. They also protect the leaders' homes and families and provide security for all Assyrian events. Their tasks are minimal, and their training is even more so.

Ninos is entrusted with a rifle. He usually carries it on his shoulder and can bring it home during his off-hours. Tonight, he is cleaning his weapon. I sit on his bed and watch him slowly dismantle and gently wipe each piece. One crucial step he omits is he fails to ensure the rifle is empty before cleaning it, resulting in an accidental firing. The bullet leaves the chamber and shoots past my head before snapping against the concrete wall, leaving a large hole. The loud noise makes me jump from the bed, terrified by the incident. The rifle barrel changed directions numerous times as Ninos cleaned it. It could have easily been aimed at me when it fired, but God's angels protected me tonight. As I said, minimal training is provided. Anyone can join the different military groups at any age and stage of life. They never turn down male volunteers as everyone is desperate for recruits to build a larger army.

In addition to the amateur armies, random wars, poverty, and lack of water and electricity, we live with something else that is even more agonizing: we do not know how long the United Nations will remain in Iraq. This unknown is, by far, the most frustrating and tormenting reality we experience daily. The UN's presence within the northern borders keeps Hussein at bay and provides us with a higher degree of safety and possibility of survival. Living in a city that is in constant turmoil with its neighbors and never knowing when the mountain people will attack is terrifying. However, despite this, it is still superior to living in Baghdad under Saddam's regime.

Rumors of the UN departing from Kurdistan often circulate, causing different shades of fear, panic, and many restless nights. Thankfully, they have yet to do so. We all know that the UN's departure will lead to Hussein marching back, regaining control of the North, and executing those who served the UN or any other American organization. We live in a higher state of stress each time they contemplate vacating.

We often ask ourselves, *"What about us? Do we even matter?"*

* * *

"Be strong and of good courage, do not fear nor be afraid of them; for the Lord your God, He is the One who goes with you. He will not leave you nor forsake you."

Deuteronomy 31:6

DUHOK - 1995

T he North has been living without electricity due to Saddam's hatred. It has been two years since we last experienced artificial lights. This is just another daily challenge that is overcome with creativity, perseverance, and many candles and lamps. Much like everyone around, I have grown accustomed to this lifestyle. A tall candle stands above my book during homework, and two candles and a gasoline lamp sit at the dinner table for supper. Nothing Hussein throws at us can hinder our resilience.

Without electricity, I must use batteries to operate my small cassette/radio player to listen to Arabic hymns and worship music; this brings me so much joy and keeps me connected to Christ. To sustain the life of the batteries, I have to use a little bit of ingenuity. Since all my songs are on cassette tapes, I use my finger or a pencil to spin the wheel on the cassette to rewind it when it's finished rather than use the rewind button. The tedious process extends the battery life and my ability to listen to music for much longer.

Along with listening to worship music, I have grown to love reading my Bible. The more I read, the more I want to immerse myself and grow spiritually. My Bible has become my refuge in times of fear. Whenever I feel anxiety growing within me, witness my family struggle with a situation, or cannot fall asleep, I reach for my Bible, hold it tightly against my chest, wrap my arms around it, and I experience immediate relief. It has become my comforter, not only in the emotional and mental sense with the powerful words and messages but also in the physical sense. Even the most cozy, most fluffy, or softest teddy bear cannot provide me with the comfort my Bible gives.

As an introvert, I prefer to stay home whenever my family leaves the house to visit friends or go shopping, giving me time to do my favorite activities. Today, there is a slight breeze cooling down the evening. The temperature in the house is too warm to comfortably enjoy my worship time, so I step outside with my Bible and cassette player in hand. My family left shortly after my usual response, "No, thank you. I would rather stay home." I sit on the tiled floor, under the grapevines, facing the large metal gates and lean against the concrete wall that separates our house from our neighbors. With my Bible tightly gripped in my hand, I press play, close my eyes, and begin singing. As I sink deeper into the Spirit, my heart full of gratitude and peace, I hear a clanging sound. Opening my eyes, I watch the metal gates rattle in slow motion. The rope we tied to the handle is being pulled, yet there is no hand. My gaze immediately travels to the large gap between the ground and the bottom of the gates. To my surprise, no feet are showing. There is no one on the other side of the gates. Shivers rush through my body as I feel a cold presence. With each passing second, the gates rattle and shake more violently.

I feel as if an invisible power is attempting to come in. I stare at the gates in awe and a little frightened. Suddenly, Jesus appears, standing on my side of the gates. He's wearing a long white robe with a red sash draped over his shoulder and across his body. He is beautiful in every way imaginable, an indescribably magnificent sight. His pierced left hand stretches out against the gates. He gently looks at me with his beautiful brown eyes and says, "Don't worry, I got you." Instantly, peace washes over me as I look into Christ's eyes, and my fear disappears. My Savior has me in His care.

I watch Christ battle who I assume is Satan. I cannot see him, but I can feel his presence and see how violently he attempts to break through the gates. This encounter lasts minutes before the Devil gives up, things calm down, the gate stops shaking, and Christ disappears.

This is not the first encounter I have had with the Devil. Often when I spend time in worship, he appears before me as a shadow in the shape of a human form, made of the blackest of blacks. He circles me when I pray and worship, pacing nonstop. Sometimes I open my eyes during prayer, whether alone or with a group, and find him circling on the outskirts. The most unpleasant interaction with him is when he silently sits on the couch across from me and watches me read my Bible. Although he has no face, I know he is staring at me; I can feel his darkness aimed at me. I find his gaze unnerving. I rebuke him in the name of Jesus, which forces him to disappear, at least until the next time.

One thing I know for sure is that Satan exists. He is continually on the prowl, looking to wage spiritual attacks, especially when threatened by the believers' work. Though his power is limited, he seeks only to kill, steal, and destroy, yet that can come in many forms. In the midst of the Devil's attempts to deter me or bring fear, Christ shows himself as my defender, the one who strengthens and upholds me.

My visions have played a significant role in my life and are one of the most remarkable ways God interacts with me. He sought me out long before I knew Him and has continued since.

It all began with the Gulf War dream, where he revealed Hussein's invasion of Kuwait as it was happening. Before reading the Bible, I had little knowledge and understanding of how God speaks to us. The gift of dreams and visions is not one that is taught in church, nor is the gift of prophecy. Our awareness of spiritual gifts, their power, and their application is limited in our culture. When there is little to no education on a matter, it is a challenge to understand the power behind it. If I had the knowledge and the appropriate spiritual tools to understand the power of the gift of prophecy growing up, I would have embraced it differently. I would have wrapped my arms around it instead of fearing it. The gift would be a blessing instead of a nightmare. However, I have come to accept this wonderful and unique gift through my spiritual growth, a better understanding of the Bible, and continuing my relationship and communication with Christ.

* * *

"God also bearing witness both with signs and wonders, with various miracles, and gifts of the Holy Spirit, according to His own will." Hebrews 2:4

DUHOK - 1995

L iving in Iraq as the minority, preaching the gospel, comes with challenges. The Assyrians are allowed to have church buildings, attend church services, and still live within the Muslim community amicably, at least most of the time. The Assyrians and the Islam, have entirely different religious views and absolutely no commonalities politically. Islam controls every part of life, from the country's religion to government power and the justice system.

Even though the two live together, I have learned that the Assyrians must use caution when in contact with those who adhere to the Muslim call. This calling is often claimed to be taken only by extremists, yet other individuals also regularly obey it and are often rewarded. Over one hundred passages in the book of the Qur'an call Muslims to take up arms against unbelievers. The Qur'an is the Islamic sacred book believed to be the word of God spoken to the Prophet Muhammad.

My family and I have deliberately decided to study the Qur'an to equip ourselves and be fully prepared to discuss it if the need emerges. Being knowledgeable in the Islamic faith allows us to compare the Qur'an to the Bible, examining the Christian faith alongside the Islamic religion.

Although the Islamic religion is referred to as the religion of peace by most Muslims—and many Muslims are peaceful—their foundation and sacred book call for them to be otherwise against anyone who is not a Muslim. Some of the passages encourage behavior that is nothing short of murder.

"Kill them [unbelievers] wherever you find them... And fight them until there is no more unbelief and worship is for Allah alone" (Qur'an 2:191-193).

"Strike off their heads and strike from them every fingertip" (Qur'an 8:12).

"Allah has purchased from the believers their lives and their properties; in exchange for that, they will have Paradise. They fight in the cause of Allah, so they slay and are slain" (Qur'an 9:111).

"Truly Allah loves those who fight in His cause in battle array . . ." (Qur'an 61:4).

"The Messenger of Allah said: I have been commanded to fight against people till they testify that there is no god but Allah and that Muhammad is the messenger of Allah" (Sahih Muslim 1:33).

We use our knowledge of the Islamic religion as a gateway to engage with our Muslim neighbors intellectually since most read the Qur'an out of religious obligation instead of fully understanding the book. When we find ourselves in a heated discussion, we draw passages from the Qur'an to gently explain Christianity, which is essential every time. We lead many Muslims to Christ while serving in Duhok just by looking deeper at their sacred book, especially regarding the passages relating to Christ.

Part of Horizons International's job is to provide medical aid where needed, especially in the surrounding poverty-stricken villages. Serving as we do in a Muslim country is dangerous, even more so in the villages surrounding the city. The Assyrian community is very small in those towns, to the point of being almost nonexistent. It also doesn't help that the police force is scarce, with most being a part of the Islamic extremists. Despite this, my family and the team have been serving in those villages for two years. Each time we visit one of these villages, we step in blindly, taking a giant leap of faith and trusting God.

Undeterred by the danger, we deliver food and medical supplies while we minister to the communities, displaying love and compassion like they have never experienced. These acts of kindness, including Mom tending to the wounded, open doors for spiritual conversations, Bible teachings, and sharing Christ's love.

Facing the unknown for proclaiming our faith is a daily occurrence, but it does not hinder us from fulfilling our purpose: to share the love of Jesus and the truth of His death and resurrection.

Most of the families cherish our visits. Their gratitude is plainly displayed in their smiles. Watching relief wash over the parents as their ill children's needs are met is both gratifying and humbling. They appreciate my mother as she gently cleanses wounds, applies medicine, and bandages injuries. She is always tender and compassionate towards all, speaking life into them as she cares for them.

Mom has been visiting one village, in particular, Nazarke, for forty-two days straight. Two preteen girls were born with disabilities. One has scoliosis, and the other has various unidentifiable ailments due to limited medical knowledge and resources in Iraq. Both girls have endured several surgeries to no avail. Mom tends to their surgery wounds daily. While doing so, she spends time with the parents and neighbors, teaching them about Jesus. These helpless parents have been very appreciative; however, some villagers have been less welcoming.

Although we understand the possibility of danger each time we visit one of these villages, we don't fully know the magnitude of this danger until one morning.

"Tell your wife she needs to stop coming to Nazarke and preaching," a stranger exclaims to Dad as he follows him to the bookstore. "If she doesn't stop, we will kidnap your daughters and kill her," he continues. The shock of this threat dissuades Dad from entering the bookstore. His flustered mind shifts to us girls and Mom. He strides home quickly, taking large steps, borderline running. He steps through the doors with a sense of urgency, saying, "We need to talk." He tells us of the anxiety-inducing news. Though we have endured hardships, this is the first time we have experienced a direct threat due to our faith and work. The disturbance of this news leaves us rattled momentarily. We are quickly reminded that the One with us is stronger than the one against us. God has faithfully protected us in the past; this is no different.

The threats do not stop Mom from continuing to offer help to this village. However, soon after the threats, Horizons obtained a medical visa for these two girls and their parents to travel to America to receive treatment and return to Iraq, and Mom didn't have to return to Nazarke again.

Though we are relieved at no longer having to worry about the threat from the village, it is short-lived.

On a cold winter morning, I step outside and immediately feel the chill air pass through my coat. I can see remnants of snow on the ground, a rare occurrence in Iraq. When it does happen, it is a light dusting that thaws rapidly. I strap my backpack on and walk through the gates like any other school day. Four houses down, I meet up with my classmate Naqia, who is outside waiting. We depart, travel to the end of the block, and turn right, marching past several houses before we reach Nina, another school friend, and a few houses farther, Salwa. The four of us stroll along, content in our warm coats and gloves.

From the corner of my eye, I notice a man following us, his left hand crossed over his body as if trying to hide a gun tucked into his unzipped jacket. He continues walking rather closely around our group, attempting to separate me from everyone. His demeanor and behavior are unsettling. I keep an eye on him the entire walk, and every time I gaze at him, his eyes lock on me. Fear stabs at me, but I keep moving forward, not wanting to alarm my friends. I shift my focus from this man to Christ as I silently utter a prayer, loud enough only for my ears to hear. "Lord, you have not abandoned me yet, and you are not going to now." I find solace as we connect with a larger group of kids traveling in the same direction. Luckily, I am in the center of the group where his attempts to isolate me fail. He continues to follow us to school with no luck. Once we enter the school grounds, he cannot walk past the two teachers waiting at the gate. For once, I am grateful for the strict rule of locked doors while school is in session. God's protection, yet again, emerges when I need Him.

School's intensity is a welcome distraction from my unpleasant experience this morning. As the final bell rings, I ensure I'm traveling with the same group of friends home. Once I step into the kitchen, I waste no time telling my parents of the incident. It is quickly decided that we will no longer travel alone, especially my mother, sisters, and me.

"For I am not ashamed of the gospel of Christ, for it is the power of God to salvation for everyone who believes."
Romans 1:16

DUHOK - 1995

The most consistent missionary group to visit our humble home is the leadership team from Horizons International. Georges and Mary are the co-founders of this organization, and they support us financially and spiritually. They visit us at least once a year, if not more, which is very encouraging, especially during our trying times. During their visits, they lead our Bible studies while also bringing clothing, hair accessories, and other personal items for us and the children in our Sunday School. During their latest trip, they delivered a set of cassette tapes of English Sunday School songs by the Cedarmont Kids. My sisters and I quickly begin to listen and learn the songs to teach them to the other kids.

They have also gifted my sisters and me with a movie, Disney's *The Lion King,* on VHS. We have no knowledge of this movie, or Disney, for that matter. Saddam banned anything American since the beginning of the Gulf War. However, in recent months, Hussein has turned our electricity back on from two to four hours daily. The timing is random, but we are grateful for the extension.

I take the tape out of its case and slide it into our VHS player, and instantly, my sisters and I are hooked. The movie is in English, which means we can only understand a few words here and there, but we don't care. The tunes are fun and catchy, and we are drawn in. We begin memorizing the songs despite the fact that we don't understand what we're singing. We love everything about the movie until the scene where Mufasa dies. Tears well up, and we cry as if we have lost someone near and dear. Mesmerized by it, we rewind the movie and watch it again and again. Except from now on, we fast forward through the sorrowful scene.

The Lion King has become my English tutor. I discovered how to turn on the captions on our small vintage television, and I asked my parents for an Arabic-English dictionary. In my spare time, as I watch the movie with the captions on, I pause each scene to search for the English words in my dictionary and memorize them. Although this exercise sounds tedious and painful, it is stimulating for me. At twelve years old, I am learning my fifth language independently. I have now discovered a path around one of the hardships I experience with the missionaries: I don't speak English. Though I am learning new words whenever we have visitors, it's not enough to be able to converse. The movie, however, is excellent in helping me learn the language much quicker. I continue practicing, and my vocabulary expands. Before I know it, I am forming sentences.

Even though the English language is introduced as a sixth-grade subject in school, amongst other subjects such as history, geography, biology, chemistry, Arabic, and mathematics, the class is less entertaining than the movie. As a matter of fact, the course is frightening. The vice principal is my teacher, and she is terrifying. She is very strict and has no sense of humor.

The only time I have ever received punishment in school was from her. Being a good student who receives grades in the nineties or higher and never misses an assignment is something I take pride in.

Having never gotten a physical beating from a teacher is even more impressive until sixth grade. Each week, she gives the class thirty English spelling words to memorize. There are no phonics, pronunciations, or even learning how to use them in a sentence; only one thing matters, learning to spell correctly. At the end of each week, she randomly calls students' names and asks them to spell various words from her list. However, she walked into the classroom last month and immediately asked everyone to stand up. She then walked through the aisles between the desks, asking students to spell words from her recent spelling list. When a student misspelled a word, they had to sit down. This continued for the duration of the class until everyone was seated. I managed to survive six rounds before I stumbled on the word "first," and I spelled "f-r-i-s-t" Scared and unsure of what was next, we all sat quietly, staring at her as she walked to the front of the room to announce the punishment.

"Each student will receive hits on the back of their hands based on how many rounds they missed," she announced as she tapped her thick round stick on the front desk. Luckily for me, I only missed three rounds. Three painful bangs, leaving my hands sore for the remainder of the day. My heart broke for the girls who failed much earlier than I as I could hear them whimper with each hit and were left in tears by the time she concluded her abuse.

Having missionaries visit us often allows me to practice my English and take advice as they help me improve it. Also, learning children's songs and watching *The Lion King* have advanced my English speaking, pronunciation, and memorization so I don't fail again.

In addition to aiding me to succeed in my English class, the Horizons team also provides us with spiritual support, something we desperately need as Christians living in a Muslim country. They pour into our lives and keep us connected and strong. At times, they bring other missionaries with them to encourage us.

One particular missionary is Laurie. She is sweet, full of love and compassion, gentle, and soft-spoken. From the moment she arrived, we instantly connected. She takes me under her wing for the week she visits and includes me in everything. We become inseparable even during Sunday School; she attends my class with me and helps Mom with the lesson. She also encourages my broken English, assisting me to improve my pronunciation and expanding my vocabulary. I am saddened by her fast-approaching departure date as I am not ready to separate yet, especially not knowing if I will ever see her again.

The night before her departure, she gives me a gold ring with a small Aquamarine stone in the center. The ring is simple and beautiful. From what I understand, the colored stone symbolizes the month of March. I'm surprised to learn there are colors associated with each month, as the concept of birthstones does not exist in Iraq.

Since students are not allowed to wear jewelry in school, I put the ring on a short gold chain, making it into a necklace, and I keep it in my backpack until the school bell rings. I excitedly put it around my neck before leaving the school grounds. Occasionally, I push the envelope and wear it during the school day with it tucked beneath my shirt.

Laurie and I have exchanged letters several times since her departure, something I always look forward to. Though my grammar is of poor quality, writing those letters helps me develop my love and passion for writing. We keep in touch for several months until written communication is blocked due to the rising disputes within Kurdistan. I lose my connection to Laurie, never hearing from or seeing her again.

For some inexplicable reason, I always feel relief when missionaries visit. I'm unsure why, but I have this easy-going feeling when they are around. I think their trips give me hope that if they can come and visit, then maybe someday, I can leave.

* * *

"Ointment and perfume delight the heart, and the sweetness
of a man's friend gives delight by hearty counsel."
Proverbs 27:9

DUHOK - 1995

Our church congregation continues to grow amid the challenging circumstances, perhaps partly due to them. I've come to learn that we often search for God when faced with our mortality. People from all four corners of the city and the surrounding villages travel to our house to attend our Bible studies. As with the staff, people are hungry for God's word and come almost daily to learn and grow spiritually. Our fellowship time together is invaluable. We pray. We worship. We fast once a month and break the fast by sharing a meal at our house. We grow closer as a church, a family, and a community as we depend on each other and support each other through all the trials of life. Most importantly, we grow stronger together in hope, faith, and trust in God through each storm we face.

Two of our favorite gatherings and celebrations as a church are Christmas Eve and Easter Eve, which are observed in much the same way. In early December, Mom found Christmas decorations, which are challenging to find in stores, especially in the North. We cut down a beautiful tree and decorated our house. The Christmas tree is displayed in the main living room, where all the Bible studies and other church activities occur. Everything is fundamental and minimal, but we love having the tree, which helps usher in the Christmas spirit long before all the holiday festivities begin. As kids, having something as significant as the tree, when not every household has one, is tremendous, and we happily gather around it on Christmas morning.

Everyone gathers at our house on Christmas Eve, where we share a meal, pray, study the Bible, and sing Christmas carols. In the weeks leading up to Christmas Eve, Mom has a great idea that she is confident will bring joy to our church members and their families.

"We should dress one of the men as Santa Claus, gather presents, wrap them, and deliver them to our church families," she says.

"That's a wonderful idea, but where will you find a Santa Claus suit in Duhok?" Dad asks.

"Leave that to me."

When determined, nothing can stop Mom from pursuing her ideas, a quality that I admire. After connecting with many neighbors, she somehow is able to locate a Santa Claus suit, despite them being hard to come by. We notify the church members of the idea, begin collecting toys, and accept donations to buy the toys ourselves. After dinner and worship on Christmas Eve, Mom asks one of the team members to dress in the Santa suit and carry the enormous red bag packed with toys. The rest of us dress in warm coats, hats, and gloves before we begin marching through the city streets, visiting church families, singing Christmas carols, and distributing gifts to the children. The kids are ecstatic, bursting at the seams, and the parents are delighted.

After a few hours of bringing cheer to the community, we return to the house for more worship, prayer, and snacks. We stay up all night playing games and creating comedy skits. Around 5 a.m., we dress in our brand-new Christmas attire and walk to the Assyrian church for communion and Christmas Mass. We only attend the end of the Mass to receive the communion and then walk back home for a short nap before beginning our Christmas morning festivities.

Our holiday celebrations don't stop with Christmas and Easter but carry into Musardel. We plan a large church picnic at a pool near the mountain. The area is part of a small resort with chairs and tables along the pool, a playground for the children, and a restaurant. It is an upscale gated area with a beautiful view. My family is able to rent the entire resort from 8 a.m. until 4 p.m., opening the celebration to our church family and friends. After renting two buses, we pack them with food, drinks, and guests and drive for an hour before reaching our destination.

Most adults jump into the pool and start swimming shortly after arriving and settling in. Like many of my friends, I have never learned to swim as I grew up without access to a body of water or a pool. So we devise a system where we take turns jumping into the pool, and an adult catches us and pulls us back out again. We keep this going for an hour or so. It is my turn to jump again. The adult in charge of catching me is not paying attention, so I drop straight into the water and sink. Panic overtakes me when I realize no one has reached for me. Desperate and running out of air, I begin flailing in an attempt to reach the surface. My lungs start to burn as I continue my unsuccessful struggle. *I am drowning.* Finally, I feel hands grabbing me before they pull me out of the water. I cough and gasp for air. I was in the water for less than a minute, yet it felt as if I had spent a lifetime. Terrified of the experience, I move away from the poolside and refuse to get back in.

Despite the incident, I do not want to waste this opportunity in a beautiful park, so I join the other kids on the playground. I can't help but smile, watching the people around me laughing and enjoying themselves. Despite our trauma and struggles, we are able to disconnect from reality and celebrate together.

"Let us come before His presence with thanksgiving; let us shout joyfully to Him with psalms." Psalm 95:2

DUHOK - 1995

Today is a big day. We will tune into Duhok's first Christian radio program in a few minutes. The first evangelical church, where Mom and I came to know Christ, launched this station. The anticipation is high, and we are grateful for their fearlessness in a Muslim country. I ensure there are batteries in my little cassette player and find the channel. I hear a drumming, marching beat at the five o'clock mark. The march gets louder, and the program begins with the song, "Hosanna in the Highest" in Arabic. Three more songs by famous artists and worship teams are played before a sermon by the church pastor is shared. The program closes with the beginning song again, signaling the end. This song has a unique marching sound, making me feel like I'm marching to the Word of God. It is encouraging to hear Jesus on the air. This is the first time an evangelist has dared to take such a bold step in a Muslim country. It is a blessing for many.

Although the radio station is deemed brave and successful, not all ventures carried out by missionaries have been as effective. Recently, a visiting missionary acquired a small store, remodeled the inside, and built shelves before opening it as a Christian library-bookstore where people from all walks of life could visit, purchase, or borrow books. On the first day of business, when the clerk reached for the door, he noticed a foreign object attached to the door handle. Realizing it was a bomb set to detonate when the door opens, he immediately called the authorities. They successfully removed it; however, because it was a Christian bookstore, no investigation was conducted to determine who planted it. Despite the unfortunate incident, the store resumed operation the following day.

The news of the potential explosion quickly spread through Duhok and the surrounding cities, but that did not prevent a small church in Arbil from pursuing their desire to launch a Christian bookstore, providing the people of Arbil the same privileges as Duhok. As the much-anticipated opening date neared, the excitement within the Christian community continued to grow. However, that excitement was quickly crushed by the tragic news that took place shortly after the launch. An hour into the opening, a man stepped in, pointed his gun at the store clerk behind the cash register, and pulled the trigger, killing him point-blank. The killer then marched out of the store as if nothing happened. Again, no investigations or arrests were made. The killer was rewarded with freedom for obeying his Islamic calling. Yet again, the Christian citizens of Iraq carry on despite the temporary fear it instilled within the community. Though in mourning, they assist the church in cleaning the store and resuming operations. Succumbing would only demonstrate that fear has won.

* * *

"Therefore I take pleasure in infirmities, in reproaches, in needs, in persecutions, in distresses, for Christ's sake. For when I am weak, then I am strong." 2 Corinthians 12:10

INTERLUDE - ASSYRIANS AMONGST ISLAM

There is a small number of families that own vehicles in the North. For one Assyrian man, owning a car has led to the worst fate imaginable.

The young Assyrian man was driving his white sedan through the streets of Duhok when he accidentally struck a young Muslim man crossing the street. The Muslim man died in the hospital later that day, and the Kurdish officers arrested the driver. A few days later, the driver was sentenced to life in prison. Unfortunately, it is a well-known fact that "justice" here is reactionary. The court system in Iraq is rigged. Lawyers work for whoever pays them the most and for those to whom they owe favors or money. Fair trials are uncommon. That is, if someone lives long enough to have a trial.

After the Assyrian driver was placed in jail, female family members of the deceased, including his mother, visited the prison, seeking to determine the man's fate since jail time was not a satisfying punishment in their eyes. The police agreed and allowed the women access to the prisoner. Rage overtook them. They strapped him down and bit him furiously until he died. He suffered a long, painful, and

284

gruesome death. After his passing, his family received his body and gave him a dignified funeral and burial.

The Islamic women who retaliated this way received no ramifications or punishment for their behavior. The concept of avenging honor is deeply woven into the culture, and their actions are seen to be within reason, given their loss. Such stories are familiar amongst villages all across Iraq. Not only do we have to survive a vicious government, but we also have to be careful living within our Islamic neighborhoods. The driver's actions were reckless and deserved punishment, but not such a brutal death without a fair trial. His outcome might have been different had he not been guilty of being Assyrian.

The news of this horrific tragedy quickly circulates in the city as the Assyrian community tries to stay calm and push forward. Retaliation will only lead to death. I have never met this individual, but his story is so powerful that it has impacted the Assyrian community.

"Be kind to one another, tenderhearted, forgiving one another, even as God in Christ forgave you." Ephesians 4:32

DUHOK - 1996

E ach and every day, Christ followers from all across the world face persecution for their faith and in some cases, even death. This is something the Apostle Paul assures us we will encounter in his writings in 2 Timothy.

Every missionary we meet tells us of their suffering, sharing stories of fellow Christians they cross paths with that experience it as well. I have read story after story of persecuted believers in the numerous books Open Doors has delivered. Facing persecution in my life creates an invisible bond between me and others experiencing similar circumstances. I find courage in that bond, knowing I am not alone.

Our persecution doesn't only come from the Islamic community but also from the Assyrians. Though they are Christians from birth, they practice faith in a ritualistic and religious sense rather than a relational one. Their church services are often conducted in the original Aramaic, a dialect most don't understand. The readings are chanted from a secondary book developed by the church instead of the primary source, the Bible. The priest is held in the highest regard possible; he is greeted with a kiss on the hand or sometimes on his ring. Additionally, Mary and other saints are honored and worshiped nearly as much as Jesus, if not more. Attending church service is an obligation to the Assyrians in place of leading others to salvation. Whereas the evangelical church conducts the studies directly from the Bible, discussions are Holy Spirit-led, and the sole purpose of our mission is to serve God and lead people to His kingdom.

Our ministry continues to grow in Duhok as we dive deeper into the Word. We encourage people to "wipe the dust off their Bibles" and read them. Even more scandalously, we encourage them to write notes in their Bibles and highlight parts of it to help them better understand and memorize the Scriptures. This is a foreign concept to most as creating markings in the Word of God is considered disrespectful. In the Assyrian culture, the Bible is holy and should only be regarded as such. The Book cannot even be placed on the ground as that, too, is a disgraceful gesture. In our ministry, however, we have pushed the limit a step further by giving each child in our Sunday School program a children's Bible. This "blasphemous act" is causing an uproar within the community. What drives everyone to the edge is the fact that we are teaching the children and the adults how to be mindful of their prayers.

In Assyrian church, the Lord's Prayer is recited at every meal. In all honesty, it is prayed during every occasion—wedding, graduation, or funeral. The prayer has become a one-size-fits-all type of prayer. However, as Christians born of the Spirit, we use the Lord's Prayer as an example of how to pray rather than just a verbatim prayer to be repeated in every instance. We believe that our prayers are conversations with God, specific to each situation and circumstance. When Jesus teaches his disciples how to pray, he doesn't say, "Pray this prayer." He says, "This is how you should pray"— Matthew 6:9-13. If we follow Jesus' teaching, then the Lord's Prayer is an example we can draw from. But, if we follow the ritualistic example, the prayer is concrete and inflexible. My family and I followed this ritualistic method of praying for many years. It wasn't until WIN and Tofiq's eye-opening teachings that we came to understand that there's more to prayer than recitation. We learned that prayer is a conversation between God and us, even when blessing our meals.

We encourage the congregation to pray from their hearts instead of reciting a memorized prayer. We teach them to speak to God relationally and share what is on their hearts and minds with Him. He does not want a practiced ceremonial prayer or for us to only seek Him when we need Him. He wants to be part of our lives and have a relationship with us. This means that we have to learn to pray through love instead of duty.

We also teach the children Assyrian, Arabic, and English worship songs, which are hummed and shared at home. Again, praising and worshiping Jesus in such a way is a foreign concept.

Another significant difference is that the traditional Assyrian church highly regards several saints, including Mary, the mother of Jesus. In August, a fifteen-day fast is held in her honor and is concluded by a particular church service followed by feasting on a sacrificial lamb. As I mentioned, Saint Georges or Dukhrana'd Mar Gewargis celebration is held in November. There is also a celebration for Jonah in February. Many of the saints have their proper fast and church service followed by a feast prepared with the sacrificial lamb to end the fast.

We, however, don't believe in worshiping the saints. When Jesus died on the cross, he became the final sacrificial lamb. He redeemed us and restored us back to God, but not before forgiving us of our sins. Continuing to offer sacrifices goes against the New Testament and the new covenant through Christ. We have participated in these traditions in our past lives, but now, our eyes have been opened, and the veil has been lifted. We can see what Christ has done for us.

Because of our beliefs, we face hardships from both groups, although, at times, it feels like the Muslims are more accepting and sympathetic than the Assyrians. We are often ridiculed and questioned in public for our faith. Some have even shunned us, avoiding interactions at all costs. But it doesn't stop there.

* * *

"I desire mercy and not sacrifice." Matthew 9:13

DUHOK - 1996

Persecution and suffering extend beyond the church community and into the school system. Each class bears much anxiety with the stresses of the strict structure and discipline inflicted upon students. At nine and thirteen years old, this is a structure Sona, and I have grown accustomed to. We have learned not only to tolerate it but also to excel under it. However, the persecution we endure at the hands of two specific teachers increases the weight of our anxiety and stressful daily school life.

Sona has been assigned to Ms. Lucy's second-grade class. Ms. Lucy is the sister of the Assyrian church pastor, and as such, she seems to take things personally and has a vendetta against my family. Though a petite woman, her roar is loud. She is open about her disapproval of the work Horizons International and my family perform in Duhok. She inflicts her distaste on Sona, ensuring the school and everyone else knows it. Despite her disapproval, Ms. Lucy is bold enough to request medicine and food from us when needed. Unfortunately, she's also bold enough to punish Sona daily, often yelling at and beating her. She finds every opportunity to make Sona's school life unbearable.

My parents have made several attempts to reason with Ms. Lucy, pleading for her to cease her punitive behavior, but it is brushed aside. She refuses to stop, telling my parents directly that she finds our work repulsive and unacceptable. Ms. Lucy feels our mission work discredits her brother and his church. Abusing Sona is her way of seeking revenge.

Moving Sona to another classroom is not a viable alternative as children cannot switch classrooms, no matter the circumstances. She has two choices: drop out of school or remain and endure the mistreatment. Though both options are terrible, the latter is best to further Sona's education and ensure she doesn't lose a school year. Even if Sona skipped a year, there is no guarantee that she would not end up with Ms. Lucy again. Because of this, my parents make the tough decision to keep Sona in school.

Though I don't experience Sona's level of mistreatment, I am not exempt from the persecution. The school pressure is fierce year-round. While school is frightening, there is one exception that makes education slightly bearable. Throughout middle and high school years, except for ninth and twelfth grade, students maintaining an average score of ninety percent or higher on every quiz, test, and midterm are exempt from the final examination for that particular subject at the end of the school year. Students scoring above ninety percent in all their classes are excused from all finals, and their school year ends two weeks early. At times, when students have a class or two with an average score in the eighties, the school rounds those grades to ninety and excuses the student from all finals. This is the school's method of extending kindness and flexibility. As for ninth and twelfth graders, everyone must participate in the final exams regardless of their scores. I have been blessed to skip my finals in the seventh grade and most of my finals in the eighth grade, except for two classes.

From an early age, the importance of education has been ingrained within me. It started with my parents, Babi Matti, and the rest of the family. My reputation is tied not only to being the perfect oldest daughter but also to being the perfect student. Obtaining anything less than ninety is unacceptable by my standards and my family's. However, in recent months, I have been struggling with English, mainly in spelling, which has reduced my overall score to eighty-eight. The same goes for my Arabic class, as my biggest weakness is Arabic grammar. Though I've always found a way to succeed, the class intensifies with each grade. Thankfully, my principal, vice-principal, and teachers have been observant enough to recognize my dedication, hard work, and perfect attendance. Their acknowledgment has convinced my teachers to round my final scores to ninety to avoid the dreaded final exams. I am beyond thrilled as my teachers share the exciting news. The relief is tremendous, knowing I have been unshackled from the agonizing study sessions and material reviews.

I am officially liberated from all exams. One more year in the books. I cannot wait to walk home, share the excellent news with my parents, and delight in their pride and accolades.

However, my joy quickly turns sour, and my enthusiasm is crushed when my Physical Education (PE) teacher, Ms. Aqeelah, who ironically happens to be the Catholic priest's sister, steps into my classroom to make an announcement. Much like Ms. Lucy, she also has a grievance with my family's mission work. She declares every student's final grade and saves me for last. She locks her eyes with mine with an impassive stare clouded with evil intentions. "Your final score is eighty-nine," her voice utters, masked with a sigh of relief.

Confused and frightened, I raise my hand, seeking permission to speak.

"Yes?" she asks.

"I don't understand," I say, fighting to hold back the floodgates of tears building up. "I have participated in every activity and every class. I joined the volleyball club and helped advance the team to compete. I also joined track and field and engaged in every event you requested. How can I receive eighty-nine?"

The brief silence that follows is unsettling. "This is my final decision," she sternly states, exiting my classroom.

My Muslim teachers are astonished by her spitefulness toward me. Like me, they can't fathom or justify her behavior. *How can other Muslim students who rarely participate in school activities due to wearing their long dresses and hijabs be rewarded a much higher grade than me?* My principal and vice-principal plead with her on my behalf to no avail. They cannot understand the adamancy of her bitterness towards someone from her own culture. Her refusal causes my other two classes, Arabic and English, to drop back down. Per government law, any rounded grades will revert back if teachers are not in agreement.

Heartbroken and crushed, I feel defeated as I cry the entire journey home. Mom doesn't take long to notice my tears as I walk into the kitchen. Her frustration quickly rises as she listens to my story, often interrupted by sniffles. Immediately, Mom and one of our team members stride to the school on a mission, looking for Ms. Aqeelah. There is a big difference between proud parents saying, "My child is fully exempt from final exams this year." vs. "My child is partially exempt." This may seem trivial to most, but to poverty-stricken citizens, taking pride in their children's education is highly regarded. It is one of the few elements remaining that Hussein has not demolished.

Upon their arrival, they team up with the principal in another attempt to reason with her and change her mind. Again, her hatred and stubbornness are overpowering any sound reason. She clearly communicates her decision and her blunt disapproval of my family's work. She does not hold back as she shares my punishment for my faith with everyone in the room.

Anxiously waiting for Mom, I pray for God's grace to soften Ms. Aqeelah's heart as I pace in the living room. With each step, the Persian rug beneath my feet is pressed with outrage. I stop in my tracks when I hear the gates open as the handle is unhinged, releasing a clanking sound. *Mom is home.* Rushing to the front door, my heart sinks as I am met with a look of disappointment and defeat plainly displayed on her face. "I have to take those tests, don't I?" Tears stream down my face as I accept my fate, walk towards my backpack, find my Arabic textbook, and start reviewing the material. There is no time to be angry. No time to mourn. I must put on a brave face and show Ms. Aqeelah she has no power over me. I will pass these tests, and I will succeed. Despite the momentary defeat, I am grateful and blessed to have only two classes to study for.

I have three classes to test for in total. English, Arabic, and of course, P.E. I review the material for the two language classes and pass the tests with a score above ninety. The day of the P.E. test arrives. I attend the class on time and in my athletic wear, ready to display any action Ms. Aqeelah requires. I am prepared to dance if it means I pass. But again, her malicious intentions shine through as she glances my way. "That is all for you. You may go now," she simply states, motioning towards the classroom door. She did not even test me. She just wanted me here for her satisfaction as she gives me a final score of ninety percent. I smile as I thank her and walk out the door. Although she may think she has triumphed, she didn't. No hateful action carried out by her or anyone else can prevent me from reading my Bible or sharing the Gospel of Jesus.

Encountering petty behaviors like this seems sad, yet we endure them for crimes we did not commit due to our faith.

As our mission work and our church continue to grow, so does the hatred and the persecution. Working for various American organizations, including the Red Cross, UNICEF, and the United Nations, has labeled us as traitors. The members of these organizations are found driving around the cities in white SUVs, with each vehicle emblazoned with the organization's symbol on the side doors. They also have the organization's flag attached to the car, waving high and proud. As they visit our home so often, with those flags displayed so openly, they have turned it into a target. Everyone knows our location, both those who appreciate us and those who seek to inflict harm. When people need directions to our house, others say, "Just look for the white SUVs with UN, UNICEF, or Red Cross flags, and you have found your destination." Although some people love the aid these organizations provide, due to religious beliefs, cultural influence, and peer pressure, they do not appreciate what these organizations stand for nor where they come from. Most people view America as a strongly Christian country, in the same manner that Iraq is strongly Muslim. With limited facts about America, the citizens have nothing but speculation to believe their assumptions to be factual.

Unlike the Assyrians and the Catholics, we conduct church services at home. We don't have the means or government permission to have a church building. Our community, be it the Assyrians or Catholics, does not see our beliefs as true faith. Their perception of us is a lost group teaching against the Bible and luring others with them. They refuse to refer to us as Christians. Instead, we are referred to as Evangelists. You may think, "I don't see anything wrong with that." You are right; there is nothing wrong with this term. However, being called Evangelist is used as an insult, not a compliment, and a form of bullying. The term is used to degrade us. Being called an Evangelist is another way to claim we have gone astray, lost our path from God, and most likely, have lost our minds.

Our ministry and preaching pose a more significant threat to the Muslims as we march into their territory and preach Jesus, drawing people away from the Islamic religion and into Christianity. With this, the pressure and persecution increase. It escalates from mundane comments and conversations to alienation by the church, cruel treatment from our teachers, and even personal threats. I am willing to suffer for my faith at the hands of the teachers or be alienated from my community. Knowing I am serving Christ and living my calling makes it all worth it.

"Love your enemies, do good to those who hate you, bless those who curse you, and pray for those who spitefully use you." Luke 6:27-28

DUHOK - 1996

During the hot summer nights, I enjoy sleeping downstairs on the living room couch while my family sleeps on the roof, which is much cooler. I revel in staying up late doing my two favorite things, reading and listening to music.

This August evening is just like any other night. Well, at least I think it will be. Minutes after stretching out on the couch, attempting to sleep, I lay flat on my back. With my eyes closed, I feel a presence sweep beneath my body, lifting me off the couch. I open my eyes only to notice that I am floating. I feel the presence carrying me, yet I can't see it. In a blink, I am transported to our last residence at Shamasha's house. I quickly realize I'm in the old family room where everyone used to spend most of their time. The presence gently places me on the ground. I find Mom and two other ladies reading the book of Second Timothy in the New Testament and discussing the second coming of Jesus. I immediately join in on their discussion, not giving a second thought to what's happening.

As we begin praying, I hear a scream outside the room. I jump up, startled by the cry, and slowly stride towards the window, gently lifting the corner of the curtain to investigate the scream. A horrific view greets me: a locust as large as the house lowers its ugly head and looks straight at me. I stare at its dark, beady eyes and feel their evil intention. It is ready to attack and excited about what's to come. There is so much repugnance ready to be poured over anyone that crosses his path. The stance of the locust reflects a horse ready to charge. It's ready for battle. Its large teeth look sharp, resembling those of a lion's. I divert my gaze up only to notice a crown resting on top of its long, dark hair. A breastplate armors the chest as if it needs to protect the locust. From what I can see, we are the ones who need protection. However, a breastplate for us may not be enough.

The locust extends one of its legs, attempting to break the window of our room as it ferociously taps the glass. An evil grin displays his desire to seize us. Although the locust's leg is much stronger than our little glass window, it cannot break through. In that same instant, as it angrily extends its leg one more time, we are taken out of the room by the same presence that delivered me there.

It is daylight this time, and I am floating above the house I currently live in. Looking around, I notice seven of us flying, all holding hands; Dad is the first, holding hands with Mom, then my sisters. Next to them are two of the Horizons team members, and I am on the end. We each have tiny, white wings on our backs, gently flapping, keeping us steady and afloat. Glancing down, I am greeted with a revolting sight of giant, powerful, hideous locusts. They are everywhere, covering the face of the earth as they overwhelm the land. It is a terrifying sight. These oversized insects have taken over the world, some even taller than the buildings and houses surrounding them. As I survey our situation, it dawns on me there are only seven people rescued. "Is this it? Is this all the Christians in the world?" I cry out. Instantly, I feel a firm grip on my hand. I look to my left and find a beautiful sight. The sky is covered with Christians flying like us, all holding hands.

With much effort, the locusts attempt to reach us but continue to fail. No matter how hard they try to attack, they are unsuccessful. Despite the fact that they are much more extensive than us, and we are well within their reach, we are safe, and it is as if there is a shield protecting us.

A great sorrow comes over me as I look down below and see people tortured and suffering with no hope of relief. The locusts seem to have the power to inflict pain upon people but not kill them. It is a horrendous sight, with many cries of unbearable suffering. I stare in shock as my gaze turns to someone I recognize. These vicious locusts are torturing a church member. He is a Christian man, dating one of the ladies working for our Horizons team. As I tightly hold onto her hand while we float, I watch her boyfriend suffer in disbelief.

Thankfully, a few minutes later, the Spirit carries me back to the living room of my house and places me on the couch, where everything seems normal again. I slide my hands against the soft couch to ground myself, bringing my senses back to reality. Swinging my feet off the couch, I feel the cool tiled floor beneath them. The room is as dark as it was when I laid down.

I hear nothing but silence.

No cries, no screams, just utter silence.

I take a deep breath as the images of the experience skip through my mind, trying to make sense of it all. *I've never seen locusts so big. What were those? How can they grow so large?* I have always found locusts creepy, but now, even more so.

It must be 6 a.m., as I hear my parents. I rush to the kitchen and find Dad at the dining table while Mom prepares breakfast.

"Good morning, Khayee. Why are you awake so early?" Mom asks.

"I had a vision last night."

"Okay. Why don't you sit down and tell us about it?"

It doesn't take much effort to get this weight off my chest. My vision has a meaning; they all do. This one seems more mysterious. I share every detail with my parents. Nothing is too big or too small. My parents have grown accustomed to my dreams and visions by now. Though they have found ways to nurture them and help me work through them, I don't know how they can help me process this one. It seems impossible to overcome such giant locusts. How can I combat the big ones when I quiver at the sight of the little ones bouncing around the fields in my neighborhood?

"That sounds so familiar. I've read that somewhere in the Bible," Dad reflects.

Breakfast is forgotten in our desire to find where Dad has read this.

Immediately, we reach for our Bibles. The sound of pages turning rings through the kitchen with urgency. No one is hungry anymore. Everyone is on a mission.

"I found it!" Dad exclaims with a grin. "It's in the book of Revelation, chapter nine."

In all my time reading the Bible, I have not read the book of Revelation. I have never found the courage to read it. Those around me have always described it as the scariest book in the Bible. I trusted their word and stayed away from it. I chose to focus on the books that I could make sense of and understand instead of the "challenging" ones. Never did I imagine the Bible describing locusts in the way that I have come to know them.

Dad begins to read the passage, starting with verse one.

"Then the fifth angel sounded: And I saw a star fallen from heaven to the earth. To him was given the key to the bottomless pit. And he opened the bottomless pit, and smoke arose out of the pit like

300

the smoke of a great furnace. So the sun and the air were darkened because of the smoke of the pit. Then out of the smoke locusts came upon the earth. And to them was given power, as the scorpions of the earth have power. They were commanded not to harm the grass of the earth, or any green thing, or any tree, but only those men who do not have the seal of God on their foreheads. And they were not given authority to kill them, but to torment them for five months. Their torment was like the torment of a scorpion when it strikes a man. In those days men will seek death and will not find it; they will desire to die, and death will flee from them."

"The shape of the locusts was like horses prepared for battle. On their heads were crowns of something like gold, and their faces were like the faces of men. They had hair like women's hair, and their teeth were like lions' teeth. And they had breastplates like breastplates of iron, and the sound of their wings was like the sound of chariots with many horses running into battle. They had tails like scorpions, and there were stings in their tails. Their power was to hurt men for five months. And they had as king over them the angel of the bottomless pit, whose name in Hebrew is Abaddon, but in Greek, he has the name Apollyon." Revelation 9:1-11

My body trembles as I listen to every word from my Father's lips. I am in shock. Each description is followed by me yelling, "Yes, that's it! That's exactly what I saw!"

I step back, mind numb, my heart thumping against my chest. Panic overtakes me like a cold wind cutting to my bone. *What am I expected to do with this? Will this vision come to life just like the others? If so, what next? God has revealed something to me before I knew of its existence in the Bible.* My mind is racing. After Dad's reading and the vivid description, the images circle back again.

Shaken and dismayed, I pull myself together to brush my teeth and prepare for the day. Although I have no appetite, with much persuasion from Mom, I force myself to eat a few bites of the scrambled eggs she's prepared.

It is almost 8 a.m., and the Horizons team will soon arrive. Shortly after they walk in, my parents encourage me to reveal my vision to them. I ask Dad to read the passage aloud before I break down the details and share the experience. They listen intently, in awe of the similarities between my vision and the Bible passage. This is my first time sharing my spiritual encounter with others besides my parents. I am nervous, unsure of their reaction. I find encouragement in their response as they praise God for speaking through me. All the while, I omit the part about the boyfriend of one of the employees being tortured by the locusts. I am still determining her response. It is challenging enough to share this with everyone, let alone adding that part to the mix.

Night falls rather quickly. It has been a long day, an emotional day. I feel restless, watching the minutes slowly pass. I can't seem to shake the images out of my head. The cries. The agonizing screams. They haunt not only my thoughts but also my emotions. Every night, I lay on the same couch, hoping for rest, begging for sleep, but sleep is nowhere to be found. Each toss and turn is met with more restlessness. I pass the time by cleaning the house, cooking, and washing laundry using candlelight. Day and night have merged. I can't tell the difference between the two as my alertness is the same, and so are my activities. I keep myself occupied as pausing leads to reliving the vision over and over again.

Sleep seems overrated at this point. A foreign concept.

It has been a week since my vision. Each morning, my parents come downstairs to find the entire house clean, breakfast ready, and meals prepped. The first few mornings seem normal, but midway through the week, my parents' concerns for my rest and health are growing.

"I can't take this anymore, and neither can you. I can't keep watching you be so distressed and tired. You are sleeping upstairs with the rest of us tonight," Mom tells me. Actually, it was more of a command.

"I'm trying, Mom, but I'm not having any luck. I can't fall asleep no matter how hard I try."

"Khayee, you can't keep going like this. You need some sleep. You will stay with us tonight, and I will play with your hair until you fall asleep." Mom knows that I can never turn down a good scalp massage. In the past, playing with my hair has been the only trick that has proven to calm me down and cause me to sleep.

Evening time, Mom leads me to the roof, where she prepares another bed for me and hangs a mosquito net around it, tucking in all the edges.

"Stay here. I need to bring your sisters. I will be right back."

I sit on my mattress, facing the neighbor's wall. Mere seconds pass since Mom stepped through the house's threshold when Christ suddenly emerges from the wall. He gracefully makes His way toward me and sits next to me. His feet are facing the opposite direction than mine, and we are face-to-face. He is less than an arm's length away.

"How many people have you shared your vision with?" He asks.

"Six. My parents and the Horizons employees."

"I need you to share this and let everyone know I'm coming. I'm on the cloud. Christians need to get ready."

I gaze into His beautiful and captivating brown eyes, unable to break the stare, in admiration of His presence. I nod in agreement. I want to speak, but my lips remain still.

He stands up and walks away, disappearing into the same wall. His words ring in my ears.

"I am coming."

I need to tell others!

I look up to see Mom beside my bed, with Rodina and Sona beside her.

"Mom, did you see Him?"

She looks around, confused. "See who?"

"He was right here talking to me! Jesus was right here!"

"Okay, tell me everything He said." she beckons. These words repeat every time I tell Mom I have seen a vision or conversed with Jesus.

I explain our brief conversation to her. She replies, "You're in luck. There's a conference happening this week. Victor Hashweh is back, and he's preaching. I will reach out to the pastor and ask if you can share your vision with the group before the sermon."

I quickly agree before I lay on my bed, staring at the dark sky decorated with sparkling lights.

I see peace.

I feel peace.

My body relaxes. My eyelids are heavy as I feel them close. Mom never had the chance to play with my hair. The peace I feel covers me like a weighted blanket.

Next thing I know, I hear birds chirping as heat strikes my skin. The sun is up. I open my eyes to find myself fully rested. I slept in. Excited, I rush downstairs, ready for the day.

Mom is gone already; she traveled to the city to find the pastor and ask him if I could share my vision with the group.

An hour passes before she comes home and tells me, "You are speaking tonight."

At age fourteen, this is my first public speaking event. I have yet to stand before a crowd of this size and share. I am excited, but at the same time, I am overwhelmed by anxiety. *What if they laugh at me? How crazy do I sound when I share my dreams and visions with others? What will they think?* My negative thoughts are quickly wiped away when I think of Christ and His request to alert the Christians of His coming.

My family, the Horizons team, and I walk to the city to attend the service. There are at least fifty people present, if not more. The excitement of seeing Victor Hashweh, the man who led Mom and me to Christ a few years ago, quickly overruns the nerves of the large crowd. He is back from Jordan, preaching at the conference. We step into the front yard, and my eyes find Victor and his wife. I quickly rush to the two and embrace them. They are excited to see me and eager to hear what God has revealed in my vision. I find courage in their presence.

Shortly after the opening prayer and worship, the pastor steps to the podium and introduces me. My nerves vibrate again; my palms are sweaty, my knees lock, and my heart thumps rapidly. I stand at the podium and begin sharing my vision, again omitting that I recognized one of the people being tortured. Standing in front of an audience is an emotional yet stressful experience. This is the first vision I have shared with acquaintances and strangers, but it's even more alarming to share with a congregation where visions are uncommon. Sharing them with trusted family is one thing, but standing alone in front of a large crowd with such a weighty message is much more challenging. After I speak, Victor steps towards me and opens up with an altar call, leading many to Christ as they accept Him as their Lord and Savior. What a beautiful evening and experience to see so many commit their lives and follow Jesus. To see the Holy Spirit shift the hearts of many through a vision fills me with joy. It also encourages me to realize there is more to my gift. This beautiful gift can connect people to Jesus. What more can I ask for?

As for the man I had seen in my vision in the clutches of the locusts, he is here today, but he doesn't seem moved by what I have conveyed. He approaches me as I step away from the podium and says, "What you shared today is impossible. You must have imagined it or had a horrible nightmare."

Looking into his brown eyes, I can see his doubt and struggle. Yet, I still don't have the courage to tell him the truth. I nod my head and find my parents. I am overwhelmed by sadness for him. Watching him suffer is not the pain I would ever wish upon anyone. Throughout my walk home, I continue wrestling with the emotions of whether I should share the truth or not. In the end, I know I must do it. It is the right thing to do and could encourage his doubting heart. We reach our home, I find his girlfriend and ask to speak to her alone. I break down and share what's on my heart and the truth of my vision. She seems to receive it well and is determined to gently tell him about it, not sparing any details.

A few days have passed since I last saw him, but he seems different at our Bible study today. He seems lighter. I approach the girlfriend, inquiring about the change. "Is everything alright?"

"Yes, everything is great. He took the news well and strives to be closer to the Lord and walk in the Spirit."

I am overwhelmed with joy listening to her share the changes in him and his desire to improve his spiritual walk. The weight of sadness I felt for him several nights ago has been lifted. Now, I feel hope and excitement for him and what's to come.

My visions, dreams, intuitions, and ability to see into the spiritual realm have become integral to who I am. Frequently, I wonder *why me. Why did the Lord of Hosts choose a young Assyrian girl?* Then I think of the spiritual intimacy I have experienced, and it reminds me of how grateful I am that God chose to communicate with me in these ways and reveal things before their time. It's an exceptional spiritual gift, and I am incredibly thankful.

* * *

"And it shall come to pass in the last days, says God, that I will pour out of My Spirit on all flesh; your sons and your daughters shall prophesy." Acts 2:17

DUHOK - 1996

The conflicts between the two Kurdish parties continue to escalate. Bombings between the territories increase with each passing night. The Democratic Party, whose territory we live in, is determined to eliminate the Republican Party. However, it is not a task they can accomplish on their own. There is someone who can help accelerate the process and quickly complete the job. Someone who has been yearning to fully access the North again. Someone with military power to provide the necessary aid the Democrats require. The cruelest human being, Saddam Hussein.

Seeking his assistance is something everyone prays against, and yet, the Democrats are desperate and foolish enough to do so.

Early August of 1996, the Democratic Party requests Hussein's reinforcement, extending an invitation for his presence and military power. Hussein, being the "gentleman" he is, always willing to help when needed, jumps on the opportunity and agrees to march to the North to assist. The aid comes with a cost, of course. One condition: once he helps the Democrats accomplish their mission, he wants full access and reigns over anyone working for the American organizations.

They can't possibly agree to such a senseless act, can they? They have to remember his vicious acts and atrocities. Yet, in their desperation to win the mindless war, they agree. They willingly sign the death certificate of hundreds of men, women, and children.

The news quickly circulates. Fear and anxiety, both familiar feelings that are all too common, crowd my mind. My skin crawls, my bones rattle, ready to scream at the horror headed our way. Mere hours have passed since my world turned dark with the dreaded news, and Hussein's military has already begun to arrive, infiltrating the Democratic region. As the troops increase in number, so does the fear among the citizens.

Torture and execution are coming.

It doesn't take long before my home is targeted. Each morning for the next few days, Dad finds threatening letters slipped under the gates. Each letter has the same message day after day. STOP WHAT YOU ARE DOING. YOU HAVE THREE DAUGHTERS, AND YOU KNOW WHAT WE WILL DO TO THEM.

The awful reality of our situation is striking rather quickly. We are forced back into living on high alert, limiting our outings and interactions with strangers and being selective of who visits our home outside the usual Bible studies. We are constantly looking over our shoulders and sleeping with one eye open, realizing death might be closer than we think.

Armin, our friendly Ethiopian neighbor from France, can easily see our distress. He operates a small aid organization in Iraq and has built a relationship with my family as he lives alone and spends many nights at our home, joining us for dinner and tea. Armin loves reading, and when he noticed my passion for it, he granted me access to all his books. He has quite a collection, considering he is in Iraq for a short-term assignment. For my first read, he suggested I start with *The Three Musketeers*. As I read the book, I was quickly swept into the historical romance. The stories, the battles, and the adventures of four heroes who take risks for honorable purposes.

"You love this book, don't you?" he asked.

"Yes, very much so. I have read it twice and would like to read it again. Would it be alright if I kept it a little longer?"

"It's yours," he whispered, followed by a wink.

"Well, I—thank you!" Squeezing the book between my hands, I quickly ran to my room to reread it.

Being the kind man that Armin is, he is troubled by our situation. With the increasing threats my family is receiving, his concern for our safety grows. Since his home is guarded around the clock, as most organizations are, he has asked his guards to oversee our house as well. His generous offer can't be turned down in such a dire time as this. Knowing we have protection provides slight relief. Unfortunately, Armin's visits and his guards' protection are short-lived. Two weeks after Hussein's military arrives in the North, his organization is retracted from Iraq. A week later, his house is vacant, our protection disappears, and my source of escaping into the world of imagination is gone. Though our God is bigger than any problem or storm we face, our fears begin to take over. The reality of the situation is looming. We fight off all kinds of negative thoughts and emotions, knowing well who holds our lives.

* * *

"For we walk by faith, not by sight." 2 Corinthians 5:7

DUHOK - 1996

The danger continues to escalate as threats persist, finding their way to our home.

Today's threat announces itself with a firm knock against the metal gates.

Dad rushes to the gates, curious who could be at the door since he doesn't recognize the man's shoes through the gap.

When he swings the large door open, he is met with a well-dressed gentleman in trousers, a button-down shirt, and dress shoes. His appearance screams Saddam.

"How can I help you?" Dad asks, recognizing the threat facing him.

"I'm looking for James. Is he home?" he replies with a cunning grin.

"James is not home right now. Can I take a message?" Dad is on high alert and knows that announcing he is James could result in tragedy.

"Yes, please let him know Jalal stopped by. I am a friend of his. We were teachers together at Miqdam High School in Baghdad. I'm visiting Duhok and wanted to say hello."

"Will do," Dad replies, struggling to remain calm.

He quickly closes the door and steps back into the house.

"That man works for Saddam. They have escalated from threats to physically coming by."

"What—how do you know?" Mom asks.

"Did you see the way he was dressed? Who walks around Duhok dressed in such attire?" He exhales as he catches his breath. "Besides, you didn't hear his dialect. It screamed Baghdad. Saddam."

"What did he say?"

"He said he worked with me at Miqdam, but I don't know him. I've never seen him before. How did he know so much about me, yet I don't recognize him from anywhere?" Dad pauses before continuing. "And how can he claim he worked with me and not recognize my face when I opened the door? That makes no sense."

"What if God blinded his sight so he couldn't identify you?" she answers in an attempt to comfort him. "What if that's another form of God's protection?"

This interaction with Jalal has startled my father and our family. A cloud of anxiety and restlessness has descended into our home. Everyone seems uneasy, walking on edge. I can see the fear behind my parents' brave faces. There is a shadow of uncertainty in their smiles and tired eyes.

Now what? We wonder.

The day is dim, and with each passing hour, more questions arise. With each knock, our hearts skip a beat, wondering if Jalal is at the door, yearning to end us.

Through these uncertain times, we are reminded of our mighty God, who has rescued us many times before. We are reminded that our God is a God of love and power, not fear and chaos. He has been our pillar, never yielding and always faithful. In those instances, we find peace and clarity. With each step of faith we take, peace grows, and fear fades.

"Pray." This is what we hear the Holy Spirit lead us to do. It is the only thing we desire to do. We spend most of the day and evening in prayer.

"Father, hear your children who have no life except through you."

The following day, another strong knock and another visit from Jalal. Only this time, he is greeted by one of Horizons' employees, Nabiel. The answer again is, "James is not home right now. Can I take a message?" The same message is relayed. Day after day, this continues.

Although my family and the team feel the peace of God spread through our house, it doesn't mean our fear has completely vanished. Satan continues to use fear to break through, attempting to disrupt our faith and trust.

Jalal's relentlessness is beginning to create panic in my family.

"We can no longer live in this house. It's not safe for us or our girls," Dad exclaims.

"I'll ask my cousin Ashur if we can temporarily live with him."

Ashur's house is nearly 5 kilometers (3 miles) from ours. Without a vehicle, we must travel on foot, walking through the city in alleys and along small streets for our safety. We avoid significant roads and drawing attention to ourselves, and in turn, we bypass Saddam's men. We take a trip to Ashur's house, seeking favor.

"Saddam's agents found us; they found our home. We don't believe we are safe living there any longer. Is it possible to move in with your family for a few days until we determine the best course of action?" Dad humbly asks, knowing this is not an easy task, adding five more members to a family of seven. Although we did it before, this seems different. Our request could jeopardize the safety of Ashur's family if Jalal finds us again.

"Of course, you can move in," Ashur quickly replies. "My house is your house." His answer aligns with any Assyrian home offering aid to an Assyrian family in need. Ashur's house and family once again welcome us with such warmth. We are beyond grateful for their hospitality and generosity. Their family has again become a blessing in times of need.

We travel back home to pack. We are each allowed one small backpack, leaving us with enough clothes for three days. Everything else is left behind. Ninos and Nabiel will remain at the house to guard it. With the need in the community, it is decided that we will continue our Bible studies in the evenings but reduce them to twice a week, leaving shortly after they are done.

As a precaution, my sisters and I cannot travel without an adult escorting us, not even for a walk to a friend's house. We journey as a group no matter where we go.

During one of our many 5 kilometer (3 miles) trips to our temporary home at Ashur's house, I can feel my frustration boiling over. The sun is high, and the heat begins to take its toll. I am exhausted and thirsty as my mom, sisters, and I travel through the small streets.

"I do not wish to do this anymore," I snap. "I can't. This is unfair." Despair is seeping deep within me. Fear hovers over me like a dark cloud, awaiting my surrender. At fourteen years of age, I am fighting for my safety and for my life.

"You're the oldest, and I would appreciate it if you could be a bit more understanding of the situation here."

"I'm trying, Mom, but I just wish we could stay in one place for a long time."

"You do realize if we stay at our house, they will come and take us, and you do realize if they get us, that means rape? Which means you will be raped. Will that work for you?" Mom replies in frustration. Her voice carries anger and fear.

I am stunned by Mom's words. They shock me and release a torrent of rage deep inside me. I cannot stop the tears from slipping down my cheeks. A terrible knot fills my throat as her words stab at my heart.

Not a word is spoken for the duration of the trip, and I have no desire to break the silence. Lost in my thoughts and my pain. *How can she utter those words to me?* Images of torture and rape flash before my eyes. *How will I respond? What will I feel in those moments if that happens?*

In a country filled with sorrow and fear, primarily due to the anguish everyone endures, stories of suffering circulate among the young and the old. No one is sheltered from what is happening and what could happen. With each story, vivid images are painted, intimate details are described, and horror is illustrated. I can't help but imagine my torment whenever I am faced with fear or reminded of the appalling possibilities. Sometimes, the scenarios become "when" instead of "if."

I have discovered through the years that life is nothing but a tale of hardships, torture is nothing but a matter of time, and death is nothing but a welcomed concept.

I understand Mom's frustration. She is operating in fight or flight. However, I did not expect such an abrupt and intense response. She is trying her best to maintain her composure amid the magnitude of our situation, yet I can't seem to escape the reality of her words.

Weeks have passed since we began our journey, traveling back and forth to Ashur's house every three days. Each of my family members bear their entire life in a small backpack, as my parents would like to travel light. With every visit home, we sort through our limited belongings, clothes, books, and toys. We then choose our favorites and heap as much as possible into the bag, and leave, again. This is the life I have grown accustomed to. Though I prayed and dreamed of a life of stability and few goodbyes, here I am, once again, making the very difficult decision of what to keep close and what to leave behind.

Amid all the packing and unpacking, amid the chaos and ongoing travels, I lose the ring Laurie gave me. As if my life is not devastating enough, I face one more loss. I have grown to love the ring, but I grieve the loss of the sentimental value more than the ring itself.

One would suppose it would get easier each time, but every time is just as difficult as the first. Building a life with little sentimental attachment to things is difficult. Whether they are good memories or bad ones, they keep us human, keep us connected to others, and give us an emotional sense of our place in the world.

Although I have our memories, I have no physical anchors tied to them.

* * *

"For God has not given us a spirit of fear, but of power and of love and of a sound mind." 2 Timothy 1:7

DUHOK - 1996

Hussein's forces rapidly increase in the North. The instantaneous invasion is followed by a declaration that is broadcast through various news outlets: "I am permitting the execution of anyone who works alongside Americans and any other foreign organizations without any ramifications. No punishment will be enforced for doing so." This terrifying incitement comes as no surprise. Many have been dreadfully anticipating such an announcement.

We are, however, surprised when an unexpected one from President Bill Clinton follows Hussein's decree. "Anyone who works for Americans or any other foreign organization, have no fear; you will be rescued."

Unlike President George Bush, whom we have learned about through the Gulf War, we know very little of President Clinton. Our lives are openly in danger. We are told we should trust him, but how can we? The concept of the President of the United States caring about us seems almost impossible. We have lived our entire lives in fear. No one has heard our cries, extended a helping hand, or even looked in our direction to treat us as human beings. We have never felt welcomed or wanted by any other country. And now, the President of America wants to save us? It is extremely difficult to believe or trust.

Could there be an ulterior motive for President Clinton's statement? Could he care enough to rescue us? With Hussein's knowledge of our whereabouts, the daily visits from Jalal, and the new alliance between the Democratic Kurds and Hussein, our lives are in grave danger.

On our knees, we are praying, seeking wisdom and discernment. We have two options: stay in Iraq, wait on President Clinton, and chance our fate or—escape again. Neither choice seems to be very promising.

"Maybe we need to contact Georges to confirm the news about President Clinton?" Dad questions while we share dinner with Ashur's family. The adults are conversing as if the children aren't present. But we are. I can hear every word. I am absorbing every word. *Which option will they choose? With my fate at stake, I don't want to miss a single part of the conversation.* "Or maybe we should contact your sister?" he continues.

Mom's younger sister left Iraq in the early eighties and resides in California.

To conduct international phone calls, satellite phones are needed. These are all located at the top of the mountains surrounding the city. My parents must take the bus to the summit and hope the telephone is in service and can make a solid connection to America. Often, these phones have a muffled connection or no connection at all. Their reliability is scarce. Thus, calls are kept short, omitting formalities and jumping straight to the point of the phone call. Hearing a family member's voice on the line is proof enough to know they are still alive.

The following day, my sisters and I are left with Ashur's family as my parents travel to the nearest mountain to make the call. Upon reaching the mountain neighboring our home where PKK resides, the connection could not be established. After several failed attempts, they reluctantly acknowledge that they need to travel to another mountain and try again.

Feeling discouraged, waiting for the bus, they stumble upon an acquaintance, Soulayman. He is a gentleman they met twice in the city during their excursions. My parents quickly learn that he also needs to complete an international phone call and is looking to travel to another mountain, except he happens to be with a friend who drives a taxi. "Would you and Madlen like to travel with us to the next location? We have space in the cab for you both."

"That's very generous of you...Thank you."

During the long trip, the four share stories of fear and uncertainty regarding Saddam's presence in the city. With each story, Soulayman is intently listening, gaining information. After several hours of travel, they arrive at the second mountain. Praying for better luck this time, Mom dials the number. On the first attempt, Mom reaches her sister. She quickly explains the situation and asks her to contact Georges to confirm the news regarding President Clinton's plan. Mom quickly throws question after question at her sister, grasping for any sort of affirmation or assurance. She asks if Horizons International is part of the plan. She asks if we're on the list to be rescued. She asks if there really is a plan in place to save us.

My aunt knows nothing of this news. She has no information to share. Hearing her confusion on the phone only increases their concerns about the validity of this plan.

The phone call does not provide the peace my parents hoped for. It does the opposite, creating more angst. "If the declaration is valid, why doesn't she know about it? Wouldn't the news be announced in America?" Mom wonders.

Soulayman and his friend offer to drive my parents back to the city. Feeling defeated and anxious, they sit in the back of the cab in silence, lost in their thoughts.

"I can help your family," Soulayman declares. "I have a connection and can get you into Syria if interested."

With so much uncertainty in the air, Mom and Dad have no other choice. It is an offer they can't refuse. They have three young daughters they need to protect.

"Great! Please write down your family's information, and I will have your travel documents ready in one week."

In desperation, Dad provides the information asked of him, including our full names, birth dates, and photos. Travel between Iraq and Syria requires legal travel documents only, no passports. This makes my parents hopeful that it should be fairly easy and swift.

A week later, Soulayman meets with my parents as promised. In his hand, he has the envelope with the travel documents. Everything looks to be in order, and our travel arrangements commence. We are moving to another country, Syria. It's time for the most dreaded task, a task I know all too well. We sift through our belongings one final time. Again, I can only travel with a small bag.

My parents arrange a meeting with the church members as we break the news to them and say our goodbyes. Everyone is struck by grief as we share our final dinner and fellowship with the group we have grown to call family. As for the church, it is entrusted to a couple that has been attending every Bible study and has been blessed with a heart of service and leadership.

Despite my exhaustion from the tears and the emotions I experienced this evening, I can't sleep. No matter how much I try to reassure and calm myself, I can't stop my mind from spinning. So many questions, thoughts, and unknowns. Although I have had a lot of experience in saying goodbye, it continues to be just as challenging as it was the first time when I was in third grade, leaving Baghdad behind.

The morning sun rises rather quickly. I have no appetite, but Mom, once again, forces me to eat to sustain my tired body for our travels. Today will be one of the most challenging as we have to say goodbye to Ninos. Ninos and I have grown close. He is my older brother. Our challenges over the past few years have knitted a strong bond between us. I wrap my arms around his neck as he embraces me, and we weep together. "It's okay," he mumbles in between his tears. "You need to be safe. I will be alright, I promise." I appreciate his assurance, but it doesn't ease my distress over his safety and well-being.

Soulayman arrives in a taxi to transport us to Zakho after the gut-wrenching goodbyes. The car ride is met with silence. I look back one final time, leaving behind everyone and everything familiar to us for the last three years. I should be rejoicing at the opportunity to escape, but instead, I ache with a grief so deep that it swells up and feels like it may overtake me.

The taxi stops several meters from the Khabur River near the Iraq-Syria border, where Soulayman's associate is waiting for us. Beside him is a small motorized boat that is covered in rusted metal. The last time I encountered rusted metal, I was left with a gruesome cut on my ring finger. Not today. I know I must be careful and ensure my sisters don't touch any part of it. Though the boat seems unstable and unsafe as we step into it, we have come too far and have no other choice. Dad loads our bags in the middle, and we are off.

The ride lasts twenty minutes before we hear and feel the boat scraping across the gravel on the river's edge. We each carefully climb out of the craft, our feet landing on dry and hot Syrian soil. To our surprise, Soulayman's associate departs rather quickly once our bags are removed from the boat. We are nothing but a shadow on the bank.

We stand on the river's edge, feeling hopeless and clueless. We stand next to a small, rundown building out in the open field. We're surrounded by tumbleweeds and dirt. I stare out into the distance and see nothing else but heat waves rising from the ground. Mere seconds pass before we are slowly approached by the heavily armed Syrian military assigned to guard the border. With the river behind us and the armed military in front of us, we are trapped. The pointed artillery facing us brings back terrifying memories of the Turkish military and their weapons. Fear washes over us as we stare down the barrels of the machine guns.

The unit commander approaches my Father and, with a stern voice, says, "I need to see your travel paperwork." Hands trembling, Dad reaches into his bag and retrieves an envelope containing everything Soulayman had given him. With a displeased face, the officer points to his guards to arrest us. They quickly lead us into the office nearby, hold us in custody, and begin asking questions. Alone and afraid, we are placed in a small, hot interrogation room that is poorly ventilated. Sweat streams down our skin as we sit in confusion, facing endless questions concerning our intentions and purpose in Syria.

"These documents are illegal," the general informs us. "You're illegally trespassing into our country."

"That's impossible. It can't—," Dad's voice quivers. "I swear we mean no harm. We were promised legal travel documents to escape Saddam."

"Your travel agent had no intention of helping you. He had an ulterior motive. He needed your personal information so he and his family could take your place on the roster for President Clinton's escape plan." He continues to explain that Soulayman had made a deal with the Syrian soldiers. While he got to steal our identities, the soldiers would allow our family to be dropped off on the border, and in turn, they received electronics while also being able to capture us. "You have been traded as a commodity."

I fight the tears of frustration as I comprehend how our lives have been exchanged for documents, VCRs, televisions, and gadgets.

In this deafening moment, our world quickly turns black. The revelation sends prickles down my neck.

President Clinton's plan was legitimate.

We missed our chance.

We all wonder, *now what?*

* * *

"So we may boldly say: The Lord is my helper; I will not fear. What can man do to me?" Hebrews 13:6

SYRIA - 1996

We are interrogated for four hours, the soldiers investigating every aspect of our lives to ensure we are not spies and mean no harm. Due to our illegal status and crossing the border without the appropriate documents, we are relinquished to a high-ranking officer in the Syrian government named Hassan. We are shocked to hear we will not be escorted to prison. Illegal immigrants are typically sent to prison, families are separated by gender, and they are usually tortured in the same manner as in Iraq. Yet, today, we receive a reprieve. God is watching over us as we are ushered into his small, white sedan and taken to his house. We are unsure if he volunteered to take us or if a higher-ranking individual assigned us to him. Regardless, we are grateful!

As he opens the gate to his courtyard, we are greeted by two women surrounded by many children. Both women are dressed in hijab and floor-length black gowns. Hassan introduces them as his two wives and tells us he has twenty-five children.

In the Muslim religion, a man can take up to four wives if he pleases. The wives tend to live together and raise their families together. This seems to be the case with Hassan and his family. His two wives live harmoniously, raising each other's children, who range from six months to twenty-five years old. They have a schedule and an agreement that pleases everyone, from house duties to wifely duties.

Hassan escorts us through a concrete open courtyard to a small room that stands to the left. "You will stay here for now," he says. With each of us carrying our single bag, we quietly step through the door and into our new dwelling. It is a little rectangular room that has a concrete floor measuring about 1.5 by 3 meters (5 by 10 feet), with two small windows facing the street. On the floor lay three foam pads covered in colorful sheets. We place our bags down and slowly sit on one of the foam mattresses, facing the door where Hassan stands. His face screams militant, rigid, and cold, yet his voice and demeanor say thoughtful, caring, and kind. Only time will reveal his true character.

"Ali. Ahmad," he calls his two eldest sons and then faces us again. "Here are your instructions as you reside in my home. You are to never walk outside this room alone for any reason. If you need to use the restroom, you need to call one of my children." He points to his sons. "They will escort you to the bathroom and back to the room. You are allowed one shower per week. Your meals will be cooked and served by my wives. If you need anything else, you need to ask my sons."

Frozen and still in shock, we nod in compliance with his rules.

"One more thing," he continues authoritatively. "I am unsure of how to proceed right now with your situation. Until I make a decision, these are your accommodations." And with that, he walks away.

We lean against the wall, facing a small, one-shelf entertainment center with a little vintage television. A picture of the Syrian president, Hafez Al-Assad, is all that hangs on the wall.

Hopelessness and depression invade the room as we face each other in complete silence. Each of us is lost in our thoughts, uncertain of what the future holds.

There is no distinction between the Syrian government and the Iraqi government. Both are Muslim. Both are ruled by dictators. Both oppress their citizens for the so-called "greater good." Both inflect fear, abuse, imprisonment, torture, and execution upon their citizens. What separates the two in this instance is—living in Syria means the fear of torture and death is no longer imminent. For the time being, we don't have a dictator here who has placed a death warrant on our heads. Though we are safe for now, we know our fate has yet to be decided, and things could change at any moment.

I am speechless, tired, afraid, and attempting to absorb our new reality when I hear—QUACK.

QUACK.

I lean to my side to peer at the entrance. "There's a duck at the door."

"A duck?" Mom asks.

"Yes. Wait, there are two chickens too."

The three birds waddle into the room, turn around, and step out. Minutes later, a goat saunters in. In awe and confusion, we watch the livestock stroll through our room in search of food. Shortly after, one of the children runs in. "Sorry about the animals. Normally, this spare room is used to house eleven of them. We will try and keep them out."

"Great, just great," Mom states in disgust. "We are living in the animal room and will dine from the same floor their animals dine from."

Much like a prison, our new room is small, confined, and has little entertainment. Resembling Iraq, television programming is limited, with most of the programs controlled by the president. Time moves very slowly in our little confinement. Each day seems longer than the one before. I find myself spending most of my time gazing out the window, either studying the dry land across the street or peering into the distance through the heat waves rising from the desert. I daydream of a life outside these four gray walls, missing my friends and church family. My family and I often find ourselves reminiscing, focusing on the positive memories and all the laughter.

It has been eleven days, and we have taken only two showers. We are sharing the space with seemingly endless children and animals. However, we are not allowed to interact or play with the children. We can hear their laughter and their cries as they enjoy their childhood.

The family continues to feed us, which we are very grateful for. Today is the first day the ladies allow Mom to join them during meal prepping, allowing my sisters and me to step outside the room and feel the sunlight on our skin.

At dinner, Hassan walks through the bedroom door and sits beside Dad on one of the mattresses. His oldest son follows him with a large tray covered with food. "We need to discuss your situation," Hassan states, looking at Dad as he reaches for the rice bowl. We surround the tray and intently listen in.

"What do you propose?" Dad asks.

"I can no longer keep you here. It's not legal. Your family needs better options." Hassan replies.

He does have an alternate option—prison. He can easily relieve himself and his family of this duty and surrender us to the local authorities. However, he chooses to continue to assist us instead.

"I agree. I don't know how to proceed from here. There is a church in the city nearby. Would it be possible to move there?" Dad asks. He had heard about this church through acquaintances in Iraq.

"I will take you to the secret service agency tomorrow morning. We need to tell them the truth and seek their counsel. Maybe they will grant you asylum. They will be the ones who approve your move to the church as well."

At his words, I feel my stomach drop. Seeking counsel from the government is frightening. We are at the mercy of another regime. How can we, as unlawful immigrants, expect a good outcome when this government lacks grace and mercy for its citizens? Not to mention, this will expose my family to a higher authority that has not yet been aware of our presence. This step could leave us vulnerable to deportation, where we would be handed directly back to the Iraqi government. Though the general has shown us compassion, we can only hope for the same from the Syrian government.

* * *

"For I consider that the sufferings of this present time are not worthy to be compared with the glory which shall be revealed in us." Romans 8:18

SYRIA - 1996

Unable to sleep following dinner with Hassan, I lay on my mattress on the floor, staring out the window at the waning moon in the late night hours. The level of anticipation is high. Dad's trip to the agency can lead to life, opportunities, and a second chance, or deportation and death at the hands of Saddam. Syria is in alliance with Saddam. If deportation were to happen, it would occur through the southern borders of Hussein's territory, not the North through the United Nations. There is much at stake, and we need a miracle.

We eat breakfast in complete silence. The extremes of emotions plague us today. Struggling one minute to repress our fear, then overcome the next minute by the desperation to survive. We find ourselves on our knees, huddled in a circle, praying and clinging to Jesus like never before.

Our prayer time is interrupted by a knock. "Time to go," Hassan announces.

"Okay, I'm coming." Dad plucks the envelope holding our identification and travel documents from the suitcase and exits the room. We continue to pray for Dad and the outcome, trusting that God is in control.

We watch the clock as the hours slowly go by. Six hours pass before we hear the front metal gates cling. "Baba," one of the children calls out.

"Hassan is home, which means they're back," Mom says.

Dad steps through the doorway. "We need to pack," he states, wasting no time. "We're moving to the small church we spoke about last night, The United Church of Christ. The government's decision is still pending."

"That's great. What happened at the agency?" Mom inquires.

"I relayed everything to them and asked if we could move into the church. The agent I worked with contacted the pastor, and they have agreed to take us in. They have a small empty apartment waiting for us. We can live there until the agency finalizes our outcome," he continues with a smile. "Hassan has agreed to take us today."

"Praise God! Our prayers have been answered!" Mom cries out.

We quickly pack our bags and rush to the courtyard. Hassan is outside waiting near his vehicle, trunk open, prepared to receive our luggage.

It takes an hour before we arrive at the church. Hassan escorts us inside, where we are greeted with smiling faces. The pastor, his family, and several congregation members welcome us with a brief tour and a warm meal.

"It was great meeting you and getting to know you and your family," Hassan exclaims, extending his right hand to shake Dad's. "I wish you the best of luck."

"Thank you for your kindness and hospitality. You and your family have tremendously blessed us." Dad utters.

Hassan nods as he departs, quickly stepping into his vehicle and disappearing from our sight.

The church is big enough to hold two hundred members. It has a large open courtyard with tiled flooring, a small game room, and a compact one-bedroom apartment, all of which are fenced in by brick walls and two large metal gates. One gate faces the church's main entrance, and the second is closer to the apartment. The church has agreed to provide us with housing, food, and the necessary toiletries to sustain us, and in return, we clean and maintain the church.

It takes little time and effort to acquaint ourselves with the congregation and adjust to our new life. Everyone is extremely hospitable and supportive. They are very sympathetic to our story and our situation. Better yet, most families have children the same age as my sisters and me, opening new playtime opportunities. Much like our church family in Duhok, we share meals and fellowship outside the church services. All the while, we are still waiting for the Syrian government to decide our fate.

* * *

"My brethren, count it all joy when you fall into various
trials, knowing that the testing of your faith produces
patience." James 1:2-3

SYRIA - 1996

A s we begin our new life in Syria, I can see the relief on my parents' faces. Though it may be momentary, pending the Syrian government's ruling, it is a welcome feeling in comparison. There is joy in the connections established, and Bible studies ensue.

I, however, am surrounded by DARKNESS.

Darkness has become my friend as I venture into yet another adventure. I often welcome change. But not this one. This change appears black. My happy personality is slowly shifting, and I am becoming more and more depressed. I've lost the will for everything, including life itself. Though once full of hope and optimism, my current outlook is bleak.

Everywhere I go and everything I do, I am followed by a black hole with my name on it; anxiously anticipating my fall. With each day, I inch closer to this hole mentally and emotionally. My being desires to exist no more. Though still so young, I have traveled a long and painful road, a road with no seeming end. Life doesn't want to hold back its powerful jabs. *How much more can I endure?*

My parents' stress has elevated as well in recent years. Their traumatic experiences have left them in anguish often. They are easily angered. Their temper outbursts unleash when in fear, primarily aimed at me. My sisters are too young to understand or endure. My every move, my every word, and my every breath are scrutinized. There is even less room for error now than there was in Baghdad. My dad and I argue frequently. The distance between us is growing as we are unable to find common ground in anything.

My mind is overwhelmed with anger. My heart is consumed with loneliness. My desire to press on is waning.

Although I have built a few friendships here in the past month, none are close enough to share my dark secret. I used to be able to communicate with Mom, but lately, she is occupied. She tends to be a good listener, but her struggles outweigh her understanding. I can see the fear resonating behind her hazel eyes. Sharing my pain with her will only add more to hers. "As the oldest, I need to lighten her load, not make it heavier," I tell myself.

I have always enjoyed building relationships with others, making friends, getting to know people, and socializing, but constantly saying goodbye is painful. It is emotionally and mentally exhausting. It creates scars that can't be erased. My sense of detachment is more substantial than my sense of belonging. Even though my God is more significant and mightier than everything I am experiencing, I have lost sight of Him and the big picture. My mental endurance has begun to crumble, slowly fading away. Gaining it back seems impossible.

It is a warm September afternoon, three weeks after moving into the church. I sit in the sunny open courtyard, overlooking the various crafts laid out, waiting to dry. The crafts are created by the women in the congregation; they paint Bible verses on white satin fabric, frame them, and sell them for profit. The ladies have been teaching me, expanding my artistic hobby. At this time, everyone is gone. Just me, staring at these beautiful creations. During my perusal, I notice one of the paintings still needs to be completed. I reach for the glittery gold glue to trace the trim of the word, only to hear Dad scream at me angrily, "What do you think you're doing?"

"I—I..."

"How dare you touch something that's not yours. These ladies have been hard at work completing these paintings!" he continues to yell, inching closer to me. I flinch as he infuriatingly slams his glasses onto the ground. Tears well up as I choke on my words. I'm fighting to open my mouth, but nothing comes out. My throat is parched, unable to make a sound. I slump back in my seat and continue to listen to his long lecture. I'm unable to speak or share how the woman who started the painting permitted me to finish the remaining word.

Every obstacle pushes me closer to the black hole that continues to grow. Its strong winds are howling, pulling me in like a tornado.

Minutes pass before Dad leaves the house. I am left alone in the apartment and the church. I step into the living room and sit on the blue cushioned chair, facing a blank white wall. The warm sun shines through the window. My dark thoughts and emotions begin to creep in, overpowering the tiny shred of hope I have remaining. The stronger these thoughts become, the weaker I get, and the more quickly I begin to surrender to them.

"What kind of life is this? How much longer can you endure?" I hear. The voice continues, *"Look around. Do you think you will survive this and have a normal life? No one cares about you."*

I listen to this voice, too powerless to stop it. The thoughts repeat themselves, slowly diminishing the little hope I have until they overtake me. I am fresh out of tears. There is nothing left in me. *I know what I have to do. I want it all to end.* Firmly pressing the palms of my hands against the chair's armrests, I push myself up and march toward the kitchen. Stretching my right arm, I pull the top drawer open. Inside, a large steak knife shines, neatly placed next to the rest of the blades, which all seem very small in comparison. The big one is calling my name. I reach for it, tightly gripping the handle with my left hand, and place the blade against my right wrist. As I begin to cut myself, I grow weak and disoriented, unaware of my surroundings and my place in space and time.

I lose consciousness.

I open my eyes and find myself sitting on the blue chair in the living room, stunned at my experience. I am afraid to look at my wrist, but I need to do it. I slowly lift my right arm, only to find it completely unharmed.

I build my courage to stand up as my knees knock together. My stomach is flip-flopping. I step towards the kitchen cabinet. Hesitant and shaking, I reach for the drawer that is somehow closed now. Pulling the handle, I find the knife exactly where I initially found it, completely clean, with no evidence of blood, as if nothing happened.

Staring at my wrist and the clean knife in the drawer, I am shocked, in part, at what has transpired, yet, a larger part of me is not surprised. God still has plans for me.

I feel God's compassion and loving presence wrap around me as I glance at my unharmed wrist. Tears well up as I declare, "God is in my corner, and it is not time for me to go yet. I accept my fate. I am spiritually saved; that matters more than anything else; death has no power over me."

I need to work through my darkness, trusting Christ in every step.

I have faith. When I have nothing else, I have faith.

* * *

"For I, the Lord your God, will hold your right hand, saying
to you, 'fear not, I will help you." Isaiah 41:13

SYRIA - 1996

No matter the anxiety that plagues me, I have to pass through the darkness ahead of me. I fix my eyes on the light beyond, the light that I have grown to love but momentarily lost sight of. Shifting my mindset is critical to survival. I am pressing into what I know—JESUS. I recognize my deeper need for Him, staying so close as to cling to His cloak, never letting go. He is all I have and the only one who understands the darkness I'm battling.

We have lived in the Syrian church for a month since our mid-September journey. There has been nothing but utter silence from the Syrian government, the pending decision still hovering over us like a dark cloud. Silence and inaction are a welcomed response, however, with a government as fear-inducing as this one.

That silence is disrupted when the phone rings.

"Hello, this is James."

I see Dad's body language quickly shift. Fear washes over him as he lifts his head towards the sky, eyes tightly closed, as if praying for mercy. His complexion pales. His body trembles as he steadies himself, holding onto the dining chair.

"Understood," he mutters and hangs up the phone.

Every fiber of my being wants to ask, "Who was that," but there is no need. I know who that was.

"Madlen!" he shouts. "Come here, hurry!"

"Why the yelling?" Mom asks.

"The man I spoke to a month ago at the Syrian agency just called..." He pauses, controlling his heavy breathing. "...They reached their decision. We will be deported back to Iraq tomorrow morning. He will be here at 8 a.m." He clenches his hands as he begins to pace.

I drop down onto the small brown couch in the kitchen, facing the dining table where my parents stand. My world turns blurry. I hear them speak, but it's muffled. I'm unable to focus, unable to decipher what's being said. The sheer terror of it all makes me unable to think. Breathing becomes difficult and requires a great deal of effort. A helpless sob erupts from all of us, reminding us of what awaits us tomorrow.

Dad quickly alerts the congregation of the verdict, and in less than an hour, panicked and shocked church members begin to fill the open courtyard. "How can they do this?" one asks.

"Don't they know what Saddam will do?" another cries.

"They don't care!" an angry voice yells.

Realizing this is our final day, we kneel beside our brothers and sisters in Christ and pray. Songs of praise and worship erupt, frequently interrupted by tearful prayers. Though I want to keep my focus on prayer and worship, I can't help but take periodic mental detours to the land that awaits—a land filled with hate and anger, a land consumed by evil, and a land that thrives on inhumane torture and execution.

I can't escape my imagination. I remember the horrific stories, stories that my brain has attempted to process over the years. We have lived near the threats for so long, but tomorrow, we will experience them. At fourteen years old, I am aware of the horror of rape and torture, but again, hearing about it and experiencing it are not parallel. Though I know our path will end in an early death, death is not the concern; our execution is nothing but a gateway to Heaven. How beautiful it will be someday to experience the presence of God and the promised eternal life without pain and suffering.

The torment is in the hours and moments leading up to death. The gruesome tactics used to humiliate and dehumanize people are beyond comprehension. Often, they force parents to watch their own children violated, tortured, and sliced into pieces before inflicting the same torture upon them. Death is a luxury when faced with such atrocities.

Today marks one of the most emotional days I have experienced so far. Though death has been chasing us for the past six years, it has never reached such close proximity. We have lived an extraordinary life despite all our challenges. We have fought the good fight and ran the race to the best of our ability. Now, it is time to let go. We know God can provide unique and calming peace amid fear, terror, and struggles. No storm is too powerful for Him to tame as long as we trust Him and relinquish control.

No one sleeps. The night is spent in fellowship and prayer.

Morning comes quickly. The long-avoided execution date has finally caught up with us. Mom and some of the church women prepare a final breakfast, which is eaten in silence, broken only by the clinking of silver on glass plates.

"There is a white van outside," one member tells us sorrowfully.

We are as ready as we're going to be. We reach for our luggage and move towards the gate as a firm knock strikes the metal barrier that has been shielding us. Upon swinging the door open, we face a Syrian government agent. "Time to go; please board the van," he commands. His voice carries neither emotion nor sympathy and yet, when two of the church members ask if they can accompany us for support, he agrees.

We say our final tearful goodbyes as we hug the church family and slowly move toward the van, dreading each step. Like lambs en route to the slaughter, we enter the van and find a seat. The side door slides shut, separating us from the church that has granted us sanctuary for the past few months.

As the engine roars to life and the van begins to move, I look over my left shoulder and peer through the back-tinted window. Though my vision is blurry with tears, I can see the congregation waving in the street. I wave back, but realize it's pointless; they can't see me through the dark windows. Defeated, I slump into my seat. The two men from the church accompanying us try to encourage and comfort us, but it is no use as my entire family weeps.

We drive for what seems like an eternity, yet it is only several kilometers when the driver tells my dad, "I just need to stop here for a minute." He brings the van to a complete stop outside of a building but does not get out.

Instead, another random gentleman walks out of the building and towards the driver's side window. He leans in, glancing at all of us before he states, "Just take them back. We will not deport them."

The driver tips his head in agreement and begins driving. To our shock, the van is turned around, and we begin heading back the way we came. I look at my parents with bewilderment, but they, too, are confused at the sudden change. Though we are desperate to know what is happening, no one dares to ask the driver.

I try to keep my hope contained, but it becomes harder as I begin to see the church coming into view, getting larger and larger with each passing second. *Is this really happening?*

My hope is confirmed when the driver pulls up to the church, parks the van, and says, "Get out."

Confused, terrified, and trembling, we shakily leave our seats, reach for our bags, and exit the van. We are equally frightened as we are overjoyed at this moment. We move quickly, pinching ourselves to ensure this is not a dream. In my excitement, I rush out of the van before the door is fully open, which causes it to slide back. With my head already out of the van, my neck is the only thing preventing it from shutting completely.

The pain in my neck is quickly forgotten as we rush out and run towards the church. Upon entering the gate, we find our church family still on their knees in the open court, praying for God to intercede for my family. Immediately after seeing us, they stand and rush over to us, praising God for intervening. In tears, we embrace each other again, except this time, they are tears of joy and celebration.

"What just happened?" the pastor asks, unable to contain his smile.

"They changed their mind!" Dad excitedly answers.

The past twenty-four hours felt like we were trapped in a slow-motion horror movie. Each dwindling minute was more nerve-racking than the one before. The feelings of turmoil and the mixed emotions are quickly replaced by relief and elation. As humans, we cannot believe what has just occurred, but as believers, we know this is the work of a mighty God who has us in His care.

We continue to live in Syria for another month. Though the government has left us alone so far, it is not guaranteed that they will

Ramina Wilkerson

not come back and deport us. We are still illegal immigrants with no proper documentation.

It's the end of November 1996, and the declaration announced by President Clinton months ago will be executed soon. Georges Houssney contacts us in Syria, informing us of the great news.

"You need to go back to Iraq," he instructs.

"Saddam is still in the North; how can we return?" Dad inquires.

"To be part of this operation, you must return to Iraq. It will not work from Syria."

Could this be? Is it possible for the President of the United States of America to concern himself with lowly lives that have never mattered before? Syria is a dead end in terms of escape, as most embassies are either closed or unwilling to accept new refugees. There is also still a chance that they could change their minds and deport us back to Iraq directly into Saddam's hands. Our future in this country seems bleak, but returning to Iraq is dangerous. We find ourselves at a crossroads again. So much unknown and so little clarity.

We have learned that with faith, anything is possible. So once again, we turn to God, asking for guidance. After many earnest prayers and a few calls from the Horizons team, my parents feel the urge to travel to Iraq. We pack our bags again and plan our trip back to the motherland, the root of all of our troubles. We know this is a dangerous move, but we don't have another viable option.

"I have fought the good fight, I have finished the race, I have kept the faith." 2 Timothy 4:7

SYRIA - 1996

A widow and her two children own the church grounds; the oldest, Michael, is twenty-five years old, and a twenty-two years old with a minor cognitive disability. The family is reserved, with the mother rarely participating in any after-church fellowship. She often walks home soon after the services, where she dwells with her children. Our apartment shares a wall with their house.

Michael is not the most outspoken young man in the congregation; he is more of a listener than a speaker. Though he participates in the gatherings and most times joins the group in various activities in the game room, he continues to keep his socialization limited. In the two months we have lived in this church, he has not spoken two words to me until today. We are in our final days in Syria, and he seems to have saved all his words for this moment.

With a quivering voice, he approaches me, "May I speak to you in private, please? I have something I need to share with you."

"Sure."

"Can you meet me in the church sanctuary?"

"Yes," I reply, feeling naive as I follow him.

He walks through the central aisle and sits on the first pew to the right. Looking at his nervous body language, I choose to sit across the aisle, leaving a distance between us.

With a trembling voice, he utters, "I would like to ask for your hand in marriage."

Stunned at his words, I stare at him. I'm surprised by his question and a bit repelled. "You want to do what?"

"I believe you and I are meant for each other. I would like you to stay behind in Syria and marry me."

In shock, I glance his way and see his eyes watching me. I find his gaze so unnerving, repulsing. I have no interest in Michael, nor do I find him attractive. A husky, tall man with a mustache, dark hair, and dark eyes. My first crush was on an Assyrian boy with fair skin, light brown hair, and beautiful blue eyes. Although many attractive Assyrian men exist, I rarely look at them in a desirable way. I have always gravitated towards the foreigners visiting who look much different than the men I am accustomed to.

I also find our age difference even more appalling. He is twenty-five, and I am fourteen. Eleven years is a large sum for a teenager, especially for a teenager with a possible bright future awaiting her on the other side. However, it is customary in the Middle East for older men to marry younger women...girls, to be exact. Still, the age difference is disturbing to me.

If I stay behind, I will never know what is waiting for me with President Clinton's declaration.

Of course, I have entertained the concept of marriage before, given my culture. I have lived most of my life watching my girlfriends marry at very young ages. I never envied them for it. I witnessed several of my Muslim friends experience the trauma of circumcision or, in better terms, FGM—Female Genital Mutilation. It is a procedure that is carried out on young girls to remove the clitoral glans, the most sensitive part of the female genitals, to provide more pleasure for the man and less for the woman. Though this practice is not conducted within the Assyrian culture, growing up around it and surrounded by horror stories can leave any female repulsed. Living in a culture heavily focused on males, I have no desire to partake in that mindset.

There is more to life than getting married. That much I know. I can sense it deep within me. I want an education. I want a life without fear and ongoing trauma. I want to enjoy my teen years before raising a family. My parents have taught my sisters and me never to concede to the pressure of marriage that Middle Eastern cultures place on young girls. They both waited, and chose to get married after school. I desire to break out of every mold my culture has placed upon me. I don't want to be part of the statistics. I yearn to be the exception to the rule. I seek independence—a foreign concept to many in the Middle East.

Michael, however, comes with a deep-rooted mentality toward marriage. Marrying him would mean living with his mother and sister, becoming their caretaker, and having a family, as is customary.

Aware of Michael's vulnerability and considering his reserved personality, I must be delicate in declining his nauseating proposal. It is taking every fiber of my existence not to burst into hysterical laughter. While screaming on the inside, *"Are you kidding me? No way,"* I compose myself. "Michael, I'm sorry; I don't feel the same about you. I appreciate your honesty, but I cannot marry you or anyone else at fourteen. I'm too young for marriage; I'm leaving with my family." Remaining calm, I continue, "I need to see what is on the other side. I need to see President Clinton's plan through. I can't stay behind and do something I do not desire at my age."

"I understand," he replies with a disappointed voice.

I feel butterflies in my stomach. They could be from the excitement of standing up for myself and what I want or from the anxiety of the situation. My movement from sitting to standing feels slow as my knees knock together.

Once I begin walking, my strides on the tiled floor are solid and loud. Each step is on a mission to escape this unpleasant experience. I reach for the massive door, swing it open, and run as fast as possible, looking for Mom.

"Mom, you're not going to believe what just happened."

"I know. I saw you talking to Michael."

"What do you mean you know?"

"He already asked your father and me for your hand in marriage, but we told him it was your decision. We didn't want to make it for you. We trust that you are smart enough to make your own decision."

I step away from her and pause to reflect on her comment. Though grateful for the trust my parents have in my decision-making and the independence they taught me at an early age, I am a little frustrated that they didn't decide for me, protecting me from that uncomfortable incident. Or better yet, warn me so I could better prepare myself. Nonetheless, I am grateful marriage is not my immediate fate, unlike many girls who have no say in their future, leaving them in the care of older men from a very young age. The final two days pass with much discomfort between Michael's family and me, specifically his mother, who had hoped for a different outcome.

We repeat our painful goodbyes and take a cab back to the Khabur River, to the very same location at which we arrived two months prior. Instead of being captured, this time, we are leaving with a sense of relief as we take a leap of faith and cross the infamous Khabur one last time back to Iraq.

At the border, we find another cab and travel to Duhok, the city that has become our shelter and our torture chamber. We reach Nabiel's home, and his family welcomes us with open arms. His parents own a house in a sophisticated and sheltered neighborhood. Understanding the danger we are in for returning to Iraq, they take the necessary measures for our protection. They cover all the windows with dark, sturdy fabric to prevent anyone from looking inside the house. They even reject any visits from their neighbors, completely isolating themselves and us for our safety. With Hussein's military operating in the city, everyone is forced to take extra precautionary steps to prevent alerting them of our presence.

"When you pass through the waters, I will be with you; and through the rivers, they shall not overflow you. When you walk through the fire, you shall not be burned, nor shall the flame scorch you." Isaiah 43:2

DUHOK - 1996

I startle awake at the feel of gentle fingers running through my hair. "Mom," I say in relief. "What time is it?" The room is still dark; the thick drapes make it impossible to decipher whether it's day or night.

"Wake up. Time to go," she responds, not answering my question. "We need to hurry; get up, please, and help with your sisters."

"Okay," I say reluctantly, not wanting to move from under my warm, cozy covers. Then, thoughts of what today means bounce into my mind. *This is it. This is the day you've been waiting for. Get moving. Today will be the beginning of a new journey as we embark on an unknown adventure.*

I wake my sisters, and we step into the bathroom to brush our teeth. I can smell the delicious breakfast prepared by Nabiel's mother. The kitchen aroma is savory. The dining table is elaborately decorated with eggs cooked two ways, sunnyside and scrambled, fresh bread, fruit, yogurt, and tea. She must have been cooking for hours as she's prepared a feast for us. We gather around the table and find our seats.

Besides the occasional sound of silverware striking the white ceramic plates, the room is silent. We are all lost in thought, our emotions elevated and mixed with sadness. Nabiel's parents are dismayed. With every bite and every breath, they are one step closer to losing their son. Nabiel, along with the rest of the Horizons team who worked alongside us in Duhok, will be traveling with us as an employee of Horizons, leaving behind everything he knows.

I finish breakfast, drink my tea, and carry my plate and cup to the kitchen sink, following everyone else. Although my immediate family is ecstatic, we can't help but feel the sadness around us, empathizing with Nabiel's family. We have had our share of goodbyes and the heartbreak that comes with them. Thirty minutes later, Nabeil's father hesitantly calls for the two taxis he had set up days before. Upon their arrival, we stand in the living room near the front door, knowing what we must do, but no one wants to take the first step. Eyes well up with tears that can't be held back. It is time. As we hug each other, it doesn't take long before the silent cries become wails that echo through the room. Each hug is tighter than the one before. This is a familiar feeling. I have become an expert in farewells.

Nevertheless, this one is strikingly different. It is higher in intensity yet flooded with peace. With our eyes red and faces wet, we very cautiously and quietly march outside and into the cabs, avoiding the possibility of alerting the neighbors. One cab takes my family, and the second holds the Horizons team. Though it is pitch black outside, both taxis arrive and briefly drive with their lights off in order to avoid drawing suspicion to us and getting us captured. We have been hiding in Nabiel's house for five days now, and today, December 5, 1996, we are on the brink of a new journey, a new beginning. As we near our destination, the morning light begins to appear, gently pushing the darkness aside. It is a welcome view as we witness the beautiful sunrise across the horizon.

Today, Zakho, the little city that has been associated with much anguish and a never-ending cycle of hope and disappointment, will be our blessing. Facing the Iraq-Turkey border, flashbacks of our Turkey deportation and the fear we felt swirl through my mind. It feels as if it was only yesterday when the Turkish military aimed their rifles at our backs as we walked across the border.

We step out of the taxi near the Turkish border, outside the United Nations establishment. A security guard escorts us into the highly secure white building. My heart bolts with anticipation and fear at the sight of armed soldiers lined throughout. I glance at their uniform; it's different. These soldiers don't belong to Hussein, nor are they part of the Kurdish military. *Who can they be? Turkey again? Or...*

Eager to get moving forward, we find a long line extending through the hall and into a room around the corner. As we reach the front, we face numerous individuals seated around a table. "Organization name?" the agent asks, seeking proof of employment with an American organization.

"Horizons International," Dad answers as he extends the envelope in hand. The agent retrieves our credentials, including the identification cards created by Horizons International.

We are faced with extensive questioning. Questions that last hours in an attempt to stumble individuals and families. Questions that can cause fear—horrible fear. Often similar, if not identical, questions are presented, expecting similar, if not identical, responses. Any attempt to prevent Assyrian families from departing is welcome here. My parents, though trembling, display wisdom and courage as they answer each question. "You can move on," the individual speaks, pointing to the inspection line several paces away.

Phew. One step down.

Searches are conducted by Muslim Kurdish individuals, and unfortunately for us, they despise Christians. It isn't hard to see that whenever they stumble upon a Christian family, they attempt to delay or prevent their departure. A Muslim female covered in hijab is assigned to inspect our bags. She probes every inch of our belongings. Nothing is left untouched. "You can't take this with you," she sneers, holding nail clippers between her fingers that she discovered in the side pocket of Mom's bag. "I have to reject your departure. This is a prohibited item." She is desperate for any possible excuse to ban our exit.

"Wait a minute! That is not true. You can't do that!" Mom cries. "We received a letter with detailed instructions of what we can and can't pack, and nail clippers are on the list of approved items."

Anxiety strikes again, and my body trembles as I silently pray, begging for God to soften her heart. No matter how afraid we are, we can't show it. We refuse to give this woman the satisfaction, so we remain calm. Mom is not giving up; she continues to gently urge the woman's attention as she points to the letter of instructions we received. Having no solid evidence to hold us back, she stamps our letter and motions us to move forward with bitterness and resentment painted on her face.

Moments later, we spot Georges in the distance, pointing towards us. "They belong to my organization," he says, smiling. Organization leaders were asked to travel to Zhako to distinguish their team members. Seeing his familiar face is comforting amid so much unknown. Being unable to communicate with officials, or anyone for that matter, is terrifying. We are being probed, prodded, questioned, and escorted, yet very little is discussed with us.

"This way," a soldier calls, ushering us to a long line of buses. We board a large and luxurious bus with tall, gray cushioned seats. "Take a seat," he continues. An eerie feeling washes over me as I sit back, looking out the window to my right. I have been here before. This bus seems much like the one Turkey used to deport us back to Iraq. It all feels proverbial, from the bus to the armed soldiers to the location.

With no concept of our fate, destination, or what's happening, concern grows within us. While peace is still present, it doesn't take much effort for fear to creep in and resound its disparaging voice, reminding us of all the times we have tried and failed. *Why should this be any different?*

This time, I remind myself, *it is different because we have God.* We can't give up. Not now. By God's grace, we shall try one more time.

With every seat occupied, three soldiers board, and the bus moves. We begin our journey with no inclination of what's next. Dad attempts to ask the soldiers questions, but silence is the only answer he receives.

"They've been ordered not to talk to us," the man in the seat behind Dad whispers.

Dad nods in thanks. We aren't surprised by the new information as the soldiers remain silent and refuse to make eye contact.

As the bus travels, I can see the sun gently disappear behind the mountains surrounding us. The sunrise I'd appreciated earlier today feels like a distant memory. It has been a very long day. We have been on the bus for four hours, it is nearly 1 a.m., and we have yet to eat or sleep. In the darkness, unable to see our surroundings, the bus finally comes to a complete stop, and the overhead lights come on.

"You are in a Turkey camp. Remain seated until you are assigned a tent," the soldier orders. A second soldier motions for our family to exit the bus and follow him. He quickly maneuvers his way through what seems like hundreds of tents. The short trip to our assigned tent feels long as each step we take, our shoes sink into the wet clay-like mud.

"This one is yours." The soldier points to the tent before us.

The tent is small, with inflated air mattresses resting on the ground. Dad lifts the side and holds it up as we crouch to enter. We set our bags on the ground and sit on the floor, waiting for further instructions. The overwhelming day filled with travel, interviews, investigations, and more travel leaves us all exhausted and yet too alarmed to sleep. The fabric of the tents may protect us from potential rain but not much else. There is little safety in cloth. It took concrete and brick to offer sturdy protection from missiles and bullets. *How can this textile withstand anything?* We hear every sound and word spoken outside our corridors as we sit silently, tired, hungry, weak, and afraid.

Footsteps approach our tent, and we hear, "Time to eat." We step outside, into the darkness, with a few lights shining through but not enough to make sense of our location or surroundings. The man points to a long line of people and orders us to join them.

As we near the front, we are each given a bowl and a spoon and then directed to the table serving soup. We receive one ladle-full, walk back to our tent, and eat silently.

So many thoughts rush through our minds, but no one is brave enough to utter them. *Is this our last meal, or are we on the verge of freedom?*

We take our shoes off and lean back onto our mattresses. We don't dare change into pajamas, too afraid of the unexpected. My eyes quickly close in weariness. Mere minutes pass when we are startled by a loud shout, "Time to wake up and exit your tents."

"What time is it?" I ask, fighting to open my eyelids and keep them open.

"It's 5 a.m.," Dad answers in his tired voice as he clears his throat.

Despite the exhaustion, we don't have the luxury of sleeping in. I sit on the edge of my nearly depleted air mattress and put my tennis shoes on. Having slept in my regular clothes makes this moment more efficient. Once we step out of our tent, we are asked to stand in the long line formed around the tents. The cold December air easily breaks through my lightweight coat. Shivers seep through my skin, down to my bones.

The line moves slowly, and once again, we are faced with a bus. We board the bus and take a seat. I lean back in my seat as I watch the rising sun casting a rosy hue across the cold, morning sky. I hear my stomach rumbling. Last night's soup did not satisfy my hunger. We don't have food; we don't have water. We don't know when our next meal is. That is, until a young, blue-eyed soldier approaches each individual and extends a brown package. "This is your meal," he says and walks to the next person.

I turn the bag around and see the letters MRE (Meal Ready to Eat) in large black font. I rip the edge of the bag open and find several pouches inside. Starving, I reach into the bag, snag the first package I touch, rip the top off, and sniff, anxious to eat. The odor quickly reaches my nose; it doesn't smell pleasant. I reach in and pull out a long, dark strip of what looks like meat. *That's odd. I've never seen meat dehydrated.* I bite into the strip; the texture feels leathery. I chew the small bite, hoping to swallow, but it takes effort. I put the piece back in the bag. *Let's see what else is in here. Maybe something edible.* I reach for a smaller package; it feels mushy. I rip the top and quickly realize this is not something I would like to indulge in. It is a yellow substance that smells like cheese. Every type of cheese I have consumed has always been in a solid form that Mom had to cut into smaller pieces to fit my sandwich. This is not it. This, too, goes back in the bag. *What's next?* Crackers, I recognize the shape and flavor. I quickly devour the eight crackers, excited I have found something to quiet my angry stomach.

Still hungry, I continue to explore my bag. I reach in again—another squishy package. *I hope this is not another unpleasant cheese.* I take my time ripping the tip, slowly testing the content by the aroma first. It smells pleasant. Different. I pull the tip-off, and I look inside; brown creamy content. I dab a small drop on my index finger and taste it. It tastes like peanuts. I look at the letters on the packet, "Peanut Butter." I've never heard of such a thing, but I'm in love with this heavenly goodness. I lean forward and ask my family if they have tasted their peanut butter, and both my parents seem unhappy with theirs, especially Mom. "Can I please have your peanut butter if you're not eating it?" Both quickly extend theirs to me.

With the distraction of food out of the way, my mind wanders back to thinking about our last day. Twenty-four hours have passed since we began our journey in Duhok with limited sleep. Nothing makes sense. We have no answers. No hint and no direction. Except for the impression that we are in Turkey, we know nothing. The drive is highly dull; the scenery is plain and dry. I sit in my seat, peering out the window, lost in my thoughts, imagining what this new chapter will hold.

As the kilometers pass, I reflect on everyone and everything I left behind. I replay my goodbyes to my friends, the tears we shed, and the memories we shared. My heart begins to ache from missing what I know, what I left behind. My life in Iraq is nothing but a memory now, and somewhere out there, my future awaits.

I look to the soldiers guarding us, the same ones who are under strict orders not to interact with any of us. Being unable to communicate causes a sense of vulnerability. It is a terrifying feeling. My life, my future, my everything is at their mercy. I have no control over the situation we are in nor of the outcome.

The bus ride from the camp lasts nearly five hours. A few jokes are shared between the Horizons team and my family, but most of the ride is quiet. Everyone is lost in their own thoughts, fears, sadness, and restlessness.

From a distance, I see a white object. As we get closer, I realize it's a large airplane—the largest I have ever seen. *There is no airport near it. No tarmac. No buildings. Absolutely nothing; how can it be parked in an open field?* As the bus nears, the airplane grows more significant in size. Confusion masks us. We are in the middle of nowhere, Turkey.

The bus comes to a complete stop before the armed soldiers usher us out and toward the airplane.

This is only the second time I have traveled on an aircraft. The plane's stairway is open and firmly placed on the dry ground. *A plane is good news, right? It has to be.* As I climb those stairs, feeling each step beneath my feet, I am grateful for the rescue but also have a hint of fear as I have no inclination of my final destination. Finally, at the top step, I board the Airbus, in awe of its enormity. I quickly find a seat next to my family, happy that I at least have a window view. Buckling my seatbelt, I watch everyone board. Each passenger that sets foot onto the airplane has uncertainty displayed on their face.

"Welcome aboard," a voice resounds through the speakers above. "This is your pilot speaking. Please remain seated at all times. If you need assistance, push the call button above your seat, and the flight attendant will be with you shortly. If you need to use the restroom, please raise your hand, and a soldier will escort you. We also ask that you try to speak quietly while in your seat. You may sit tall to converse with people around you, but do not stand up unless necessary."

He concludes his short speech, and to our disappointment, he does not mention our destination. The airplane begins to move quickly, and memories of my first flight rush through my mind. As the engines roar, I can't help but feel excited as one of my favorite parts of flying is coming up, the lift-off.

Six hours into our flight, the pilot's voice rings through the intercom again. "We are beginning our descent into Dubai. This is a two-hour layover—just enough time for the plane to be refueled, restocked, and cleaned. You are to remain in your seats. We will depart for our next destination after our brief layover." I feel a glimpse of hope. I know we are farther away from Iraq. However, we are still in the Middle East, in a Muslim country. Safety still seems uncertain.

I gaze through the window, watching all the planes directed in and out of the gates, watching people freely roaming outside and enjoying the fresh air. I'm jealous of their freedom. All the while, our airplane is being cleaned as we remain seated. I watch strangers pushing food through aisles while others vacuum. Two hours pass, and we begin the journey to our next unknown destination.

After five more hours in the air, we are feeling trapped and restless. The pilot speaks again, "We have another layover. This time, we are descending into Colombo, Sri Lanka." The pilot proceeds with the exact instructions as before: no standing, no moving, and so on.

We watch a team of people walk through the plane to clean it and restock it with what looks to be an abundance of boxes of drinks and food. More than before. The aircraft is fueled and ready. Again, we lift off into the unknown. Concern and anxiousness with a hint of relief settle in. Though I don't know where I'm going, one thing I know for sure, I am traveling further away from Iraq and the Middle East with each layover.

Jetlagged, tired, restless, and unable to sleep for long periods, my legs cramp, and my butt is numb from the constant sitting. I'm exhausted, and my mind is racing; *where are they taking us now?*

Finally, after a sixteen-hour flight, the pilot's voice resounds through the airplane. "Please fasten your seatbelt and prepare for landing. This is our final destination. Welcome to Guam."

"Where the hell is Guam?" This is the first response I hear from the adults around me. Having never learned about America, its history, or geography, I have no inclination to where Guam is and who it belongs to. Hussein's hatred for America ensured our knowledge didn't expand beyond the Middle East.

Upon landing, I stand up from my seat, legs shaky from sitting for so long. I am excited to feel my blood flow through my body again as I step into the aisle, preparing to exit the airplane that has become my shelter for the past thirty-one hours. I feel a bit apprehensive as I walk down the aisle, unsure of what's ahead, yet I feel an overwhelming peace and anticipation about what lies on the other side of the airplane walls. I stroll toward the door and the open-air stairs. Immediately, I am startled by the racket coming from below. As I focus my sight down the long stairs, my eyes are shocked at the beautiful scene before me.

Uniformed soldiers are lined up on both sides, from the bottom of the stairs all the way to the hanger bay, creating a pathway for us. We stride between the two lines as they welcome us with cheers, clapping, and smiles. Some are even holding stuffed animals for the children. Still clueless of our whereabouts, we reach the end of the line and face one of the military generals who smiles as he welcomes us and proceeds with my favorite statement of all time:

"WELCOME TO AMERICA. YOU ARE ON U.S. SOIL. YOU'RE SAFE NOW."

* * *

"Be still, and know that I am God." Psalm 46:10

EPILOGUE

I clutched my Bible tightly, pressing it against my chest, feeling the familiar comfort of its weight as I walked alone to the little chapel on the Anderson Air Force base in Guam. At least, I thought I was alone until I felt a presence around me. When I looked to my right, there He was; Christ was walking alongside me. His silent presence was powerful and profound. He didn't have to say anything for me to feel His companionship and His love. Knowing He was right by my side was comforting. I was not alone.

I walked that .8 kilometers (.5 miles) in complete silence with a big smile—a smile of peace and gratitude on my face. We climbed three wooden steps, side by side, to reach the chapel door. I reached for the handle and gently pulled the door towards me. As soon as I entered the small, one-room chapel, He departed. Everyone was already inside waiting to start the Bible study when I walked in, confused as if I had lost something.

"Are you okay?" asked Mom.

"Yes, I'm just looking for Him."

"Who?"

"Jesus! Did you see Him walk in? He was here a second ago."

"No, Honey, you walked in alone."

Little did I know that that was the last time I would experience His physical presence—His presence filled with warmth, love, grace, and absolute shalom.

The U.S. Government launched Operation Pacific Haven to rescue Iraqi citizens who worked for American organizations. The operation took several months to execute and landed us in Guam, an American territory island outside Australia. After living in Guam for three months to complete our medical exams and begin our immigration naturalization process, we officially descended to the United States on March 12, 1997. We arrived in Denver, Colorado, my future home, before moving to Idaho twenty-three years later.

My journey in America came with its own set of challenges. At times, it felt even worse than Iraq. Although I had been an immigrant before, this time, it felt different. I was no longer on the run, which should have provided relief. It did to an extent, but the uncertainty created a brand-new fear. The country that had repeatedly rejected my family and me was now welcoming us with open arms. It had saved us in a miraculous way that required no visa, passport, or money. I was beyond grateful and relieved to be here, and yet, with very little English and no cultural understanding, I was expected to survive and thrive. The culture shock I experienced was overwhelming and physically, emotionally, and mentally painful. All of that brought on anxiety, depression, and loneliness. I found myself smiling at school and around family but crying myself to sleep when alone. But that's a story for another time.

I can tell you today that despite everything, I knew I had a purpose. I knew I was brought to America for something bigger than myself and the dark world growing around me. I also knew that because of that purpose, I had to change. I had to pull myself out of whatever I was going through by relying on God—and I did. He gave me the strength to turn my life around, overcome my depression, and conquer my anxiety and loneliness by forcing myself to become more extroverted, make friends, and start a new chapter in my life. I had a calling, and I needed to fulfill it. God didn't bring me to America for me to waste my opportunity.

Each of our lives is a story full of adventures, challenges, tears, and triumphs. With each page, we learn, we grow, and we adapt. My story and the road I have traveled have shaped me into who I am today. Never once have I looked back and wished I had a different life. If given the opportunity, I would choose this life all over again. It sounds wild, but it's true. I am grateful and blessed to have had the life and the experiences I've had so far, and I cannot wait to see what else God has waiting for me.

My early life felt like it was always under an ominous shadow. I believed that because I was born in a war, I was going to die in one. Looking back now, I see an additional shadow. A shadow of pure love that covered me from childhood until this very day. It makes me think of a Scripture I love in Psalm 91:4, "He shall cover you with His feathers, and under His wings, you shall take refuge; His truth shall be your shield and buckler." Thus, I will gratefully and humbly walk in His shadow and in His truth for the remainder of my life on this side.

* * *

"It is to your advantage that I go away; for if I do not go away, the Helper will not come to you; but if I depart, I will send Him to you." John 16:7

I dedicate this book to my Heavenly Father. You designed my life and purpose before my existence. You chose me and placed your favor upon me before I knew you. I am humbled and grateful for your abundant love that led to my salvation. Thank you for your faithfulness.

Jesus, my Lord and Savior. My sweet friend. My heart leaps whenever I think of your magnificent beauty standing before me many years ago. Not only did you reveal yourself to me, but you physically protected me and walked with me when I needed you the most. I yearn for the day I will see you again.

Although I am the physical author, this book is only possible with the actual author, the Holy Spirit. You are the ultimate inspiration behind this memoir. This is your story. Each memory holds a significance only you understand. You smiled as I laughed, held me when I cried and comforted me while I found healing. Thank you for guiding my every step, speaking so clearly, and sharing your heart so the world can hear YOU.

Acknowledgments

"As iron sharpens iron, so a man sharpens the countenance of his friend." Proverbs 27:17

Writing this book has been a journey in itself. Reliving my past was an emotional rollercoaster, from momentary depression to endless tears and laughter. Pushing through those emotions and overcoming all the challenging circumstances would not have been possible without the people with whom God has enriched my life. So many have blessed me, spoken truth into my life, and even boldly offered constructive criticism when necessary. Your words and actions have helped shape me into the person I am today, and for that, I am grateful.

To Charles: My best friend, security blanket, and rock. You have been my biggest inspiration for this book. Since our first date, you have encouraged me to put my story into writing. Thank you for never giving up on me and the book, even though it took me fourteen years to take your advice and finally start writing. I appreciate your patience, especially during this process. You grieved with me when I cried and joined in my laughter as I walked through my past. You have been gracious and supportive, always lifting my spirits even during my most profound, darkest moments. Each day with you only gets better. I would not be the woman I am today had it not been for your love.

To Amnisty and Addiley: No words can express the delight and joy you bring to my heart. Thank you for being patient through this project. I want to acknowledge your sacrifices and understanding as I spent so many hours attached to my computer. Your smiles and energy brighten my day. You keep me on my toes and inspire me to be better every day. I love sharing my childhood stories with you and answering your questions. I love you to the moon and back.

To my parents: You have endured so much in your lifetime. No parent should watch their young girls suffer as you did, but you kept a brave face, kept pushing forward, and provided us with a normal life to the best of your ability despite our circumstances. Thank you for everything you have endured and for finding ways to keep our family safe.

To Sona and Rodina: You have been my rock, the best support system, and the most amazing editors anyone could ask for. To say you are remarkable is an understatement! The memories we share are priceless, and the bond we built through our challenges is unbreakable. Words can't describe how grateful I am for you two and everything you have done for me and my family. Our past has made us who we are today, and I would do it all over again if it means I get to have you as my sisters again. You are wise and strong. You speak the truth when I need it and see me through any warfare.

To my family, aunts, uncles, and cousins, near and far: You have been an inspiration through this process. Thank you for all the memories we have built together and for giving me a fantastic childhood regardless of our situation. I love walking down memory lane with you over tea and cookies. I am grateful God chose you as my family. To the resilient women in my family, you are strong and persistent. You don't give up no matter what life throws your way. Thank you for being an example.

To Horizons International Team: Thank you for allowing God to use you to impact others across the world and for your discernment and obedience to the Holy Spirit. Your impact on our lives and the lives of many will be greatly rewarded in Heaven. Thank you for being a light when we needed you most.

To Open Doors and other missionaries: Thank you for sacrificing so much to love others. To love strangers like your brothers and sisters. Thank you for allowing the Holy Spirit to guide you. You have changed more lives than you can imagine.

To Matt Eng: You have been a blessing since you walked into my house without knocking. You have been supportive, a soundboard throughout this painful process, and a shoulder to cry on more times than I'd like to admit. You have challenged me when I needed it and pulled me out of my darkness when I needed it. I am grateful for the adventures we have shared and look forward to many more.

To the powerhouse women who have walked alongside me and pushed my spiritual growth. Kathy Schissler, Amy Moilanen, Ashley Hulley, Amanda Deich, and many others. Thank you for pouring into my life and helping me overcome obstacles I never thought possible. You speak the truth that's wrapped in love. Ashley, thank you for your gentle touch in this book.

The team at Mainspring: thank you for your prayers, love, and support and for rallying around me and building me up when life got tough during this process. Thank you for demonstrating Christ to everyone around you in such a beautiful way. A special thank you to James Du Plooy, Sy Ruiz, and Paul Boorujy; you are an excellent example of Christ's light that shines consistently in this world.

Danielle Patridge: Thank you for the time you invested in this project. I value and appreciate our time together. Your support, understanding, and patience have been greatly appreciated, especially during the unforeseeable circumstances that took place during this process for both of us.

Geoff Safford: I believe one of the reasons God brought you to Colorado for such a short time was this book. You walked into my life at such a time, and even though you didn't know me well, you still took the time to invest your effort into this project and help it come to life. I am grateful for the time we spent together and the discussions we had. Thank you for your Christ-like heart of service.

A special thank you to the Wood family for your love and support. I love you guys beyond words. To all my friends, brothers and sisters in Christ, and church families, especially North Ridge. Thank you for speaking Christ into my life, cheering me on, and praying for me and this project. You know who you are!

To Liz Enlow: Thank you for your sweet time and your insight. You are a gem, and I'm lucky to know you.

To the beta readers: Thank you for your yes. Thank you for sharing your honest opinion and your heart. I am grateful for your time and love to conclude this project.

There aren't enough words in all the languages combined to express my gratitude to the *BRAVE* men and women of the U.S. armed forces who risked their lives not only in fighting wars in Iraq but also for rescuing me, my family, and so many others, and who served in Guam as we transitioned to America. I wish I could meet each of you, shake your hand, and say, "THANK YOU!" You may not know this, but you have been part of something bigger than life. Your service and sacrifice save more lives than you can imagine and provide opportunities that otherwise would never have been possible.

A special thank you to the man who introduced me to my first Disney Princess, Cinderella. Chaplain David Cannon, thank you for your love and support during our days in Guam and beyond. Your love, encouragement, and faith were much needed during the uncertain times of transition.

To President George H. W. Bush: You were one of my biggest inspirations growing up. I wish I had the opportunity to grow up under the presidency of your stature. I am thankful for your boldness to step in and declare war to stop Saddam Hussein. I admire you so much that I almost lost my life praising you. Rest In Peace, Mr. President.

To President Bill Clinton: You saved my life! In my wildest dreams, I never thought the President of The United States of America would take a minute to put Operation Pacific Haven in place to rescue me and my family. Thank you for presenting me with an opportunity and a second chance at life. To experience safety and freedom were things I didn't understand until you came along.

To President George W. Bush: Thank you for all you have done. I hope you know the magnitude of your work has impacted the lives of many. I appreciate and admire you beyond words. Thank you for being the President who launched operations that led to the capture of Saddam Hussein. This was an unbelievable feat.

To you, the reader: Thank you for saying yes to this book. Thank you for allowing the Holy Spirit to take you on this journey. I pray that you found courage in this book and realized you are stronger than you think. No matter the circumstances, you can overcome anything. Possibilities await you; all you have to do is say yes.

* * *

"A friend loves at all times, and a brother is born for adversity."
Proverbs 17:17

Made in the USA
Monee, IL
07 October 2024

66750706R00218